INTO THE WIND

A YOUNG FAMILY AND
THE AUSTRALIAN PILOTS' DISPUTE
AS TOLD BY AN '89ER

PAUL EDGLEY

We acknowledge the Traditional Owners of the land on which we publish books, the Quandamooka people and pay our respects to Elders past, present and emerging.

Please note that some names have been changed to protect personal privacy.

Published by Boolarong Biographies
an imprint of Boolarong Press
38/1631 Wynnum Road
Tingalpa Qld 4173
Australia.
www.boolarongpress.com.au

First published 2021

A catalogue record for this book is available from the National Library of Australia

ISBN: 9781922643100 (paperback)

Edited by Jacki Ferro of Raw Memoirs www.rawmemoirs.com

Typeset in Amiri 12pt by Boolarong Press

Cover image: Boeing 747 over the North Pacific on the way to Anchorage by author. Back Cover: Brisbane by author.

Cover design by Boolarong Press

Printed and bound by Watson Ferguson & Company, Tingalpa, Australia

FOR SHAR

ACKNOWLEDGEMENTS

I want to thank my wife and children for all their encouragement, and for putting up with me over the years it took to jot all this down. There were times we could be out and I'd suddenly yank the ever-present pen and notebook from my pocket, and scribble another thought. And other times, jumping from bed in the early hours of the morning, and firing up the computer to tap in another change. Not to mention suffering the shades of those unique moods born from the inability to find an elusive word. And a special thanks for the years of feedback, suggestions and sometimes conferences as we fixated on computers resting on the upstairs desk, pouring over the many discarded drafts.

I'd like to thank Morna Kenworthy for her encouragement. Morna's husband, Bill, was one of Ansett's most senior Captains who was killed in a tragic accident during the Airline Dispute. Morna attended every court hearing and demonstration throughout her difficult times and kept and updated her files and records over the last three decades. Morna is also writing about the Dispute and over the years we've compared notes, with Morna providing quotes and pointing to references that were beyond my computer skills. Morna lives in Melbourne and despite the fact we've never physically met, this has made no difference to our friendship fostered through the wires.

I am grateful to Jacki Ferro, of Raw Memoirs, for her patient and thorough editing. Not every thought I tapped into the computer, despite my sometime protests, was needed to tell this story.

Thomas Lynch is a Senior Solicitor with Kay and Hughes in Sydney and is also a volunteer with the Arts Law Centre of Australia. One of my passions is music and I thank Tom for his time and generous advice. Tom suggested how best to weave the soundtrack behind the words into the narrative without infringing on the creative talent and originality of the artists I so admire.

Dan Kelly of Boolarong Press is another I wish to thank. I appreciate Dan's frank telling it like it is (I don't think there'd be much interest in a story with a backdrop from 30 years ago), and later his thoughtful, furrowed brow and broad smile in the small upstairs office at Boolarong Press, and then a few days after this, his email equating to — what the hell, let's give it go.

And last but not least I'd like to thank my friends and colleagues, the '89ers. There were times it felt as though the whole world was against us as our families stood shoulder to shoulder, each taking care of the other. Some of us have passed further into the blue that filled our lives and many have now hung up their hats and coats. I only hope that by telling my family's story, I have at least in some way told all of our stories. No matter where we go or whatever we do, this event from so long ago has forever bound us. To each and every one of you — Sui Generis.

PROLOGUE

In 1966 when I was 11, I flew with my school to Canberra. While the day turned out even better than our school organisers imagined, it was significant in another way. After the Ansett-ANA Lockheed Electra dropped us back at Sydney airport, I made a decision. As I walked to the terminal, I paused and looked back at this magnificent aircraft. One day, I vowed, I would become a pilot.

I didn't much enjoy school and my lack of effort was reflected in school reports. When I expressed my desire to be a pilot, the school career counsellors shook their heads. In my final two years of senior, I played drums in a rock 'n' roll band. Concerts and the music of top international and local acts became my world. Bruce Springsteen and Bob Seger were favourites and I remember gigs savaged by AC/DC's pulsating aggression, and Angels' concerts where the crowd chanted in response as Doc Neeson's musical question lingered. It was always great to see their faces again. Our band latched onto the idea of becoming rock stars. It could be a long haul to reach the top and while it worked out for AC/DC, it didn't for us.

After finishing school, I started working full time with my father who was a builder. Since my early teens, I'd worked weekends and school holidays with Dad, and for my 18th birthday he gave me a special gift — a hammer, the same as his, and a nail bag. These have travelled with me on every journey since. Whenever I grasp the hammer, I remember my dad's caring ways and wise sayings, often housed in the slang of his time.

A couple of years out of school, our band broke up, so at 21, I decided to chase my dream to fly. After gaining my Commercial Pilot's Licence, I took to Highway 1 in my blue Holden panel van. I planned to drive from Sydney to Perth, stopping at every airport along the way, in search of work.

In South Australia, I struck some luck. In my first job, I flew fish-spotting aircraft for the tuna industry based in Port Lincoln. When the tuna season ended, I returned to Sydney and after upgrading my qualifications set course for Darwin, accompanied by my good friend, Ari. I could fill a section of a book (and have) on Darwin and 'The Territory', but it's here that luck for both Ari and me changed for the better. We both landed jobs. Ari started with the Darwin Aero Club, then moved to Arnhem Air Charter, and I slotted into Northern Territory Air Charter (NTAC). Two major events occurred while in Darwin. I met my partner Sharon, and after amassing enough flying hours and experience, I was granted a final interview and accepted into Ansett Airlines of Australia.

When Ari and I had left Sydney, the first tape I slotted into the much-used cassette player was one of my favourites. The sound of rubber against bitumen knitted with the rich harmony as Bob Seger's '*Against the Wind*' spilled from the van's rear mounted speakers. I'd always been conscious of which way the wind blew, and this song seemed to depict my life since I began pursuing aviation. But the winds that buffeted my old blue panel van as we cruised down Highway 1 were nothing compared to the tempest that erupted in 1989. Australian pilots had felt goaded for many years prior, and believed that the airlines were only waiting for an opportunity to attack our professional association, the Australian Federation of Air Pilots (AFAP).

My generation marked the era of anti-Vietnam War civil unrest, and many of us didn't wish to go 'All the way with LBJ'. Generally, we had a rebellious attitude towards officialdom and this, in turn, is reflected in my choice of car. The panel van became a symbol of our rebelliousness, as we took a tradie's work vehicle and turned it into a surf wagon. We grew our hair long, and this rankled our elders no end. This clash of ideologies formed the backdrop to the pilots' dispute, because opposing two of the most powerful business people of those times, and the Government, and the ACTU, became just another instance where our generation challenged the established order.

But the pilots who protested were not solely of my generation. The 1,647 pilots involved in the dispute ranged in age from their early twenties through to their late fifties. Many older pilots were more conservative, both politically and in their attitudes to life. While they may have swung a tad to the right, the tactics of our adversaries were too much for even the most staid of my senior colleagues. We marched in the streets as one.

The dispute involved Australia's two major domestic airlines: Ansett and Australian Airlines, as well as regional carrier, East-West Airlines, and the air cargo company, IPEC Aviation.

While many may remember our troubled times as 'The Pilots' Dispute', this is because the victors control the narrative and, not to put too fine a point on it, we pilots, the '89ers, lost.

In industrial terms, our 'limited industrial action', or 'go slow' paled in comparison with the turmoil caused by airline management and owners, the Government and the ACTU, along with the focus of a media empire run by the person who owned 50 percent of Ansett.

As the alliance of pilots who were involved, we refer to the event as 'The Airline Dispute of 1989-90', as the airlines' industrial baton far outweighed our short-lived campaign of restricting our working hours to match those of airline executives.

This story is that of an ordinary pilot, a 'grunt on the ground', and how a young family navigated what became one of our country's most bitter industrial disputes. The magic involves how such a diverse group held firm against the gale force winds that changed each of our lives forever.

This book, book 2 in my memoir trilogy, begins as I left Darwin to commence my airline career. In December of 1981, I boarded an Ansett Airlines Boeing 727. My new company's aircraft lifted from the Darwin runway, taking off into the wind as I headed home to Sydney. A short time after, I trekked further south to begin this next stage of my aviation life in Melbourne, on the 4th of January 1982.

CHAPTER 1

> 'To live is to face the storms and not cower before them.'
>
> *Last Night I Dreamed of Peace,*
> *The Diary of Dang Thuy Tram*

Trouble had been brewing for years. Older pilots lamented how things had changed since the Reg Ansett days. I'd joined since, but I did notice the aggression towards us in the last couple of years. Ansett General Manager, Graeme McMahon, was like an attack dog who felt that, for pilots to be productive, they should load the baggage. Any chance to denigrate, he'd take it. One of the most important phases of flight is pre-flight procedure, especially in new aircraft. A wrong figure entered in the performance calculation could result in insufficient thrust for take-off; flight management computers were just as prone to a fatal error as any other computer.

Everyone had their part to play as we worked together to make our company viable. The baggage handlers' job was no less important than any other, but we pilots needed to be in the cockpit. Manager McMahon's aggression displayed outwardly what was occurring within. As with all things in our company, nothing happened without Sir Peter Abeles' oversight.

Our AFAP (Australian Federation of Air Pilots) pilot leaders approached the companies again. The meeting on the 17th of August between management and staff broke down. The airlines held one position. They were like a broken record: commit to the Accord, or else. We didn't know it then, but we were wasting our time. The plan was already hatched, even down to taxpayer-funded subsidies for the airlines.

My unease was relieved, but only slightly. We didn't go on strike. I thought all in our company should be treated equally. If executives grabbed a 40 percent hike, with some pocketing even more, then why not highlight this by working the same hours?

On Friday, the 18th of August 1989, Australia's domestic pilots commenced a campaign of limited industrial action. It's important to note that our action did not involve Qantas pilots; in 1989, Qantas pilots belonged to a different association, and they only flew international routes. Our alliance of pilots worked for Ansett, Australian Airlines, East-West, and Ipec (a freight carrier). From that Friday in August, we only worked office hours, between 9:00 am and 5:00 pm. Up until then, nothing was sacred, and we were required to work any hour of the day or night, on every day of the year.

Limiting pilots' working hours disrupted the airlines' flight schedules and caused inconvenience. During our campaign, the flying public adjusted their plans and, for the most part, passengers made their journeys. As always, bland statistics never tell the full story and, while people generally did get to where they wished to go, in many cases, the reduced timetable was an inconvenience.

On Sunday the 20th of August, ministers and airline officials once again joined the Prime Minister in a meeting that was held in the Hyatt Hotel, Melbourne.

> "The chain of events, in order, started with suspending pilots who refused to work as directed; shutting down the airline system; issuing writs for damages against individual pilots and the Federation; sacking pilots and offering to rehire them on terms which isolated the Federation. It was agreed that the only way to tackle McCarthy's diametrically opposed position was to hit pilots hard and fast until they capitulated."

This quote comes from *Sky Pirates: The Pilots' Strike that Grounded Australia* by journalist Brad Norington (ABC Books 1990). Pilots were offended by this book's title and felt Norington's label belonged to our antagonists. Mr Norington provided an expert rendition of the technicalities around what had begun, but when analysing the length, width, thickness and weight of the plank, why not examine the morality of forcing someone to walk it? While this vessel may have dazzled, the heart of the matter remained hidden inside. As if a pirate was so enthralled by the intricacies of the chest's decoration that he failed to open the lid.

I did not wish to renew an agreement with which I disagreed. Australia wasn't a totalitarian state or ruled by military junta. In our democracy, people do find themselves diametrically opposed. Did Mr Norington, or anyone attending this meeting, consider that forcing capitulation, and Australia's liberal democratic freedoms, were also diametrically opposed?

The phone rang. It was crewing; I had a trip. I didn't know what to say. Eventually, I asked for details. It was a flight to Melbourne. Was I refusing this duty? As I had spent much time on reserve, I knew the crewing officer. I remained confused, and he took pity.

> "The flight's down for 4:00 pm, so you won't be going; you guys made sure of that. I just have to ring everyone, and get you all on record as refusing."
>
> "If there's no flight, then there's no need for me to crew it." I wasn't going to run down the runway flapping my arms, but this response didn't quite satisfy.
>
> "Look, I've got a lot of people to call, so could you just say what you're meant to say and be done with it?"
>
> "I refuse to crew a flight that's not scheduled to fly."
>
> "I guess that'll do. See you when all this is over."

Sir Peter Abeles' income was income, Bob Hawke's income was income, airline executives' income was income, and judges' income was income. The Prices and Incomes Accord was a farce when it came to prices, and also when it came to incomes. 'Income', for Accord purposes, meant ordinary peoples' wages and salaries.

Our former Federation executive, Len Coysh, had recently joined Ansett, becoming the Industrial Relations Manager for aircrew. He liaised with Ian Oldmeadow of personnel. Mr Oldmeadow became a driving force.

In a previous meeting, Ian Oldmeadow, as if strutting on hind legs, made it clear that our claim was preposterous. Past productivity was in the past — more fool Australian Airlines pilots for helping out in hard times and introducing a new type — and bad luck if inflation had eroded take-home pay. Wages and salaries were framed within the Accord's guidelines, and weren't open to discussion by individual unions or associations.

The third point emphasised my central gripe with the system. We'd drawn attention to skyrocketing executive remuneration. Why was there one rule for them and a different rule for everyone else? As pointed out, this comparison was clearly absurd — executive remuneration was not subject to the Accord.

In the Industrial Relations Commission (IRC), arguments between the powers that be and staff flew to and fro, but the commission was not all that impressed with the fact that we were not all that impressed with the commission. If ordinary people joined together and elected representatives who worked through pay and conditions with employers, there wouldn't be a lot to do here. This fact was possibly not lost on Justice Maddern. Justice Barry Maddern had taken over when Justice Peter Coldham retired from the IRC. He was appointed by Bob Hawke in 1986, after being recommended by his ACTU friend, Bill Kelty.

The companies argued — well, Ansett argued, and the other airlines meekly followed Abeles' lead, that as a registered union, we came under the umbrella of the IRC. Under the IRC, we should submit to the Accord's guidelines. The first statement was correct, but the second involved a leap of faith. The Accord was an agreement and not the law. If it was, there'd be no need for all the coercion for us to submit.

Before my time, the Federation of Air Pilots had registered with the Australian Conciliation and Arbitration Commission. Our hours were similar to shift work, but with differing responsibilities. We didn't fit into any particular pigeonhole. The officers of the commission coined a term, 'Sui Generis'.

At school, I had studied Latin. At the end of term exams, I failed with the distinction of not one question right. Red-faced, I left the class. I am not the one to translate but, as I understand it, Sui Generis equates to 'Special Case'. Within the commission, a tribunal was set up to deal with our situation. But, in 1989, the Conciliation and Arbitration Commission was abolished and replaced with the Industrial Relations Commission.

Justice Maddern was fast losing patience. We pilots were directed to resume normal hours by 4:00 pm on Monday the 21st of August.

I felt it a reasonable request for my representatives to speak on my behalf, directly with my employer. Actually, I felt it a democratic right. If Peter Abeles presented a case where the company needed us to pull together, in good faith, I would accept a lesser salary. Although, he may have found this a little hard to justify, with his own pockets overflowing. We could suggest he tighten his belt along with everyone else, and do his best to get by with a paltry couple-a-mil. With more in the kitty to be shared, I felt, then everyone could be afforded the opportunity to keep up.

Bill Kelty, the ACTU secretary, injected himself into the mix. Bill's ACTU cap wasn't the only one he wore. The Federal Treasurer appointed Kelty to the board of the Reserve Bank. I wonder if he sat with Peter Abeles at the monthly meetings?

If we negotiated directly with our employers, then the haunting spectre of a wages breakout threatened. But then, how had the mushroom cloud of executive remuneration not led to a wages explosion? Swaggering, this union leader gripped the helm he now shared with the government and airlines, Jolly Roger raised and cannons manned. On the sea of Australian industrial relations, the ship of parliamentary pirates (maybe a good name for a book), and all on board, swigged their rum and salivated at the thought of plunder — the enemy's rowboat off the bow.

Those at the helm argued that sharing the wealth generated by a company more equitably would increase costs, and add heat to the economy. To me, conversely, that strategy looked 'revenue neutral'. Besides, it was hard to imagine anything adding more heat than the naked greed and excess currently pumping rocket fuel into the furnace.

The question was not of adding heat, but of how the benefits of work were distributed. If ordinary people were given a fairer share which they then spent on the everyday things of life, then perhaps "a recession we had to have" may have been avoided. Employers and employees working together could then achieve the ideals touted by the Accord, which were going undelivered.

The IRC, in lockstep with the ACTU, joined with the government and airlines and morphed into a multi-headed monster. Fiery threats spat from indistinguishable orifices (or is that 'orifi'?). 'One rule for them, and one for the rest' may have been the norm in Edwardian England, but it wasn't in line with the spirit of our country. I didn't subscribe to their *Upstairs, Downstairs* philosophy, and I didn't work after five on Monday the 21st of August. Nor did any other pilot.

The newspapers railed against us. Considering who owned half our airline, I felt that some reports smelt a touch of the fox guarding the henhouse. While certain journalists bypassed even basic research, others recycled old insults. 'Greedy fat cats' and 'lemmings to the cliff' were rehashed ad nauseam, as if journalistic birch.

We were warned. We had taken industrial action and had to accept the consequences. Anyone who stomped down this same path could expect the same treatment. Just two days earlier, *The Australian* reported, 'Industrial chaos hits Vic'. Trains stopped, power was shut off, the wharves lay idle, and threats were coming from metal workers. On top of this, Simon Crean, the president of the ACTU, listed several demands. A special conference to discuss the latest version of the wages system was scheduled for the 7th of

September. As Mr Crean directed, "Until that time, no union is to give a commitment."

Anyone who thought pilots working the normal hours of a large section of the community was any different to stopping the nation's fuel, halting exports and imports, shutting off power, or causing damage on building sites was a babe in the industrial woods. If we engaged in such thuggery, then we could expect the same harsh treatment.

With a downturned mouth, as if he'd just bitten into the sourest of lemons, and using the same logic as if addressing the football team "and its members", Prime Minister Hawke expressed his ire:

> "The simple position with which we're faced is that we have an organisation, the Federation of Air Pilots and their members who seek to put themselves above and beyond the community by an unacceptably greedy grab for remuneration."

Perhaps, the more than 30 percent destined for his own pocket had slipped Hawke's mind, as if a melting Snowball, and with not the slightest thought of glass houses, Mr Hawke spent less than two minutes totalling his position. Maybe, his system of thought was focused on what was written on Australia's barn wall, in need of a quick revision.

Even with the old commission abolished, pilots must have still been considered 'Sui Generis'. We didn't take sledge hammers to aircraft, shut off the nation's power supply or threaten to bring our country to its knees. That said, by restricting working hours, we blew any claim to being viewed as 'pure as the driven snow'.

During this period, aircraft only flew executive hours. Well, not quite, as we also worked weekends, but this still proved inconvenient. The inconvenience imposed by our actions, however, did not approach the weight those in the ACTU brought to bear on our country's legs.

Later that day, the 21st of August, Justice Maddern cancelled our awards. It took more than a year and a Royal Commission to deregister the Builders Labourers but, for us, our agreement ended after just days. Who would have thought that possible?

John Raby, another pilot association executive, attended the hearings at Nauru House, a Melbourne skyscraper on Collins Street. The view from the IRC floor was striking, and it illustrated, in part, the industrial chaos hitting Victoria. From this vantage point, Captain Raby observed the results of the current shipping dispute:

> "The whole of Port Phillip Bay was covered in ships swinging at anchor which couldn't get into the Port of Melbourne."

Hitting hard and fast, also on the 21st of August, Bob Hawke declared war on us, and the airline companies sent out letters. The letters required our commitment to full services by 10:00 pm the following evening, or face dismissal. I'd had better days.

Over the next two days, events sunk in. It took a few phone calls to those more well-versed, but a pattern emerged. Cancelling our awards had cancelled any recourse through industrial law, opening the way for common law.

I wasn't yet aware of the meeting in the Prime Minister's office on the 15th of August. Had I been, I probably would have noted that things were progressing much to plan. Union heavyweight Bill Kelty vetted new pilot contracts. Nurturing the newborn document, he not only gave his stamp of approval, but lent his name. The leader of the ACTU and purveyor of individual contracts; how ironic was that?

Sir Peter Abeles occupied the left seat, Rupert Murdoch handled paperwork, the government and ACTU positioned on each wing, and the IRC scrambled when needed. Somewhat outgunned, both 'precarious' and 'situation' were two words that complemented each other, in our one sentence.

To communicate, each AFAP branch set up a telephone chain. Pilots were divided into groups of roughly a dozen people. When a message came through, the leader called each in the group.

On the afternoon of the 23rd of August, the phone rang. A special briefing was scheduled at the Federation office. My report time was set for 8:00 that night. Wondering what this was all about, I faced another problem. I didn't know where the Federation office was. A phone call remedied this and that evening I drove to Breakfast Creek in Brisbane.

I arrived as a group left the venue. I asked one of them what was going on. Ashen-faced, Brett said it was best if I waited for my briefing. The Federation rep, Brian Henderson, who was up from down south, gathered our group together. We moved to a small room off the foyer.

Henderson started by outlining events so far. I guess it was his way of settling us down. Next, he detailed several professions, including the politicians, who'd scored big pay rises. Did they really believe no one would think, 'what a double standard'?

The tide seeding in my gut crept outwards, then upwards. Each breath I drew deeper, with each of Brian's words, sharper than the last. With our industrial awards shattered, the doors to common law thrust open:

> "We have reason to believe the companies may commence serving writs against individual pilots tomorrow morning."
>
> The room fell deathly silent.
>
> Our rep continued, "We've spoken with our legal advisers, and their opinion is a person can't be sued by a company if that person is not an employee of the company."

If the room felt quiet before, the air now hung so thick that a Paul Keating insult would have trouble cutting through it.

As a precaution, our resignations would be held, and only submitted if the companies signalled their intent to serve these writs. With the seriousness of the situation hitting home, Henderson asked if any of us had anything to say, any questions or suggestions.

A Captain I had recently flown with asked, "If we all resign, then what's to stop the companies picking us off one by one?"

> The answer was simple and one I took comfort in.
> "We will all resign together, and we will all go back together."

Our only protection was us. If we all stood as one, each pilot and family linked in an unbroken chain, then each ensured the safety of the other.

CHAPTER 2

A light breeze skimmed the T tail of the 727 as it lifted off the Darwin runway. The hush power of the three JT8Ds whispered as we climbed. From my window seat, I took in an uninterrupted view of Darwin Harbour's blue waters.

Returning home would take mere hours as opposed to the usual long drive. In place of crossed fingers, I had an appointment with a destiny I'd chased since setting out on that first trip, driving down Highway 1. Casting my eyes towards the flight deck, I peered down the long, cylindrical cabin. Outside, the wet season's cumulus built higher skyward and I wondered where fate's eyes would rest, and what the future might bring.

The Brisbane stopover wasn't long, but it was long enough to remind me of its uniqueness. Strolling across the tarmac to the old, arch-roofed terminal, I remembered my first time here. One short visit since had served to reinforce the relaxed and casual atmosphere.

Brisbane to Sydney took just over an hour and, on approach, the crew dimmed the cabin lights for our evening arrival. A ferry twinkled its way home from Manly as, through the left windows, skyline colours of orange, red, green, and a smattering of blue turned the city lights and structures into jewels, with the Harbour bridge a tiara on the quay. Dad had often marvelled at the ingenuity of the bridge's design. Well before the days of computers, engineers had poured over blueprints using longhand and slide rules to design our graceful 'coat hanger'. During construction in the 1920s, 16 men had lost their lives. Dad recounted the story of one who cheated death. Apparently, he had dropped his hammer before falling. His tool broke the water's surface, allowing his survival.

Across the quay, my eyes fixed on the magnificence of the Opera House. White floodlit sails jutted into Port Jackson. The Sydney Harbour Bridge and Opera House are not only synonymous with this city, but as internationally renowned icons of our country.

Although only young at the time, I remember the controversy surrounding this iconic building. The architect, Jørn Utzon, was something of a dreamer, incapable of realising his vision. This false narrative was pushed by a government that, if not for a trade union's Green Bans, would have savaged much of our city's heritage with wrecking balls.

The Boeing touched down smoothly in a light crosswind. Mum was there to meet me. We hugged and I asked how she was.

"I'm fine, how about you? Congratulations!"

My length of absence was less than the last, but the hugs and handshakes were just as ardent. Preparations for Christmas 1981 were in full swing and, as usual, our relatives spent the day with us.

I needed to make arrangements, but most hinged on the car arriving. I'd planned to unload my gear, then drive on to Melbourne. When I had left Darwin, the trucking company estimated the car's arrival would coincide with my return to Sydney. Unfortunately, the truck had needed to drop off trailers along the way in Brisbane. When I rang, the freight company advised that my car would arrive in a few days. This left very little time before Christmas. While this was bad news for me, it was not so for the truck driver who decided to head home for Christmas. My car would spend the festive season with his family. Up in the Territory, flying to remote outposts, I often crossed paths with long-haul drivers as they traversed outback roads in their Kenworths, Macks and Peterbilts. Truckies worked long and hard, and felt the same affinity with their rigs as we pilots did with our aircraft. Despite the inconvenience, I wished him well for Christmas.

I called Ansett and they issued a ticket through Sydney's Oxford Street office. Now I'd make my way to Melbourne by jet, and return on the first weekend, to drive the car down then.

Christmas arrived, together with our relatives. Chicken, ham and pork joined the potato and green salads, along with beetroot, fresh bread and apple sauce washed down with a few festive drinks and good cheer. The Liberal party were in power and, while this did not sit well with Uncle Bede, Uncle Alex was pleased. Whenever conversation, even vaguely, headed in this direction, comments turned to the weather. It was agreed that the day was pleasant, with the coolness appreciated after the many, far hotter Christmases of the past.

The time between Christmas and leaving for Melbourne provided a good chance to catch up with friends. I visited Gemma and Paul. Paul and I had been best friends through school and we'd met Gemma in our senior years. While I was up in the Territory, they'd become Mr and Mrs. I dropped by to see Liz. Liz was another friend I'd known since our school years and often afternoons melted into evening as we chatted. The last time Liz and I had spent so much time talking was before I'd left for Darwin in May 1980.

> Her Mum joined us and asked if Liz had told me her news.
> "No, not yet," Liz replied. She turned to me. "Carl and I are getting married."

The couple had been together since our early years out of school. I wished them well. The years were rolling on, and we were all taking our next steps in life.

Paul arranged a get together of our former rock band members at a local pub. It was good to catch up with these friends, and laughter and reminiscing filled the evening. While renewing old friendships and spending time with Sydney mates, I couldn't help but think of those left behind in Darwin. I didn't know I could miss a place so much, not to mention the friends.

The new year of 1982 marked the start of a new phase. On Sunday the 3rd of January, with just under 2,000 hours in my Pilot's logbook, I left for Melbourne. The Travelodge next door to the Ansett training centre was too expensive for a week's stay, so I found a small motel with a shuttle bus to the airport and unpacked my few belongings.

On Monday morning I reported for my first day with Ansett, together with 20 others. Ushered into a classroom in the training section, our initial training would commence in Melbourne. After that, we would take up our basing. Before training commenced, however, we needed to be sorted by aircraft. Usually, intake pilots filled slots on the most junior type, the F27 Fokker Friendship. Due to Ansett's rapid expansion and vacancies left by promotions, however, several positions had opened up on other types.

Which aircraft each pilot was assigned depended on two major factors that would dictate what happened throughout our careers — where we were prepared to live, and our seniority numbers. Seniority was based on joining date. As our course was filled with 21 new recruits, Ansett sorted us further, by date of birth. Looking to the future, the company recruited pilots across a broad age range. This, we later learnt, was to spread out retirements. They certainly took a long-term view.

Our most senior classmate was 29, and he'd flown Mirage fighters in the RAAF. The next, at 28, was a long-serving General Aviation (GA) pilot with turbine experience. Following him, and 27, was another experienced GA pilot. Next on the list was another from the Air Force. He flew the BAC-111 with VIP Squadron. The following numbers went to three pilots with many GA twin hours. And I slotted in below these. Together we made up the 'senior citizens' of our intake. The youngest recruit of all was just 20 years old.

The time came to exercise the privileges of our brand-new seniority numbers. Most vacancies were on the F27, however, a couple of slots were open on the F28 and one on the Electra. Ansett had developed a unique way of referring to the types. The Boeing 727 was easy. As it was the only Boeing, it was known as 'The Boeing'. Later, when other Boeings joined the fleet, they were known by model numbers. The MacDonnell Douglas DC-9 was 'The DC-9' or just 'The Nine' and, to those who flew it, it was 'The Diesel Nine'. There were two Fokker types. The F27, with its turboprops, was known equally by this designator, 'The Friendship', or simply

'The Fokker'. The F28 Fokker Fellowship was a jet. Although just as much a Fokker, it was labelled simply 'The F28'. The Lockheed Electra L-188 was immediately recognisable as 'The Electra' or 'L-188', and it was launched at Ansett as a passenger aircraft.

At that time, the Two Airline Policy stipulated similar departure times and it also dictated the same aircraft types for both the commercial Ansett-ANA and the government-run TAA (Trans Australia Airlines). Although it had begun as a domestic airline between Queensland and the Northern Territory, Qantas, at that stage, was a purely international carrier. Airline founder Reg Ansett preferred the Electra, but TAA differed. Eventually, a compromise was struck, with Qantas somehow involved, which resulted in three Electras delivered to Ansett.

My partner Sharon and I had discussed where we preferred to live. Coming from the laid-back lifestyle of the Territory, we didn't want to live in either of the big city centres. The F28 was based in Perth, but we were warned only to bid if we had turbine time. New recruits usually commenced on the turboprop and then, after building experience, transitioned to jets.

We submitted our bid sheets. The F28 slots went to our most senior member, along with another from a previous intake. The L-188 was awarded to our high time, turbine experienced classmate. The F27 operated from three bases. With some bids successful and others not, the rest of us filled positions in these three cities.

We spent the remaining three days of that week reviewing a subject we'd all passed, Basic Gas Turbines. The following week, with those on other aircraft-types moving to different classrooms, we began our F27-specific training. Ground school was held during office hours and, after class on Friday afternoon, we were free for the weekend. On that first Friday evening, I returned to Sydney.

My car had arrived, so Dad drove me to the yard where we were reunited. Back home, I unloaded my gear and set the stereo up in the lounge room. I wouldn't need it for a while, so I figured that Mum and Dad may as well use it. I had wanted to take something home for Dad. Before dropping the car at the Darwin transport depot, I had stopped at a bottle shop. With my gear unloaded at my parent's place, I leaned in to the small space behind the seat where I kept my old hammer and nail bag.

> "I've got a couple of beers here, Dad. Maybe we can pop 'em in the fridge for later."
> "Sounds like a good idea."
> I slipped the first bottle from the protective towel. Dad's eyes nearly popped out of his head at the size of them. "What are they?"
> "Darwin Stubbies, NT Draught."
> "Good drop?"
> "Yeah, I like it."

After a quiet night, early next morning I packed essential items and set off down the Hume Highway. Given the 1,000-kilometre haul, there was plenty of time for cassettes and reflection. Training would be tough, but once through I could look forward to a long career. When senior enough, I could fly jets, with the security the airline provided. This last point was a relief as, unlike when I left for Darwin, now I wasn't the only one to consider.

Until I had started to fly, I was Sydney-centric. Everyone I'd met and every place I had visited since had not only added something, but had changed how I felt about other places. Dwelling on this, I picked up the highway to Melbourne. My old hometown of Sydney, once the centre of my universe, had become a nice place to visit. Where would Sharon and I settle? The job security was comforting. As the saying went, "A job with Ansett, is a job for life."

Arriving late afternoon, I booked in at a motel. The next day, I needed to find somewhere to live. A senior classmate, who was from Shepparton in Victoria, was also staying at the same motel. His wife was due to arrive shortly and, on the previous Thursday, I had tagged along as he looked for somewhere to rent. We visited Sunbury, north-west of the airport, and Greg took one of the few places on offer. That Monday afternoon, I returned there in the hope of renting one of the other houses.

"Mate, you should've taken one then. They're gone now," the agent said.

The rental market was tight, and it took until Friday, and many visits to estate agents, before I secured a flat in Moonee Ponds. Two bedrooms and a bathroom, a standard layout — I signed before I'd even seen it. It was somewhere to live, which met the requirement for our time in Melbourne. I took the foam mattress from the car and, together with a couple of pillows, sheets and a blanket, my bed lay on the floor of the main bedroom. The few plates and cutlery from home joined the fold-up card table and two director's chairs I'd recently bought. These completed furnishings.

The five-week module covered every facet of aircraft systems. In years to follow, ground schools would become computerised, and teaching and assessment would move to a screen, backed up with practical lessons in fixed base simulators. In the 'Chalk and Talk' times of 1982, however, we sat in a classroom, and our instructors guided us in person. We studied the function of engines, electrics, hydraulics, and pneumatics, and the workings of landing gear and flaps, and all that went into the makeup of this aging aircraft. Despite their age, the F27s were kept in excellent condition and were the workhorses of regional Australia.

Our course participants included a wide range of pilots who, like me, had moved around. Despite varying experience and ages, it wasn't long before we felt a bond. Our former VIP squadron member told of transporting Prime Ministers and senior government figures, and our youngest shared stories of trips around Moorabbin. As always, there was another Paul. His last name sounded a little like anus, so he became affectionately known as 'Paul Bum'.

The F27 was a complicated aircraft, especially when it came to the electrical system. My feelings towards electrics hadn't changed since my days on building sites, which, unfortunately, didn't coincide with Ansett's view. The machine had two generators, each fitted to an accessory gear box attached to the engines. These generators provided electrical power. This, I felt, provided a good explanation but, sadly, it fell short of the depth required. On high power settings, the engines spun at high revs, and on low settings the opposite. This wasn't a good thing when it came to generating stable electrical power. Skilled boffins devised a system based on planetary gearing. This converted the varying engine revolutions to the constant speed necessary for generators.

To emphasise this, our instructor, an engineer on loan from that department, wheeled in a trolley with an old, constant speed drive unit. With the casing cut away, the planetary gears were visible. The electrical system used alternating current and direct current (but without the driving rhythm I associated with AC/DC). Bus Bars, Transformer Rectifier Units, Inverters, and all manner of switching featured in this delivery of electrical power. Our manuals showed numerous complex circuit diagrams indicating electrical flow, with breakers open, and then closed.

One classmate was earning a reputation. He asked many questions and delved into great depth. He worried and stewed over every aspect. He fussed like a mother hen, so became known as 'Mother Steve'. To one of Steve's complex questions, our even-tempered instructor replied, "Look, you're pilots. You don't have to build one." We all breathed out a collective sigh of relief. "You only need an overview as to how it works, and what to do when it doesn't."

The overview provided an understanding of the system's operation, especially during an emergency. Some problems required an immediate response, such as engine fire or severe damage. These were known as 'Phase One Emergency actions'. We memorised these and executed them in a timely manner. Lists of emergency drills were kept in a booklet, the *Quick Reference Handbook* (QRH), next to each pilot station. After completing the memorised tasks, we referred to the QRH.

Mother Steve was at it again. He wanted to know the tiniest of details.

Our instructor, exasperated, replied, "OK, when it comes right down to it, the F27 electrical system functions using one simple principle, PFM."

There was an audible groan. Why did everything have to be abbreviated to three capital letters?

We all looked to him, and he looked back at us.

"None of you seem to understand, so I'll write it on the board."

In big letters the instructor wrote P, underneath F, and on the bottom, M. Next to 'P', he wrote *Pure*. Against 'F' went a descriptive qualifier, which applied to the last letter, *Magic*. With this, the function of the F27 Fokker Friendship's electrical system became crystal clear.

Ground school was structured to enable pilots to commute from their bases. Monday start times and finish times on Fridays allowed for travel. I was in Melbourne, but others who were changing aircraft types were travelling from different bases. Ansett would shortly introduce the Boeing 737-200 (Advanced), phasing out the DC-9. This was an interim measure until the more modern 737-300 arrived. Later in 1982, the first Boeing 767 was due. In addition, long range variants of the 727 formed another part of this comprehensive fleet upgrade, so the training centre was a hive of activity.

By the end of our second week, we had completed several exams. I was especially excited as Sharon was due that Friday afternoon. After ground school ended, I had a few hours to wait before the Darwin service arrived. Rather than return to the flat, I dropped by Essendon airport. With my new ID card, I could access the tarmac. Passing the time, I wandered around a rich assortment of aircraft.

IPEC was a freight company. Jimmy, one of my former NTAC colleagues, had a job with them, flying the Argosy. I spent time checking out this big old turboprop. This, the last aircraft produced by Armstrong Whitworth, used the same Rolls Royce engines as the F27, but it had four of them.

A task needed my attention. While not urgent, it would become so. I'd been thinking, and had considered several options. My leaning was towards the traditional. There were fads, others came in and out of fashion, and certain choices could be quite original. We had agreed that, if a girl, I could suggest the name and, if a boy, Sharon would have first choice. Names are such that, I found that if I liked a person, then I usually liked their name. I was conscious too that consideration lay not only with those giving, but to the one receiving, as this decision would last a lifetime.

The Argosy's doors stood open. I climbed in, mounted the ladder, and sat in the cockpit. After checking out the instrument panels, I cast my eyes outside over the expanse of aircraft. Scanning the range, from single engine trainers to sophisticated business jets, I settled on my choice. A feeling somewhere deep inside, something I couldn't quite put my finger on was, perhaps, intuitive. I felt that we'd have a girl. If so, and with Sharon's approval, my choice would be a favourite, Rebecca.

The time came to return to Tullamarine. The Boeing taxied in. Several passengers marched up the aerobridge and Sharon came through the door looking radiant.

We hugged. "How are you? How was your trip? You look great."

Her hand touched her gently protruding tummy. "Good. And the trip was fine, just a little long."

Walking back to the car, she asked, "So, where do we live?"

"Not far from Dame Edna."

"Eh?"

"The flat's in Moonee Ponds."

Sharon had lived in Melbourne before, so she knew the layout.

"I'm sorry, but we don't have much in the way of conveniences. It's unfurnished. We can get some things tomorrow."

"Have you been cooking?"
"Nah. Ansett has a canteen at the airport. Other times, it's been takeaway."
This comment was met with a frown.

Back at the flat, Sharon unpacked while I grabbed something for dinner. Next morning, we visited a shopping plaza. Completely lost, I drove while Sharon directed. The first item on our list was a refrigerator. In an electrical shop, a bar fridge was on display. This sufficed, so I handed over my card. We wheeled it out to the carpark and loaded it into the back of the van. We bought a few more things and returned to the flat.

To celebrate Sharon's arrival, we had planned a night in Melbourne city. Remembering my last attempt at city driving, I was reticent.

"We can take the tram. It's easy," Sharon suggested.

The night was warm, so we wandered around. With Sharon still leading, we strolled past shops, arcades and eateries, by larger buildings that sprouted water features and fountains. We found a small restaurant for dinner, and Sharon then guided us back to Moonee Ponds. After a Sunday drive, before we knew it, the weekend was over.

CHAPTER 3

Battling our way through ground school, my classmates and I had been at it for over a month. In mid-February we completed our final exam and progressed to the next phase, Emergency Procedures. We would become familiar with fire suppressant, portable oxygen, survival equipment, smoke flares, and signalling devices. In addition to classroom exercises, we joined the new flight attendants for 'ditching routines'. The company booked a local swimming pool, where we learnt how to evacuate and launch life rafts. We swam in heavy overalls, with life jackets over our clothes, and boarded the rafts from the water.

Over the following week, we were scheduled for sessions in the Link Trainer. A basic simulator, the Link Trainer had limited movement and looked like a black, oblong box on scissor jacks. As we practised letdowns and approaches, the trainer's computers recorded our progress with a stylus on a barrel drum.

We also rode the jump seat on scheduled services. After eight sectors, we could commence aircraft endorsement. In the meantime, we studied our *Quick Reference Handbooks* and other manuals. We were expected to know the Phase One emergency items by heart, with a working knowledge of all other procedures.

From Melbourne, the F27 ran to Tasmania, regional Victoria, and the South Australian port of Mount Gambia. For the first time, I dressed in my brand new uniform and sat behind the Captain and First Officer in the extra cockpit seat. Alex, the FO, briefed me on the route to Devonport and then Wynyard, with return to Melbourne. This was exciting in itself, but it was also my first visit to Tasmania.

The junior flight attendant, Michelle, introduced herself and asked where I'd be based.

> "My Dad's a Captain there. You'll probably get to fly with him."

The timing of endorsement training depended on our base. Most trainees bid for Sydney or Melbourne but, as Sharon and I had agreed to shun these two big cities and there were four vacancies at the third base, I opted for one of these. Two of my base colleagues were Melbournians and the other was from Perth. All three requested Melbourne but, being the most junior, they missed out. My age placed me in the top half of our intake, so I experienced the more pleasant side of the system.

Melbourne was alright, but Sharon had warned me that the winter weather could be miserable. For Melbournians, grey skies and bitter winds were normal but, for a Territorian, the cold was a major negative. To me, Melbourne was similar to Sydney in that people were all pent up, and they rushed around as if there was no tomorrow. In the Territory, no one gave a second thought to all the unimportant things. Life for those in these two great southern cities, it seemed, was viewed in the opposite way.

Sydney was beautiful. I viewed it as one of the most beautiful cities in the world (although I hadn't yet travelled beyond our shores). Of the photos I'd seen of major metropolises around the world, none came close to Australia's harbour city. The problem, though, was the same as in Melbourne — this manic pace. There was no way a sedate amble through Smith Street Mall in Darwin could be replicated in the human pinball machines of Pitt and Bourke Streets.

Sharon was born in Nowra when her dad was in the Navy and, with me from Sydney, we were typical of many who thought of themselves as Territorians. If we couldn't live there, we wanted to live somewhere smaller than the two big capitals. Brisbane would have been ideal, and the closest to our adopted lifestyle. Unfortunately, Brisbane wasn't an F27 base.

We met in Ansett's Melbourne crew room, an upstairs section of Tullamarine Airport. Four Check Captains were assigned to instruct the eight trainees for this session of endorsements. An F27 waited in the northern Tasmanian city of Launceston, and our group was rostered to position down there shortly. During this meeting, we learnt another aspect of Ansett culture. The company operated on a first name basis. The most junior First Officer addressed the most senior Captain by their first name. Superintendent Command and Intake Training Captain Raby was one of the four instructors, but he only answered to John. Now I understood why friends who had joined earlier referred to the Chief Pilot, Captain Theunissen, as Henry.

Different companies had differing philosophies. Qantas, I heard, expected Captains to be addressed as such. If familiar, this could be substituted with 'Skipper', and, if best friends, perhaps 'Skip'. It made little difference as long as the pilots on the flight deck communicated. Given the choice, I preferred 'The Ansett Way'.

Stephan and I were sequenced together. Sharing endorsement training we'd be known as 'crash buddies'. We were assigned to Captain Derek Scherer's care. Derek had emigrated from Austria as a teenager. He still possessed a partial Austrian accent, so this mix with his adopted country's accent proved interesting. He'd also embraced the language, especially the more colourful aspects.

> "C'mon you two. We've still got time. We'll go downstairs and get the bloody walk around out the way."

Dutifully following our Captain, we progressed through various corridors, down lifts, and along passageways that resembled a rabbit warren behind the public areas of the airport. On the tarmac, an F27 was between flights. Derek led us around, pointing out what needed to be checked, and how, before flight. He was economical when it came to words, spoken in his interesting accent. If he said mate, it sounded like 'mite'.

When I had started out on the building site with my Dad, I was exposed to regular use of the 'F' word. All the trades let these fly, but this was especially so when drainers turned up. Theirs was a family business, handed down from father to three sons. They dug their trenches and fitted their pipes, while turning the air blue. Within half an hour, there was more profanity than in Kevin Bloody Wilson's *I want to be a builder* skit.

Dad had explained to me that swearing was not all that necessary, except in extreme circumstances (and I can remember one or two). It would appear that our Austrian instructor Derek's father had provided no such briefing.

> "What types did you fly before?"
> Stephan answered, "The BN2 Islander."
> I added, "'Beechcraft Barons and Cessna 402s."
> "At least you've flown twins," Derek replied. "But still, should be f…ing interesting."

On arrival in Launceston, instructors and trainees arranged to meet for dinner. Next morning, we were up and out at the airport early. Derek gave his briefing. Today focused on 'general handling'. Stephan opted to go first, and took the right seat for take-off. Raising the gear as commanded and bringing the flaps in, we were underway. Derek handed over to Stephan. Through turns, climbs, and descents, Stephan felt the weight in the controls.

> "It's not a light twin, mite," Derek advised.
> After Stephan completed his routine, we changed seats. Grabbing the yoke and initiating a turn, I had the same feeling.
> "What'd ya bloody expect?" Derek commented. "It's not a bloody four-oh-two."

Taking note of Derek's guidance, I wrestled the monster, and managed to execute the planned exercises. Lesson complete, we headed back to the airport and Derek took control. I lowered the gear and ran the flaps as we came in for a silky-smooth touchdown. If the aircraft landed like this, perhaps it wasn't as hard to manage as I had imagined.

The following day, by the end of my sequence, I was feeling a little more comfortable, but the controls still felt heavy. Swapping seats, it was Stephan's turn. After completing the session, we returned and handed over to the next crew. On the way back to the hotel, Derek was talkative.

> "You'll get the hang of it. It's just another bloody aeroplane."

The next day, with more handling came a change. The controls felt less weighty and more normal. As we anticipated turns, they became easier, as did other manoeuvres. We returned to the airport to practise circuits.

> "You're driving, so you may as well do the landing," Derek said.

We motored around the pattern. Derek pattered and I hung on, managing to stay ahead, but only just. I called for gear down and the last stage of flap. Over the threshold, I gently reduced the power. *BANG*! The whole aircraft shuddered and shook as, rejected by the bitumen, we bounced back into the air. Derek grabbed the yoke and coaxed it to the ground. Here we learnt not only of his embrace of the language, but his inquisitive nature.

> "What the f--- were you doing?" To this, he added, "You forgot to flare."
> Well, not really. I was just about to …

The F27 was not the only one shaken as we lined up on the runway. On my next approach, I flared higher and, when the wheels contacted the surface, they stayed there.

"That's more bloody well like it."

During the next few circuits, landings became progressively smoother, for both Stephan and me, and soon we needed to fit in with the normal traffic at Launceston. On one run, Derek was just about to tell me about an approaching jet, but I'd already commenced the turn. From the corner of my eye, I caught a fleeting smile. At the end of our final session, we taxied in. As well as the local language, Derek was up with Australian history too.

> "Neither of you are Kingsford bloody Smith, but Rome wasn't built in a day. You'll become more polished with experience."

By this final session, Stephan and I had come to realise that Derek was born into a culture that was perhaps more direct than ours. His briefings were thorough, and he always bought us an evening beer. He was apt to call a spade a shovel, but Derek's bark was worse than his bite and, in the briefing room, he signed the forms. With another hurdle cleared, we were relieved and grateful for Derek's kind words. On the 28th of March, we qualified for our brand new Airline Transport Pilot Licence, emblazoned with Second Class F27 Fokker Friendship endorsement.

The next phase was First Officer Line Training, which would commence in our base. Back in Melbourne, we didn't have time to spare. While we'd remain on our initial salary until our 'Clearance to Line' check, we were on the payroll, at $13,151 per annum.

Sharon and I had given notice on the flat before I left for Launceston and, as I needed to report to base the following day, we planned to leave on the 30th. Marcus, a young classmate, suggested we travel in convoy, so the next morning, we met and commenced the drive. The car and I had travelled this route before. Guiding the machine to the open road, I was reminded of earlier trips. This life we'd chosen would be spent, in varying degrees, defying the wind, but the choice of music today was Sharon's.

At nearly 27, I had spent much of the past seven years with my panel van, tracking over vast swaths of our country. Marcus followed in his Toyota Celica, and Sharon sat beside on the bench seat with our other little passenger. The van purred like a kitten, as usual. The Ansett subsidiary, Airlines of South Australia (ASA), was expecting four, brand-new First Officers. My friends Dominic and Stephan flew across and, before the sun set on this March day in 1982, we all arrived into the City of Churches.

CHAPTER 4

"This sure is a wide street."
"Yep, the widest of any Australian city."
"What's it called? I didn't catch the name."
"King William. We need to turn left up here. It's the way to the airport. We can look for somewhere to stay the night."

With Marcus still following, Sharon and I found a pub, so we took a couple of rooms. Next morning, we drove the short distance to the airport. Sharon waited in the car. Marcus and I approached the Ansett information desk and were directed to the Airlines of South Australia offices at the right of the terminal.

Captain Tony Mooy, the Operations Manager, welcomed us, "Have a seat."

Our files lay on his desk. We needed to change our ID cards to reflect the new basing, and our licences were still being processed. In the meantime, we could take 'jump seat' rides. In usual Ansett fashion, we were both scheduled for flights that afternoon.

With just three aircraft, the ASA section of Ansett was compact, with an operations counter and three Dispatch Officers, Bob, Dean and Don. Beside were desks for the Ansett Traffic Officers. This crew handled ground operations for jet services and the ASA F27s.

ASA's Administration Manager Ian Bucham (shortened to 'Buck') sat in the centre of the admin area. Past Buck's office was the crew room, which housed the pilots' mailboxes. Both ASA and Ansett Mainline crews could use this room to relax between flights.

Returning to the car, our priority was finding somewhere to stay. Thankfully, the rental market wasn't as tight as in Melbourne, and the agent showed us through a couple of flats. One on the ground floor of a block in Kurralta Park, next to the Anzac Highway, was not far from the airport. As it had no steps to climb and a small front courtyard, we signed the paperwork. Partly furnished, a bed stood in each of the two bedrooms, a loungeroom sofa with coffee table filled the living room, and a small fridge meant that our bar fridge could revert to its original purpose.

After unloading our few possessions, I needed to return for my observation flight. I changed into my uniform and we drove back to the airport.

My first flight was to Whyalla. I'd met the First Officer before. Geoff had joined Connair in 1979, and had worked with Northern Airlines until they folded. Then, he flew the Nomad with Northern Territory Aerial Work (NTAW). I had first bumped into Geoff on the Darwin tarmac because their hangar was just up from NTAC's. He had transferred to Ansett in August of the previous year.

After showing me where to sign on, they took me upstairs to the Department of Transport (DOT) briefing section. We checked notices relevant to the flight and were briefed on weather affecting departure, destination, and alternate airports. Then, we worked on and filed our flight plan. Back to the office and then the tarmac, I accompanied Geoff on his walk around.

In the cockpit, the Captain set up for departure and Geoff listed procedures as they readied the aircraft for flight. This was good experience for my fast-approaching time in the right seat. The flight attendants arrived, and the two girls were as friendly as everyone else in this close-knit operation. One of the many First Officer responsibilities was to complete the load sheet, and Geoff gave a practical demonstration on the turnaround.

On return to Adelaide, I changed aircraft. The FO was another I knew. Brett had been a class ahead at the Cessnock flying academy we both attended in NSW's Hunter Valley. I once lobbed a lift home with him in his GTR XU-1 Torana, which he aced in record time. There was a story he was pulled over just out of Cessnock (momentarily exceeding the speed limit). The cop's initial volley was laced with sarcasm.

"OK, son, let's see your pilot's licence."

Returning the Officer's serve, Brett produced his Flight Crew licence. The rumour was, it didn't help matters.

Back in Adelaide I picked up my new roster. My line training was scheduled to commence on Sunday, the 4th of April. It was evening by the time we arrived home. Sharon had found a supermarket, so we used our basic cooking utensils and shared our first meal, in our new home, in our new city.

Geoff and I weren't the only former Darwin pilots to bid for Adelaide. My friend Dave had requested the same. Dave and I had worked together at NTAC, and he joined Ansett on the intake ahead of me. I guess he and his partner, Coralee, had the same discussion as Sharon and me. He'd recently been 'Cleared to line', so it'd be good to catch up with them.

Over the next few days, we found a laundromat. We'd need to think about buying a machine. I set the second bedroom up as a study using the card table for a desk. As there was no dining table, we moved the furniture back to the loungeroom at mealtimes.

The day arrived for my first 'line flight'. I was assigned to a Training Captain, Jim, who'd guide me through to 'checkout'. This training usually took six to eight weeks, depending on sectors flown and individual progress. I would forever think of him as Captain Jim, but he'd only respond to Jim. As I was trainee, a 'Safety First Officer' was rostered for the first few sectors. Sitting in the jump seat, he provided an extra set of eyes in the cockpit. Our first flight was to Kingscote, before returning to Adelaide and then up to Broken Hill. Jim did the flying, while I became familiar with my FO backup duties.

The next day, the sequence was Port Lincoln, Adelaide, Whyalla, and back to Adelaide. Now accustomed to my right-seat duties, Jim passed control to me. Aircraft, passengers, and crew rolled down the runway. After the odd bump from the nosewheel and concave centre lights, we broke free and lifted into the air. As we turned onto our outbound track, the machine responded to the control wheel, with light pressure on the rudder. I relaxed, or perhaps was a little less tense, during cruise, and then commenced descent. Gripping the wheel with my right hand and adjusting throttles with the left, I entered the circuit.

While I was too busy to look, I could sense a small farmhouse to the left of Runway 19. With the gear extended and a high-pitched dog whistle whine, this now familiar airport was combined with a not-so-familiar aircraft. My first landing was a little harder than I would've liked. Jim reinforced what I was just learning. The aircraft handled differently when loaded with passengers and luggage.

On the final stretch returning to Adelaide, we found time for casual conversation.

> "Where'd you fly before?"
> I gave a brief outline of my time in Darwin.
> "You must have had twin time to get that job. Where did you start off?"
> "Actually, my first job was here."
> "South Australia?"
> "Yep, Port Lincoln. I started out fish spotting."
> Jim listened as I told him how a stranger's tip at Parafield led to the lucky break in Lincoln.
> "So now you're back."

The next day took us to Whyalla and Broken Hill. The following day involved the regular charter flight to Moomba, with a Whyalla return. Moomba is a company town associated with the gas and oil fields of the Cooper and Eromanga Basins. Almost due north of Adelaide, Moomba didn't have permanent residents; we flew workers in and out. These sectors, each taking two hours, were viewed as ASA's 'long haul' flights.

On the way up, I asked Jim how he came to be here.

"I'm originally from Adelaide, but started in the airlines with Ansett-ANA. I flew the DC-6B as a First Officer, based in Melbourne. After about three years, there were positions going with ASA. It was a chance to return home, so I transferred back." Jim reached forward and adjusted the heading bug. "ASA operated DC-3s and then the Convair 440. I flew both. When they introduced the Friendship, I was upgraded to command."

Jim had since been further promoted to Training Captain. I spent this month and most of the next benefiting from the depth of his vast experience and infinite patience.

On the fifth day, after flying up to Broken Hill and back, we left Adelaide for Kingscote and, on our return, flew across to Lincoln. This final stretch capped off the longest working sequence in the ASA roster.

Walking to the terminal in Lincoln, load sheet tucked under my arm, I was greeted by a surprised Karyn. Karyn was an Ansett traffic officer who had lived with her sister in the same Port Lincoln block of flats I'd shared with my fellow fish-spotting pilot friend, Greg. On my first trip, I'd asked after her.

"What are you doing here?"

"I'm with Ansett." I guess this was sort of obvious. "Sometime after I last saw you, I went up to Darwin, built up more hours, got the airline job, and here I am."

"So, you were the pilot asking about me," Karyn smiled.

I sat behind the counter and filled in the figures while Karyn passed on numbers regarding passengers, seating, baggage and freight, in order to calculate the take-off weight. Next, I needed to check the balance of the front and rear lockers, to check if any items needed moving.

"Have you seen Greg?" Karyn asked.

Greg had returned to Melbourne and joined a newly formed cargo airline.

"I saw him at Sydney airport a few weeks ago. He flies DC-3s with SETAIR, a freight company based at Essendon."

I asked after Karyn's sister, Elizabeth. She was fine. Her husband was still working on the tuna boats, and her good news was that they now had a baby boy. It was time for the passengers to board, so Karyn and I said our goodbyes, but would see each other regularly.

The rostering system, like everything else, worked on seniority. A month's flying was known as a 'Block', and was published ten days before the end of the month. Captains bid first and then, when allocated, First Officers. Some Captains preferred certain days off, or morning or afternoon flights, or had other inclinations. FOs could not only bid along these lines too, but, as the Captains' blocks were already out, they could opt for a particular Captain. If positioned towards the upper end of the list, life could be agreeable. If you were a junior, well, with the passage of time things would improve.

Jim's block, which was now mine as well, had days off coming up. Sharon found a hospital and arranged for her check-ups. If all went according to plan, our baby was due in a little over two months. My first free day coincided with Sharon's medical visit. Looking up our new street directory, I plotted a course to the east of the city.

Fullarton Road was a main thoroughfare in Rose Park, with the hospital on the corner of Grant Avenue. Sharon would be a while, so I took my manuals. While waiting in the car, I used this time to study. With so much to learn, I barely had any time spare.

Approaching the hospital, the main road felt familiar. I thought back to the first time I had visited this city, and smiled.

"Why are you smiling?"
"I was just thinking."
"Thinking what?"
"You never know what the future will bring."
"No, but why would you think that now?"
"I remember being here before, but driving in the opposite direction. The next day, I drove to Port Lincoln, which led to us to being here now."
"Yes, I suppose so. But if you don't get in the right lane, you're going to miss the turn off."

Ah ... I wondered if our little one would inherit its mother's particular blend of philosophical practicality.

That night, I made a call. Mike was the Chief Pilot for Port Lincoln Tuna Processors when a young guy had shown up in a road-grimed Holden panel van, and a brand-new pilot's licence. Mike answered and, after reminding him who I was, I asked after his family. How were Anne and the boys, and how was the farm? After assuring me everything was bubbling along nicely, Mike asked what I was up to.

Mike also mentioned Brian's accident. The familiar rawness tugged at my heart. Brian and I shared a room as we slogged our way through flying school, with the irony that when I gave fish spotting away it created a vacancy that he filled. Witnesses had heard an engine "spluttering and misfiring" as the aircraft flew overhead, desperately struggling to reach the airport. Not that it made any difference, but he had survived the impact. Hopefully knocked unconscious, he had drowned when the Shrike sank. On this sad note, we wished each other well and hoped to catch up, perhaps on one of my trips across.

Back at work, I did the majority of the flying. Jim took an occasional sector, as I still needed to practise backup duties. Days passed, with hours spent at the controls and evenings and days off devoted to slogging my way through the books. Jim guided me and suggested areas of focus, but it was simple: I had to gain a good working knowledge of the 'Ops Manual', along with other

Ansett publications. Practically, I'd need to handle the F27 to a high standard and perform all approaches within tolerance.

The other area requiring strict compliance was *Standard Operating Procedures*. When I flew single pilot, I did what had to be done, when it had to be done. In airline flying, this was prioritised and documented. For every phase of flight and every action, standard procedures were followed. The last time I'd studied this hard was before I had left for Darwin, upgrading my Commercial licence with Senior Commercial theory.

Any action needed the other pilot's confirmation, and everything was completed meticulously, as set out in manuals. Previously, I'd operated gear and flaps, managed fuel, talked on the radio, and flown the aircraft, all at the same time. At times a handful, this was very different to operating as a crew.

At the end of the month, Jim invited me to his home. He took me through the manuals, making sure I discussed any queries, away from the pressures of our work environment. I thought this was kind of him, on his day off. Over and above a Training Captain's duty, this emphasised Jim's dedication. At their home, Mrs Evans offered cups of tea and coffee and made lunch. Even though she wasn't an Ansett employee, she insisted on the protocol.

"Please, call me Yvonne."

During lunch, Jim talked about his career in the RAAF, then charter flying with South Australian Air Taxis, and instructing at the Aero Club before flying with the airline. During his years as a junior First Officer with Ansett-ANA, he flew with numerous Captains who had passed on their knowledge and added to his experience. When he transferred back home, he stepped though the aircraft types and upgraded to command.

This was the strength of the Australian system. Starting in General Aviation or the military, pilots progressed through their careers. Moving up through the ranks, they accumulated knowledge and experience. This vast repository was then passed down to young and keen newcomers, equally dedicated to pursuing their chosen career.

I thought of the overseas students who'd trained at the Cessnock Academy. Their airlines had a different approach. Trainees started from scratch as ab initios. The cost of this training was borne by the company, and pilots returned to commence their airline careers. Our airlines not only saved this expense, but benefited by recruiting pilots who already held professional licences. Cadet schemes had operated in the past, but nowadays young applicants had already demonstrated aptitude and commitment, and were experienced in commercial or military operations.

Jim and I continued in this tradition. In what became common practice across all Australian airlines, Jim's Ansett Training Captains had given their free time. Together, these extra efforts, along with those of engineers, flight attendants, air traffic controllers, and all those on the ground vital to operations, had created the safest airline system in the world.

In the movie *Rain Man,* Qantas was singled out. The reference wasn't quite correct as Qantas had its share of crashes, but these incidents happened before the jet age. Taking this into account, Qantas was not alone in its unrivalled safety record. The Dustin Hoffman character could well have expressed a desire to travel with any Australian airline.

CHAPTER 5

The weather turned cooler. For Sharon and I, anything below 28 degrees was out of our comfort zone. This would be our first winter for some time and, as Adelaide was in the south of the continent, the mercury dropped into single digits. We looked on the bright side. There weren't that many days that were both cold *and* miserable. Neither of us had much in the way of cold weather gear, so we invested in jumpers and other warm clothes. The car's heater hadn't been used for years but, fortunately, it still worked, eventually. We bought a couple of electric heaters and set one up permanently in my study room, and the other in the lounge.

Towards the end of April, I had several free days, so we ventured into Rundle Mall. Don Dunstan, a somewhat flamboyant past Premier, had led the transformation of this vibrant, pedestrian shopping precinct. All the big department stores were here — David Jones, John Martin's, and Myer, along with numerous specialty boutiques in the arcades. In a food court in an underground section, we found a Middle Eastern outlet that sold a delicacy called Shawarma. Shavings of marinated lamb from the spit were wrapped in pita bread with salad. This mouth-watering delicacy became a regular feature of our following visits.

As training progressed, I became more comfortable with the aircraft and route structure. The heavy monster I had first experienced in Launceston had been tamed, and it not only felt normal but enjoyable to fly. Jim loved it. With a smile he told me that, along with the Convair, 'The Friendship' was his favourite, and this was not to say that he didn't have a soft spot for the DC-3 and DC-6 too. With far less experience, I too looked back fondly at my former aircraft. Each had its unique characteristics.

The staff of ASA were a mix. Some senior Captains had joined the company when it was known as Guinea Airways. Founded in Adelaide in 1927, Guinea Airways operated Junkers for remote mining enterprises in Papua New Guinea. In the 1930s, the airline moved back to Australia, acquired more modern aircraft, and flew between Adelaide and Darwin, with a host of intra-South Australian routes. Taken over by Reg Ansett's company in 1960, the name was changed to Airlines of South Australia.

These senior airmen contrasted with the four latest and most junior arrivals, beginning our careers. Jim sat towards the middle of the Captains' list. My friend Geoff from Darwin would shortly become the most senior FO. Being a small port, there was frequent movement within the ranks. Several would shortly leave for Ansett Mainline, so my position as number four from the bottom would improve.

At the electrical store, I helped the assistant wheel our new purchase to the car. He and I lifted it into the tray. Parking out front of our flat, I managed to ease the load down to the footpath, but it was too heavy to carry inside. I tried to 'walk' it in, but couldn't. As I pondered the situation, someone called out, "Hey, need a hand?"

In April, another Ansett intake had commenced. These new recruits had completed initial training and recently transferred to their bases. Several senior FOs were moving to Mainline, having picked up jet slots, so they made way for the seven new faces in our office. On the balcony of an upstairs unit, the youngest two of these new pilots looked down. Without time to answer, the pair descended the stairs, and the three of us positioned the new device in our bathroom. This marked the end of our visits to the laundromat. Our young friends, Huey and Robbo, had gravitated to the same block, more than likely for the same reasons Sharon and I had.

So far my instrument approaches had been simulated, but as we headed to Mount Gambier, the cloud base was reported as 'on limits'. Jim advised this was common for Gambier and, if we couldn't get in, we'd return to Adelaide, our alternate. We descended into the grey murk and over the VOR, our primary radio navigation aid. I flew the sector entry and positioned for the outbound leg. Jim called altitudes as I configured, and descending inbound and through 500 feet, we were still in the soup. Jim called "Approaching Minima".

My hands tensed, ready for the missed approach, but as we were about to hit minimum altitude, the runway lights and slick black bitumen popped out of the gloom.

After shutdown Jim turned to me, "There you go, wasn't that fun, there's nothing like the real thing!"

By late May, I had completed my hours and sector requirements. My check was scheduled for the 28th, with the Deputy Operations Manager, Captain Grant Mason. The route was the afternoon Port Lincoln–Kingscote–Broken Hill shift, with a night return.

Every check in an airline career is important and, without sounding too dramatic, an adverse result can mark the end. No matter how many years a career spans, it is only thought of in six-monthly intervals. Of all these checks, two stood out. The first was 'Clearance to Line', and the second was the 'Initial Command Check'. One day I hoped to be a Captain, but that was a dream years in the future. Achieving it would also depend on today's outcome. A failure, followed by another, would end my ambitions before they had even started.

Arriving early, Grant met me outside his office. My stomach tightened and my hands felt damp as Grant attempted to lighten the mood.

"How'd you manage to score this?"

This check was considered a difficult sequence. Over the six sectors, there'd be the chance for an approach using each of the radio navigation aids.

In Grant's office, he mapped out the day ahead. He'd fly the first sector executing a 'DME' arrival into Lincoln while checking my back up. If satisfactory, he'd hand the rest of the day's flying over to me. We proceeded to the briefing office. He asked questions about weather forecasts, documents, our flight plan and air traffic control.

At the aircraft, he followed my walk-around checking method, and enquired as to the function of various external items. In the cockpit, Grant set up for departure. My clammy hands operated gear and flap levers and on the DME arrival I called distance and altitude. Distance Measuring Equipment (DME) was an Australian invention. Coupled with lateral guidance, it allowed a stepped descent with safe terrain clearance. For lateral guidance, at Lincoln we used the ground-based Non-Directional Beacon (NDB), coupled with Automatic Direction Finding (ADF) cockpit equipment. The ADF needle pointed to the NDB station and we used this to track the designated inbound course.

After landing, Grant followed through on the load sheet while I double-checked each of my figures. We resumed our seats.

"It's all yours."

The F27 needed an accurate descent profile. It didn't have speed brakes, and engine torque had a minimum setting. Every thousand feet, we made a mental calculation. Five times the height to descend, plus five miles to slow down. My trainee friend Marcus later pointed out that, allowing for zeros, half height plus five was an easier calculation. If trending high or low, we needed to adjust early. Allowing for the wind, I flew a visual, straight-in approach to the shorter Adelaide runway. A fraction high to start with, we stabilised and touched down within the zone.

At Kingscote we performed an NDB approach. Our charts had specific outbound and inbound legs that allowed us to let down for a low-level circuit before landing on the gravel strip. This was always demanding, but I'd flown it, within limits. Throughout the day, Grant fired questions,

"What's the max TGT for start?"
"Nine thirty."

On the night arrival into Broken Hill, we used the 'VOR' for the approach. VOR stood for Very High Frequency Omnidirectional

Range. This was one time we were grateful for the three-letter abbreviation. The VOR cockpit instrument used a course bar to indicate track and, like the NDB, it allowed for a non-precision approach. Lining up with the runway, we landed. One to go. On the return, it was time for dinner. With trays on our laps, we ate at our stations. Jim had been thorough in all aspects of training, and he had even given me advice on this. "When you're eating, he won't ask questions. Drag it out as long as possible without being obvious." Grant was once an FO. He would've had a Training Captain just like Jim. Without overly lingering, I didn't gulp dinner down. Meals were a luxury. Not only this, but they provided a choice. The only stipulation was that each pilot had to choose a different meal. Jim always asked me, "Would you like the chicken or the beef?", to which I always replied, "I don't mind; either will be fine." He was such a gentleman. This could result in further deliberation, as Jim was also partial to either.

Our senior flight attendant swept the meal trays away and Grant launched into discussing flaps. This progressed into questions, as most discussion on this day had. "What system powered these secondary flight controls?", "What do you do if they fail to run?", "What if they are only partially extended?", "What if they extend on one side only?" While this was referenced in the QRH, Grant delved deeper.

> "What's the angle between sets for flap asymmetry protection?"
> "Three degrees."
> "What's the approach speed for a 'flaps up' landing?"
> "150 knots."

This last question brought us close to descent point. I briefed for a straight-in 'ILS'. The Instrument Landing System is a precision runway approach that projects a radio beam along the extended centreline of a runway, for lateral guidance, and another giving slope guidance, usually set at an angle of three degrees. I flew it with the comfort of no questions, and ended by executing the second smoothest landing of the day.

Back in the office, I sat opposite Grant. He laid the form on his desk. Progressively filling in each item, he made comments. Perhaps, I could have done this differently or maybe that another way. I could have been more expansive on some answers, and it would be an idea to have another look at the electrical system. Jim's advice had even covered this phase. "At the end, when you're de-briefing, make sure you take notes. No matter how well you do, the Check Captain will always have something to say." I took this as good advice, along with all given to date. "It doesn't really matter what you do with them later, it'll make a good impression at the time." As I scrawled notes, Grant, now on the last item, ticked the box.

After signing the form, the Captain passed it across for my signature.

> "Congratulations."

Following every check or test came a rush of relief. This, my first airline experience, was no different. For the next two years, I'd wear the junior First Officer's single gold bar on my jacket and epaulettes. After these, another gold stripe would be added. With seven in the airline, the three gold bars of the senior First Officer lay ahead. Command, and the fourth gold bar, would depend on seniority, but even that was coming up quickly these days in Ansett.

Marcus flew a different route and was checked on the same day. Stephan was checked the next day, and my other friend, Dominic, was checked the day after. We were all cleared to the line.

One flight remained for the month and, as I shared Jim's roster, we flew together. But this time it was different. On the 31st, we took off for Port Lincoln and Moomba, not as trainer and trainee, but as Captain and First Officer. On this flight, Jim had one last piece of advice.

> "Fly with as many Captains as you can, and learn something from each."

Jim's gentlemanly approach combined professionalism with consideration, and he was polite in his dealings with everyone. No matter what the problem or difficulty, he calmly worked through it. When the time came for me to once again fly from the left, I hoped to be as cool and calm as Captain Jim, or 'Gentleman Jim' as he was known throughout ASA.

ASA's four newest First Officers spent June on reserve. Airlines run day and night throughout the year, so this necessitates a certain flexibility that allows for unforeseen circumstances. Aircraft break down, sometimes the weather causes a diversion in destination, and crew members occasionally become ill. As a result, airlines don't only employ enough crew to fly the aircraft; they keep extra staff in reserve to cover these and other unforeseen events.

To keep aircraft flying uninterrupted and on schedule, airlines adopt one of two systems. Ansett used the 'Reserve Block' system. Flying was divided into blocks, and the remainder were scheduled with 'reserve coverage'. Reserve coverage or standby duty was not popular, and it was usually assigned to the most junior pilots. There was also a financial consideration. Part of our salary included 'a flying credit', but this was only awarded after a two-year qualifying period.

Other airlines managed a system of 'Composite Blocks'. With this system, every pilot was allocated some reserve flying, perhaps two or three days each month. To me, sharing the standby flights seemed fairer, as it did to any pilot saddled with a reserve roster. Ansett had adopted the North American Bidding System years earlier and, while we all agreed seniority was the best and fairest way to determine promotion, I felt that allocating flying and reserve could do with tweaking. Stuck on the ground 'standing by' felt like the rough end of the pineapple, when all I wanted was to fly.

To celebrate my check, Sharon and I booked dinner at a restaurant. After carefully extracting a heavily pregnant Sharon from the car, we walked the short distance. Three young musicians played classical music as we relaxed over our meal.

The next day, the phone rang. An extra flight was scheduled for Port Lincoln. I'd need to report that evening. The South Australian Captain had originally joined Ansett Mainline. He had transferred back to upgrade to command, and he'd been called off reserve as well. He gave me the sector.

> As we turned onto base, he said, "A little more."
> Tightening the turn, he then called for even more, so I tightened more. This resulted in a close turn to final. After we landed, he lost his cool.
> "Why did you fly such a tight base?"
> "I thought you wanted me closer. Didn't you say to turn more?"
> "No, I wanted you to widen out. That's why I said more."

He could have been more specific. I felt our positioning wasn't bad to start with. After several flights, I found him a bit of a control freak, and I didn't ever warm to him.

My birthday arrived and Sharon and I celebrated with a roast dinner. It felt like the coldest day I'd ever known. We'd certainly moved from one extreme climate to another. Our little flat on the ground floor felt like an ice box, even with both heaters on.

On the 13th of June, I was called up for a flight to Moomba. Paired with one of the most senior Captains, at sign on, he talked as if we were old mates, and once in the aircraft, he combined his experience with personal consideration. His daughter was a Melbourne-based flight attendant. As we chatted during cruise, he referred to his wife as 'Mama'. Apparently, Mama could be quite the wet blanket, pouring cold water on many exploits my Captain had planned over the years.

The next day, I was called for a Kingscote and Lincoln. Perhaps, the extra flight was due to the public holiday. Gentleman Jim was the Captain, so we were together again. Even on reserve, I picked up sectors. The pilots of ASA devised a system where each Captain and First Officer 'donated' a couple of days' flying each month. These sectors went into the kitty, as it were, and were given to the guys stuck on reserve.

Jim was the Branch Chairman of our pilots' Federation, the AFAP. He and I discussed the system. I felt that, as each pilot was already swapping a couple of days for reserve, these sectors could be incorporated into the blocks. He agreed and told me that this issue was raised before every contract renewal. It didn't matter to the company; they only cared that the flights were covered, so the system was gripped by inertia.

The following day, I was called up for a Whyalla flight and back. The Captain, from Melbourne, was newly upgraded. He was religious and talked about his life since becoming 'born again'. I stuck with the tried and trusted, and made no comment. The day turned out pleasant enough, if a little God-bothering.

CHAPTER 6

It was around three o'clock the next morning when Sharon woke me. As I shook the sleep from my eyes, Sharon gripped her pillow. "We have to go to the hospital."

Instantly awake, I sprung from the bed. Then she added, "There's plenty of time. I'll have a shower and get ready. You do the same, and then we'll go."

At four in the morning, with no traffic on the road, it was a quick trip. I helped her to the reception. We took the lift to a small room, then I left to park the car. On my return, she'd been moved. When I entered her new room, she lay on the bed with nurses helping.

Sharon's contractions were still far apart. The doctor dropped by to check on her. All I could do was stand around feeling useless. As much as I wanted to, I could do nothing to help. The contractions became stronger and closer together. She was having a hard time, which made me feel even more useless. I held her hand. The doctor administered gas and then asked if I'd like to wait outside.

A nurse showed me to the waiting room. Sitting on a chair near the coffee machine, my mind wandered. After her father left the navy and took up his position with the wireless technology company AWA, Sharon, her dad John, and her younger brother Lindsay, lived in Papua New Guinea. Before that, they'd lived in Townsville and Collinsville in Queensland, Geraldton in Western Australia, and, preceding their move to Darwin, spent a stint in both Sydney and Melbourne.

Sharon's nomadic life contrasted sharply with my stable existence. I thought of my married friends who'd grown up in Sydney. Living within a 10 kilometre radius of each other, they'd developed strong bonds and, coming from a similar environment, they shared a certain outlook.

While Sharon's way of doing things was often different to mine, this was balanced by our personalities. We could both be stubborn and unconventional, and we both embraced the rebelliousness of the era of our upbringing. While we disagreed on some things, we seemed in harmony on what mattered most, or, at least, what mattered to us. Our life, at this stage, was not only another example of our shared values, but of how we both threw propriety to the wind. Dad may have thought marriage and children had a set order, and that we were "putting the cart before the horse", but neither of us cared for convention.

The sun rose. I had a rough idea that a woman's labour could last from six to twelve hours, perhaps longer. I started to pace. It was like one of those old movies where Groucho Marx has ever-ready cigars in his top pocket, except I had no cigars. Back and forth, up and down the corridor I walked, never too far from Sharon. In between, I sat and read. I read all the magazines from cover to cover, without taking in a word, and then paced some more.

My beeper was clipped to the inside of my right pocket. Somehow, I'd remembered to bring it. In the days before mobile phones, we used these pagers. When called off reserve, we had two hours to report for duty, so the beeper allowed us to move around rather than remain confined, waiting by the phone at home.

While today was a reserve day, I intended to call in sick. Neither passengers nor staff would appreciate someone in such a heightened state at the controls.

It was after lunch, although I couldn't have eaten even if I'd thought to. A nurse came into the waiting room.

> "You can come now."
> I'm not sure what I was thinking, or what expression marked my face.
> She added, "Everything's fine."

In the room, Sharon sat quietly on the bed, propped up with several pillows. In her arms, a white blanket enveloped this little bundle. Sharon smiled and held it up. A nurse moved in, and handed the bundle over to me.

I held this little person in my arms as gently as I could. A few strands of brown hair poked out from the blanket. Two beautiful blue eyes, melanin yet to take effect, looked deep into mine. It was like a mighty force rushed over me. I'd never known such feelings. Without crying or movement, these two eyes did not stray from mine. This small face had such an inquisitive look, as if asking, "So, what's going on here?"

A beautiful little princess had entered the world. She was ours and, with her in my arms, an instinct to protect her engulfed me. She'd need to be looked after and cared for in every way. This feeling of responsibility was only outweighed by the joy brimming inside. Eight days before, I had turned 27. Sharon would turn 24 in November. Now we were three.

Sharon needed to rest. Later that day, I picked her dad up from the airport. I looked on as John held his first grandchild. He was just as bewitched as us. John stayed for three days before leaving for Sydney where he was taking a course on a new piece of avionics. Each day we visited the hospital, and each day I carried my beeper. So far, it hadn't gone off.

On the fourth day, the beeper beeped. A new flight was scheduled. It wasn't yet on the blocks, so it had fallen to the reserve crews. Ansett Air Freight had begun a night service to Melbourne using an ASA F27. Peter Abeles' speciality was freight, and this new service was instigated to take advantage of people willing to pay the higher cost of overnight airfreight. My flight was rostered for the following evening. As I checked in, I met with the junior Captain. Geoff had flown the Boeing out of Melbourne and moved to ASA for his upgrade. He was methodical and polite at briefing. If I didn't mind, he'd fly across, and I could fly back. Geoff was a popular name at the time. Not only this Captain and also my FO friend, it was shared by the third member of our checking staff. The aircraft was VH-MMV ('VH' denotes Australian registration). Special seat packs allowed parcels and other items to be placed inside. Using the passenger aircraft for freight was only temporary, as ASA would soon add a 'QC' (Quick Change) version to the fleet. The floor of the new aircraft was strengthened, and seats were fitted on secured pallets. During the day, it would fly passengers, and at night with the seats removed, it became a freighter. The night flight was a shock to many ASA crews. Shared throughout the blocks, a pilot averaged one or two of these 'all-nighters' a month.

Geoff took off and we headed for Melbourne. On arrival, he flew the ILS and then taxied to the freight shed. Here we joined the Electra crews (known as 'the Wombats' — perhaps due to their nocturnal lifestyle and eating habits), as their cargo was loaded and unloaded. After we parked, I ambled across to the closest aircraft. The cockpit was huge, with a set of throttles for each pilot. Checking the clusters of instruments, I thought back to the day when, as an 11 year-old, I had returned from a school excursion. Shuffling towards the terminal, I paused and looked from the tarmac back to Reg Ansett's first Lockheed Electra. All those years ago, my eyes had fixed on the flight deck windows, and a spark of determination was ignited.

Sadly, all things must pass and, a year and a half later, the L-188 performed its last flight (Wombat 3, 31st January 1984). On this flight, the wombat mascot could be seen shedding a tear, along with the many crews who can often be heard today extolling the virtues of this 'gift to pilots'.

The turnaround was several hours. Freight was arriving on other aircraft. Geoff led the way to the terminal. With our ID cards, we could rest in the Ansett crew room. When our aircraft was ready, they'd call us. After managing a nap, we returned to the machine. On arrival back in Adelaide, I flew the ILS and landed, and we taxied to the freight shed. The shed was further down the tarmac, by the hangars and close to our carpark. It was just after 5.30 am.

Walking to the car, I passed a semi-trailer being unloaded. It was unusual — neither the truck nor trailer had markings.

Arriving home, I went straight to bed. A nap in Melbourne wasn't a night's sleep, and I'd need at least a couple of hours before visiting the hospital. Sharon was being discharged at noon, and I planned to be there at least half an hour before.

At 11.30 am I was still tired, but this was made up for with excitement. I carried in our new bassinette containing a tiny nightdress, singlet, sheet and blanket. There were forms to fill before we were free to go. It was cold as we left Queen Victoria Hospital. Sharon walked beside me and, in my right hand, I carried the bassinette. Empty on the way in, Rebecca now lay inside, dressed in her nighty, and warm and snug under her pink blanket.

In our bedroom, the bassinette stand held a bassinette which, in turn, held our baby girl. Learning about babies was a fairly steep curve. Rebecca needed feeding every four hours, and our limited supply of clothes and nappies meant washing every day. I was tempted to go back to the shop for more. Night feeding involved me bringing Rebecca to Sharon at the first cry. Feeding happened in two stages and, after the second feed came the nappy change. A back rub followed, resulting in the obligatory burp. With baby returned to bassinette, we could all sleep for the next four hours.

This sounded good in theory. Our bundle of joy, however, needed training. Sitting in a cold and darkened lounge room, she drifted off in the upright position. After ever so gently inclining her at forty-five degrees, she'd come back to life. Rocking started again and, after a while, both baby and parent returned, exhausted, to the bedroom. Dad referred to our method as "making a rod for your own back", but we were new at this. Unlike the Fokker Friendship, babies didn't come with a manual.

With my check out of the way, I dropped by admin. We were granted a travel benefit, but I neither knew how to apply nor use what was known as a 'Green Ticket'. ASA's Admin Manager, Buck, advised that, after prioritising passengers, positioning crew, anyone travelling on company business, or anyone on standby, spare seats could then be allocated as Green Tickets. The Green Ticket (printed on green paper) had no priority, and if the journey covered several sectors, you risked being offloaded to any port along the way.

Buck explained that, after issue, I'd need to 'list' for my preferred flight. 'Listing' was like an unconfirmed booking. At the airport, I'd have to wait until the flight closed. Even with the last-minute scramble to the gate and the risk of being 'bumped' off a flight, Green Tickets were a valued privilege. There was one other advantage. If the extra seat in the cockpit, the jump seat, wasn't being used then, at the Captain's discretion, pilots could ride there. With this clarified, I had another query. In a thick South Australian accent and with his right hand held up as if he were a policeman at an intersection, Buck said, "C'mon, you know the rules."

This was only my second time in Buck's office. I had no idea there were rules. Buck rose and moved to a filing cabinet against the back wall. He lifted up a cardboard box and placed it on his desk. It had a slit in the top, like a money box. On the front in black Texta it read: SLUDGE FUND.

> "One question per day."

Buck pointed to the box. It seemed my second question would cost me. I took a note from my wallet and slipped it through the top. He now produced a ledger that I could imagine Ebenezer Scrooge scrawling in, and he entered my name, rank and employee number.

> "Now that you're officially a Sludger, what did you want to know?"

I noticed the other pilots' names in the journal. As I left, he placed the list back in the drawer and returned the cardboard box to the cabinet.

Although I'd completed training, I wasn't out of the woods. In July, I'd complete a flying block before undergoing my 'Consolidation Check'. This one final check would confirm that I was up to standard.

Reserve Blocks were the least popular, but there was also a 'least popular' Flying Block. Supervising pilots (Check Captains) shared a roster. Combined with office duties, this roster ensured that they did a certain amount of flying each month. Each Check Captain was a pleasure to fly with, but that added word in their title brought a certain pressure when sitting beside them. In July, I scored the Supervisors' Block.

With Rebecca's arrival and being on reserve, I hadn't kept up with all that was happening. On the 1st of July 1982, I flew a Lincoln–Moomba sequence with Tony, the Operations Manager. He was in a serious mood.

> "How far up the list are you?"
> With the April intake, I was 35 numbers from the bottom of the Ansett seniority list.
> "You know the economy's turned."

Since joining Ansett, I'd lived in a cocoon. I barely watched TV or read a newspaper. All I read were manuals, and my chief concern was the arrival of our baby, along with the need to pass my checks. I wasn't big on the economy. I remember Dad talking of credit or "money squeezes". He'd also spoken of "downturns". Growing up, these were just words as, apart from things being a little tight and the need for cutbacks in our household spending, Mum and Dad had shielded us from money worries.

Tony told me that the economy was "going into recession". Another word, but its meaning started to bite with what followed.

> "The July intake was cancelled."
> This was the first I'd heard of it.
> "Also, the October intake. In fact, all recruitment's on hold."
> After several years of continual intakes, I'd come to think of the process as normal. It wasn't one of those 'good news' days.
> "Are you still in contact with your old GA company?"

Northern Territory Air Charter no longer existed. Like so many light aircraft companies, it had gone to the wall. My former boss Graham had done his best. What I had thought at the time were unusual maintenance flights were part of his last-ditch efforts to save the business.

A few days later, I flew with my old F27 Check Captain, Grant. He was concerned. Apparently, it was only the inertia of such a big company that had given us jobs in the first place. *All* intakes for 1982 should have been cancelled. The concern now was how this oversight would be corrected. I was worried sick and rumours were rife. My dream was turning into a nightmare. Not just affecting the last two intakes, the number of those possibly to be retrenched increased to 50. This would include my pilot friend from Darwin, Dave. Since checking out, Dave and I had been in frequent contact. Dave rang Santos. If worst came to worst, perhaps, we could still catch the F27 to Moomba. Two weeks on and two weeks off in the oil and gas fields wouldn't be ideal for a young family, but it was better than being unemployed.

I hadn't yet met the third of our supervisors. On the 14th of July, Captain Geoff Harris and I were scheduled for Mount Gambier. On meeting him, Geoff showed the same concern as the others. On our flight down, Geoff passed on all he knew. He confirmed the plan to retrench between 30 and 50 pilots. If only 30, I'd hang in there, just. As we were to fly together regularly, Geoff agreed to keep me updated.

Not only the other pilots, but the flight attendants were concerned. Although we had been with ASA for less than six months, we were very much a part of this branch of the Ansett family.

Later in the month, when the three Check Captains were busy, I flew again with Jim. He was worried, but assured me that the Pilots' Federation would lend support. Unfortunately, if we were laid off, not much could be done, apart from ensuring that, when the economy recovered, we'd be given jobs again, and in the rightful order of seniority.

On the last night of July, I flew with our youngest Captain, Jeff, on the Melbourne freighter. Jeff's father was a senior Captain in

Melbourne. Unfortunately, news from the main base wasn't good. Retrenchment numbers were still rumoured to be between 30 and 50 pilots. Jeff could yet face disruption. Any backwards movement would mean he'd lose his command and be bumped to a different base.

August 1982 marked a noticeable change to economic conditions. Back on reserve, I flew only three times. My check was scheduled for the middle of the month with Captain Geoff Harris. News was that the company was offering early retirements and leave of absence.

In September, conditions worsened. I crewed just one flight. The schedule was cut back and sitting on the ground waiting for the phone to ring or beeper to beep was frustrating.

I'd become a regular at the baby clinic. The sister weighed and measured.

> "How long is it before a baby sleeps through the night?"
> "Somewhere between three months and a year. It all depends on the baby."
> In the waiting room, a mother with babe in arms and a toddler in tow arrived. She looked worn out. The small boy was about to speak when she held up her hand.
> "No more questions."

Apparently, little people wanted to know stuff. "Why is the world round?", "How come frogs are green?", "Do fish drink?" Maybe, Mum had adopted Buck's daily limit.

Mum, Dad, and my sister Maree hadn't yet met Rebecca. I had a weekend off, so I decided to take Rebecca to Sydney for the day. Checking flights, I found spare seats on the direct service. The evening flight back also had seats available. Sharon bought infant milk bottles and, with my small esky in hand, we walked the concourse to the staff counter. Sharon felt uneasy. This was the first time she would be apart from Rebecca. I promised to call her when we arrived.

> "Take it easy. You've got the whole day to yourself. Do whatever you want."

Walking to the 727, I pondered how times had changed. My daughter's first ride in an aeroplane was at just three months old. In Sydney, we arrived at a standoff gate. While crossing the tarmac, I sighted Mum, Dad, and Maree in the window. Mum looked especially excited. As soon as we walked into the building, Mum eased Rebecca from my arms into hers. Dad looked on as we met for the first time on such terms — both now fathers.

As if to show how life is full of coincidences, my friend Paul, who I'd last seen in Darwin, walked into the terminal. Paul and I had shared a desk when studying our Senior Licence subjects in a Bankstown classroom. There, I'd also met my friend Ari. Not long after that, Ari and I had set out for Darwin together. Paul was still with CSR, flying the Lear jet, but he had been upgraded to Captain.

At home, Mum took charge while I called Sharon. She planned to go to the city and would take my beeper, in case I needed her. I assured her that everything was fine and, once again, urged her to take it easy. Mum produced a pink dress that she had spent hours crocheting. Before checking the fit, it was feeding time. Mum warmed the bottle and knew exactly what to do, as I guessed she would. First bottle finished, burping complete and nappy changed, it was time for a sleep. Mum lay down pillows before laying Rebecca on my old bed. Rebecca took no time to drop off.

In the family room, we sat and talked. Dad was having a hard time with the recession; it was the worst he'd known, and building was one of the first industries to suffer. I knew another. It looked as though Dad would have to let his apprentice go. Mark had been with Dad for several years and losing him was something Dad hoped to avoid, but the time was fast approaching when there'd be no choice.

Mum arranged to visit Nana and Auntie Pat on the way to the airport. In the late afternoon, we set out. Rebecca was overwhelmed by the new faces, and she clung to me. Outside, we took a group photo. Nana sat with Rebecca temporarily on her knee, Mum knelt to the left and I knelt to the right as four generations were captured with an Instamatic. Auntie Pat gave Rebecca plastic knuckles, originally for a game called Jacks. This was a game played before my time, but I was grateful because, on the return flight, the bright colours kept her occupied. Our daughter was already exhibiting her strong will and, when awake, she needed to be amused.

Arriving home that evening, Sharon took Rebecca. I asked her how she had filled her day.

> "I spent time at the mall. Then I strolled by the river, and read in the afternoon."

The more senior FOs left. The irony was that coupled with insecurity came advancement. I moved up the list to rate a Flying Block. The block was with John, the young, religious Captain. We flew our flights and got on well. For ear protection, ASA had noise-deadening headphones, and we used the intercom to communicate.

Towards the end of September, we flew the Melbourne freighter. On the way back, it was my turn to fly. Feeling tired and sitting quietly, the Captain's voice came through the headphones.

> "Do you believe in God?"

At this stage, I believed in peace and quiet. Not wishing to engage in a philosophical discussion I felt neither could bring anything concrete to, I replied that my views were probably not as firm as his, and left it at that. We continued on to Adelaide in companionable silence.

Shortly after, John accepted the offer of a year's leave of absence. This move, I felt, was very Christian of him. He went on to attend religious college and, on completion, qualified for some form of clerical office. His leave, along with that of many others who opted for a year away, was very much appreciated by the remaining pilots. A number of senior Captains took early retirement so, when the numbers were finally crunched, we, the junior pilots, were spared.

Word came from the very top. With retirements and leave of absence, transport magnate and joint Managing Director of Ansett Transport Industries, Sir Peter Abeles, advised that these staff changes alleviated any need to retrench. However, there'd be no recruitment, and promotion would grind to a halt but for us, the 30 to 50 from the bottom, this news was "Manna from Heaven", as my religious Captain may have put it.

Three years prior, in 1979, Sir Peter Abeles and Rupert Murdoch had combined their empires in a hostile takeover bid when Thomas Nationwide Transport (TNT) and News Corporation took Ansett. Sir Peter's bid earlier in the decade, together with South African-born entrepreneur and corporate raider Robert Holmes à Court, had failed.

Aviator and Founder of Ansett Transport Industries, Sir Reginald Ansett, wasn't new to takeovers. The minnow Ansett had swallowed the giant Australian National Airways in 1957 to become Ansett–ANA. In 1959, Reg Ansett orchestrated the NSW company Butler Airways' absorption into Ansett Transport Industries. Guinea Airways was likewise absorbed in 1960, and MacRobertson Miller Airlines, based in Perth, joined the fold in 1963, with Queensland Airways enveloped in 1966. Over time, air freight, TV stations, hotels and passenger buses were added to the business, along with other interests. These included package holidays and, by 1947, Catalina Flying Boats were transporting tourists. In 1968, the name changed to Ansett Airlines of Australia and, in 1969, Reginald Miles Ansett became Sir Reg. With company expansion, Sir Reg's personal holdings dwindled, and poor decisions in the 1970s left the company exposed, paving the way for the takeover. Sir Reg had passed away in December 1981.

While both tycoons were billed as 'Joint Managing Directors', it was rumoured that Rupert Murdoch was only interested in the television stations. Peter Abeles wanted the airline to integrate with his transport network, and for day-to-day operations, Sir Peter ran the show with little happening outside his knowledge. I was grateful to Sir Peter. An axe hanging over my head had been flung aside. With his rotund shape, ill-fitting suits, cardigans, grey and thinning hair, Hungarian-Australian accent and comical Ronny Barker-type glasses, he was like a father figure.

After receiving this good news, I was in our crew room as a Brisbane crew signed on after a layover. The Captain, who was very senior, asked,

> "How's the Country Club treating you?"
> As a regional operation, despite early mornings and late returns, the South Australian base didn't have overnights or all-night 'red eye' flights that characterised some Mainline routes. This lifestyle, other pilots joked, was more in keeping with a Country Club. To us, though, ASA was not so much a club as it was a big family.
> "Great," I replied. "Especially since Sir Peter took pity on us."
> He frowned and took a breath. "Son, if you think Abeles gives a tuppeny stuff about you or anyone else, you've got a bit more growing up to do."
> I wasn't expecting such a reaction.
> "All he cares about is his interests and his interests only. I'm pleased you weren't retrenched. The reasons, though, were purely financial."
> The Captain I was flying with arrived. "He doesn't seem all that fond of Abeles."

There was something about the Brisbane Captain. He had that 'I've been on this planet a good many years more than you' look, and a certain wisdom in his eye.

"You know he's right about one thing," my Captain remarked.

"What's that?"

"The reason you're still here has nothing to do with the goodness of anyone's heart."

My colleague then ran through the six months of training I'd recently completed. From uniforms to an empty F27 flying around Launceston, the investment was considerable.

"Don't forget, you guys are on the lowest pay scale. You don't even rate flying credits. Some may not have returned, maybe leaving for jobs overseas. If so, Ansett's investment would be lost forever. When called back, most of their endorsement training would need to be repeated. Keeping you on, even with minimal flying, was the cheapest option. It was bean counting."

Whatever the reasons, I was happy to still be flying the Fokker Friendship.

CHAPTER 7

We'd been in our flat six months, the length of our lease. Summer was approaching and Sharon suggested a change. She liked light and airy, and she thought our ground floor flat was dark and dingy. For several days, Sharon took the car. Adelaide was surrounded by parkland and four terraces. A townhouse was available for rent on the edge of East Terrace near Victoria Park. Although more expensive than our current flat, it was affordable. The lounge room had full length glass windows, fulfilling Sharon's requirement, and overlooked a small front yard. Beside the kitchen, a small dining room with a spiral staircase led up to two bedrooms. The main bedroom featured glass windows across the front, the same as downstairs, with a narrow balcony. We moved in the following weekend.

Around this time, a court case in Darwin was nearing its conclusion. In August 1980, a young family had visited Uluru (the Aboriginal name for Ayers Rock), for a camping holiday. Parents, and their two young boys were shocked, when during the evening of the 17th, their baby disappeared from their tent. An initial Inquest agreed with the mother that a dingo had taken her baby. A second inquest, however, overturned this decision and led to a murder trial. Expert witnesses testified that handprints were evident on the infant's jumpsuit, and the rips were consistent with scissor cuts. The baby's matinee jacket was never found, and blood was detected in their car.

As our baby lay snug and protected in our new home, I wondered how anyone could harm someone so defenceless. If they had, no punishment could be harsh enough. Lindy Chamberlain was convicted of murdering her daughter Azaria and given a life sentence. Michael Chamberlain was convicted as an accessory after the fact. No motive for the crime was ever offered. But the story did not end there. Opposing expert testimony was neither given credence nor widely reported. Hairs found on the jumpsuit, and the rips, were consistent with that of a canine. The 'blood' in the Torana lacked haemoglobin. Dingoes in the area were not shy, benign creatures. In the weeks before the baby died, Rangers had become concerned and had warned tourists of the dangers. Although Aboriginal trackers identified dingo tracks outside the tent that appeared to drag an object, this testimony was not accepted by the courts. The Chamberlains maintained their innocence and exhausted all avenues of legal recourse.

In 1986, when climbing Uluru, a British man fell to his death. When retrieving his body, police found Azaria's matinee jacket lying outside a dingo lair, around 50 metres from where the baby's jumpsuit was recovered years before. Evidence mounted supporting her innocence and, in 1987, Lindy Chamberlain was released. In June that year a Royal Commission exonerated the Chamberlains.

In 2012, a final coronial Inquiry issued a new death certificate recording Azaria Chamberlain's death as "the result of being attacked and taken by a dingo". They'd since made separate lives, but with shared grief, and with the legal ordeal over, the tragedy and trauma of the past 32 years could only be overshadowed by one greater. Lindy and Michael Chamberlain's baby daughter had lost her life, and was lost to them forever.

November arrived along with Sharon's birthday. We celebrated with 24 flickering candles atop her chocolate cake. My block was with the senior Captain I'd flown with once before. We were flying the Whyalla — Broken Hill sequence.

> "G'day, mate. I've had a few days off. Mama didn't seem all that upset to see me off this morning."

Moustache just short of a full handlebar, and hair with flecks of grey from under his cap, the Captain stood at least half a head taller than me. His uniform cap, at slight tilt, was different to mine, its emblem from a previous era. We wore a plain navy tie, yet his had a gold stripe and the lettering 'ASA'. Above left pocket and pinned to my blue shirt, I wore my blue and gold Ansett wings. His were silver, with lettering as on his tie and cap.

He shared how he'd started with Silver City Air Taxis out of Broken Hill and moved to airline flying as the last of three pilots recruited by Guinea Airways before it became Airlines of South Australia. He hadn't updated his uniform, and no one was going to tell him any different. He was very much 'What you see is what you get'; the real McCoy — Keith.

> "How about I take it to Whyalla, mate?" The Captain decided who did the flying. Usually, we flew leg for leg, thus sharing the sectors. I flew back. Preparing for the next departure, I realised that this would also be mine; as would the flight out of Broken Hill.

Progressing through the month, this remained the pattern. No matter how many sectors, Keith only ever flew one. Along with his relaxed attitude, this was how he nurtured young pilots. On entering the cockpit, Keith removed his uniform cap and produced another. White, it read 'Airlines of South Australia' across the front.

Keith completed the 'after take-off' checklist.

> "Let us know when you want the gear down, mate."

Keith kept a close eye, but allowed me to make decisions. This was his mentoring way and by the month's end, he'd boosted my confidence. Keith became a favourite, and many times, I'd bid with just one aim — to fly with him.

In December 1982, I flew with another senior Captain, who became my other favourite. At sign on, Lionel was quiet and polite. A few years from retiring, he was a little taller, with his grey hair turning to white. Lionel's serious demeanour was broken when he accidentally entered a flight plan figure in the wrong column.

"I've been doing this for years; you'd think I'd get it right by now." A huge smile accompanied.

As the month advanced, I learnt that Lionel's greatest source of amusement was his own perceived folly. During our first few flights, he didn't say much as we did several short hops to Kingscote and crewed a Melbourne freighter. On the 10th of December, we flew Lincoln–Moomba. On the long sector, the Captain opened up. I told of my time in South Australia and then the Territory.

"Did you fly out of Darwin?"
"Yes."
"Have you heard of a place called Fenton?
"I flew there once."
Lionel was surprised. "Towards the end of the war I was based there. What's it like now?"

We compared Lionel's once vibrant air base, about 200km south of Darwin, with the derelict airfield I had visited, where weeds grew through cracks in the pavement. Lionel described the many buildings where both US and Australian squadrons were once stationed.

As our long day drew to a close, we arrived to find a notice on the board:

Annual Sludge Fund Event
Aviation Institute
Saturday 18th December

Until now I had no idea of the intended use for the many dollars that I, and every other pilot, had added to the small box in Buck's office. The Aviation Institute was within the airport boundary. It had a bar, club facilities and a BBQ area, which we hired for the day.

At the door stood Buck with his list, assisted by his office workmate, Colin. As each name was ticked off, we were presented with a plastic name tag. ASA was a small operation. Everyone knew each other, so this made me smile. The rest of the card was taken up with the word: SLUDGER. I'd been with ASA for just nine months. This day, spent with friends and colleagues, reinforced the feeling of family that made ASA such a unique entity. I, like every other Sludger, wore my badge with pride.

It wasn't just the atmosphere, but the flying that attracted me to ASA. The F27 was a great aircraft, and our route structure offered many challenges. Night approaches into outports were basic, with no path indicators, precision guidance, or auto-flight systems. Many were what we termed 'black holes', with nothing more than runway lights. After departing from a capital city airport with all the facilities, we adapted to basic navigation and approaches at smaller airports. Kingscote was still gravel, and Ceduna was the same as in my fish-spotting days — a dirt strip with a hump in the middle. Sometimes, the wind was so strong at Lincoln, we landed on a grass cross-strip. In the company of fine people, it was a pleasure to go to work.

The next day, on the way back from Lincoln, Lionel asked what I was doing for Christmas.

> "We don't have any plans."
> "Would you like to spend the day with us?"

We'd flown together for less than three weeks and our conversation was basically polite, so I was surprised by his kind offer.

On Christmas morning, we drove to Fulham, a suburb close to the airport and not all that far from Henley Beach and the house I had visited years before, on my first trip to Adelaide. Lionel met us as we pulled up, and Mrs Edwards greeted us at the front door.

> "Please, my name's Joan. Whenever I hear 'Mrs Edwards', I always think of Lionel's mum."

Inside they introduced us to their many relatives. Joan and Lionel had a daughter and son, twins, just a little younger than me, and another daughter who was older. Cousins, nieces, nephews and friends gathered in the Christmas spirit. Scott arrived shortly after. Scott was among the latest intake, and Lionel attended to his line training. Not only did we know Scott from Darwin, but when Sharon first started flying in Melbourne, he was her instructor at Moorabbin.

Turkey, chicken, with stuffing and all the trimmings, were followed by pudding, custard and coconut ice. Rebecca spent most of the morning with Joan, and after lunch, it was time for her sleep. She drifted off as we sat with Joan and Lionel. Scott joined us, and as we chatted, Joan told how she and Lionel had met.

> "On my way home from work, I passed by the church. On Thursdays beautiful organ music came from inside, so I always paused to listen. One day I sat on the steps. Shortly after, the music stopped, and Lionel walked through the door."

Lionel took a keen interest in young pilots. Not only did he have his own mentoring style, like Keith, but this day marked the first of many visits to his family home. Scott hadn't flown to Fenton but, working with Air North, he'd heard of it.

Lionel spoke softly, "It was towards the end of the war. Fighting on the now Indonesian section of Borneo centred on the township of Balikpapan. Our wing had temporarily transferred from Fenton to Morotai, a northern Indonesian island."

Theirs was a night mission. A Liberator took off but, tragically, the aircraft failed to return. The next night, another took off. This aircraft also failed to return. The mission, still a priority, meant that the next evening another bomber was dispatched. This crew was also lost. On the fourth night, Lionel and his crew were assigned the mission.

> "We completed our briefing and walked to the aircraft."

The four Pratt & Whitney Twin Wasp engines coughed and spluttered, then settled into rhythm as they taxied to the runway. Cleared to line up, they held in position for take-off.

> "Sweating in the cockpit, we sat there. Each of us fidgeted and looked from one to the other. The engines ticked over as the minutes clicked by."

As Lionel calmly spoke, it was as though a cold and clammy weight first settled on my chest, then grew fingers to grip my throat, then crept to tingle the back of my neck. Tongue paralysed in my mouth, I could only wait for him to continue.

> "The navigator leaned across and reminded us that we'd already burnt 20 minutes of fuel. Then, the Base Commander came on the radio. The mission was called off, and we taxied back."

I thought of that hot Territory day when I'd flown to Lionel's old base, 36 years later, in a light twin. But this memory was eclipsed by another. Years before I was born, our country was bombed and our way of life was under threat. It wasn't possible to feel any greater admiration for this man and those like him. Raw courage was buried deep within. When Lionel held the yoke of the B-24 Liberator with one hand, and throttles in the other, he was only 19.

CHAPTER 8

Sharon and I did our sums. For just a little more than our rent, we could afford a mortgage on a small house. On exploring Adelaide further, we found a large park in an eastern suburb. With a public swimming pool, it had only one downside; it was a convenient area for people to walk their dogs (which also proved convenient for the dogs). In later years, rules were introduced, but as we wheeled Rebecca's pram around the grass expanse, the day was marred by the need to clean our shoes and the pram wheels afterwards.

While this desirable suburb was disappointingly out of our financial reach, we drove along Greenhill Road to get there. Turning left for our park visit, Sharon surmised that, if there was a Greenhill Road, then more than likely there'd be a Greenhill. After a morning at the park, Sharon and Rebecca veered left instead of right. Sharon's logic proved correct. The small suburb of Greenhill sat where the hill peaked and turned off the main road. The following weekend, under Sharon's guidance, I sat at the wheel as the car climbed the hill. There were two houses for sale. From the outside, I could tell they fitted the four-bedroom, two-bathroom specifications that Dad aimed for when building. Unfortunately, both exceeded our budget.

We returned the following Saturday. At the end of an avenue, a block of land was for sale. It looked over the main road and across the valley, with glimpses of the city in the distance. The owner must have planned a house, as the sloping block was cut with a level portion that included a concrete water tank. Greenhill lacked sewerage and water, with only electricity and telephone offered as basic services.

We called the agent. Sometime after completing ground works, the owner had changed his mind and was keen to sell. I worked out the square metre cost of what was termed a 'first homebuyers home', and added the amount for the land. The problem was finance. We didn't have any.

This wasn't an insurmountable obstacle, however, and the agent suggested we make an offer noting this as a condition. His office closed in the afternoon for the weekend. Would we like to drop by his home tomorrow and complete the paperwork? We were reluctant to intrude on a Sunday but, as his family was grown, he and his wife would be happy for us to visit.

The agent's house was in the older suburb of Norwood and was what I'd describe as 'Federation style' (this, through the eyes of someone who'd grown up in Sydney). After crossing the ample front veranda, we rang the doorbell. The real estate agent and his wife, in their mid-60s, immediately made us feel at home. We settled in their lounge room, with a plate of freshly made scones with whipped cream and strawberry jam, and cups of tea and coffee. The agent explained the intricacies of the contract, and that he would present our offer the next day.

We'd driven up the hill that morning, and after walking the block once more, decided this is where we wanted to live. The sounding wind rippled through the gumtrees, and dappled sunlight shed varying shades of green and brown. Trees and bushes lined the valley wall opposite; it already felt like home. The following morning, Sharon took the call. Our offer was accepted.

While several project home companies offered entry level designs, my bias was towards smaller builders. Dropping into the agent's office, I asked if perhaps he knew any. Two young carpenters, formerly from a major firm, had recently started a business. I remembered two young 'chippies' a generation before who had done the same in Sydney. They showed us sketches. One, with a basic 'L' shape, fitted the cut of our land. With a lounge and dining room, family room, three bedrooms, a kitchen, bathroom and laundry, the lounge room window would overlook the valley. The car's recent luxury of a carport would be short-lived. Their quote was competitive and we liked the layout, so we gave our conditional acceptance, based on securing finance. I added the land contract to the house quote, and gathered my salary slips.

Back when I had needed to upgrade my licence, the Commercial Banking Company of Sydney came through. But the CBC didn't have an Adelaide branch, so I called my lifelong bank with which I'd long held but little used a savings account. This bank was established back in 1911 by Andrew Fisher's Labor government. The bank's brief was to care for the common welfare of ordinary Australians. Not only was it staffed by men and women dedicated to serving the public, it was owned by the Australian people.

The loans officer welcomed me. I quickly explained the amount we needed. The bank worked on a formula. Repayments could not exceed a certain proportion of earnings. The bank officer frowned.

> "Do you have any other income?"
> "No. I earn a salary with some allowances."
> "Have you got any other pay slips?" More frowning.
> "I thought you guys made more."
> "No, that's it. But I won't be a junior First Officer forever."
> His was a common misconception. Contrary to popular myth, my pay slip could never be mistaken for the Chief Pilot's. After being cleared to the line and now in my second year, my pay had increased. I was on a little more than $18,000.
> "I'm really sorry. But my hands are tied."

While disappointed, I understood. In my job, too, there were things you could do and others you could not — and never the twain shall meet. As I prepared to leave, he added, "I shouldn't really be saying this, but the building societies cater more to first home buyers. Maybe you could give one of them a try."

We looked up Adelaide Permanent and made an appointment. Sharon and Rebecca came with me. While I presented the same documents, it was as though we'd entered a different financial world.

> "Your salary's on the lower limit but, as you're with Ansett, I don't see any problems. Give me a couple of days and I should have confirmation for you."

Within a week, we had our loan. With the land contract executed and building agreement confirmed, we were rapidly moving towards a home of our own. The builders would start mid-February.

After spending January 1983 on reserve, in February I rated a flying block. It was with Geoff; the young Captain I had first flown the Melbourne freighter with. For a First Officer and the rest of the crew, the tone of the day was set by the Captain. A thoughtful and considerate skipper made a day at work enjoyable. Captains came in all shapes, sizes, and temperaments. Occasionally, if sitting beside one not so inclined, a trip to Moomba could feel like an Atlantic crossing. Fortunately, most were like Geoff.

The day approached for the builders to start. Our excitement built, along with the temperature. Adelaide was a place of extremes, and it was shaping up to be a sweltering summer. We longed for our 30^{0}C Darwin days. Adelaide was pushing 40, but I had the day off, so we thought we'd drive up to see the first sod turned.

That morning we closed all the doors, windows and curtains in an attempt to keep the stifling air out. We set up Rebecca's baby bath in the lounge, to splash and keep her cool. The wind picked up and the mercury rose. I tuned into the radio. Normal programs were interrupted with news flashes and bulletins. Bush fires had broken out in Victoria and South Australia. They raged out of control. Tinder dry land from years of drought fuelled fires fanned by strengthening winds.

Reports became worse. In Victoria, people had lost their lives. Near Adelaide, the Mount Lofty area was savaged by a firestorm. The sky turned from blue to a murky greyish brown. The air smelt of smoke and ash.

When we thought the reports couldn't get any worse, they did. More people were killed, with houses and property torched. The Adelaide Hills became an inferno. Then, another report came through. Greenhill was ablaze. The Country Fire Service was doing all they could but, even with superhuman efforts, the fires raged wherever the winds fanned them. We didn't bother the builders. The start date for our house was no longer important. People suffered greatly. Houses could be rebuilt and possessions replaced, but the loss of a loved one was for all time.

A week after the fires, we drove up the hill. Our lush green neighbourhood was now blackened and charred. Down our street to the right, we gazed at the outline of discoloured concrete and scattered bricks where a house once had stood. To the left, the sunroom of a home was now a mass of seared timber and bricks. Amazingly, the rest of the house was saved.

Driving up to our block, we could only stare. Slowly, we walked across our land. It would be a long time before we would again hear the wind call through the trees, and it was hard to tell if their blackened hulks would ever recover. Checking our water tank, it seemed intact. From what would be our backyard, we looked to the rear of the house we'd first seen with a For Sale sign out front. Next to this home had stood another. All that remained was a cindered, vacant lot.

As we returned to the car, our future neighbour stood in what was left of his front garden. I wound the window down to say hello. A look of distaste engulfed his face.

> "Having a good sticky beak?"
> "We're checking our block. We'll be your new neighbours."
> "Sorry. I really can't see the need for rubbernecking. There've been so many."
> I couldn't think of any response.
> Then, in laconic tone, he added, "Welcome to Greenhill."

Looking through the car window, there was nothing green about this hill. On 'Ash Wednesday', the 16th of February 1983, 75 people lost their lives. 28 died in South Australia and 47 in Victoria. This was the first time the authorities had called a state of emergency. We descended the hill in silence.

The builders commenced in March, and once again, I rated a flying block. By now, pilots who were moving out had left. With operations trimmed and adjusted to economic conditions, and with the more senior FOs gone, my seniority improved. This month I was not only flying a block, but was awarded the block I had bid for. It was with Keith. We flew our flights, the lion's share with my hands on the controls. Our block included several trips to Moomba, providing us a chance to talk. Keith loved sailing. He must have been one of those 'elements' people, of the sky and sea. He owned a sailing boat, but Mama often had something to say if he spent too much time on the water.

When not long out of his teens, Keith had signed on for a voyage with the Pamir, a commercial sailing ship. Loading grain from Port Victoria in the Spencer Gulf, Keith joined the crew bound for Falmouth in the UK. On the 11th of July 1949, they rounded Cape Horn, the last time for a vessel of this type.

> "Mate, we were the last Cape Horners."
> As he told the story, this 50 something year old, flecks of salt and pepper from under his white cap, had in his eye the glint of a young boy off on the adventure of a lifetime.

1983 was an election year. As the campaign progressed, I sensed the mood for change. Keith felt it too, but was apprehensive. He hadn't warmed to the new opposition leader, and neither had I. To me, he appeared combative, with a superior attitude. From beneath his dark, wavy, boofed-up hair and downturned mouth, he often snarled responses to questions. On the 5th of March, Australia headed to the polls. That evening, the news heralded a new government. Labor had ousted the Liberals and a new Prime Minister was heading to the Lodge.

The months passed, and in June, we celebrated two birthdays. I didn't feel any older, but birthdays can't be denied. Where had all the time gone? As I'd completed more than a year with Ansett, we decided to take this month as leave. First, we visited Sydney. My old home town was just as cold as Adelaide, so we packed warm clothes in the many bags we now needed when travelling with a little one. As well as family, this trip was a chance to catch up with old friends. Gemma and Paul invited us to dinner, along with Liz and Carl. As we ate, Rebecca slept in the spare room, but she was not alone. Liz and Carl's daughter was three months younger.

We caught the train and ferry and explored Sydney, as through the eyes of a one year old. At home Mum, Dad, and Maree fussed. Rebecca was very much the centre of attention. Wheeled in the stroller by her Nana, Grandpa dug out long packed away toys, and Auntie Maree provided tickles.

Sharon prepared a bowl of steamed vegetables. As I fed our infant daughter, much of this vitamin-enriched sustenance was ejected. Sometimes gently eased away with the tongue, other mouthfuls exploded back at me in an impressive spray. My coaxing of "Here comes the aeroplane" was met with her version of the jet engine. Even so, I managed a success rate of about one in three. As I proceeded, Dad became progressively uneasy. Shifting in his chair and visibly agitated, he could restrain himself no longer.

"Aww, c'mon. Can't you see she doesn't like it?"

My jaw dropped and I raised my eyebrows. Remembering threats of "No sweets unless you finish", and "Eat it now or you'll have it for breakfast", my eyes levelled to meet his. There was no need for words as he caught my drift. While Dad's tune had changed, his defiance remained. When it came to his little granddaughter, well, things were different.

We spent the second half of our holiday in Darwin. While the depths of winter raged down south, Darwin bathed in the glorious midst of the dry. We swam at Berry Springs, and walked along Casuarina and Mindil beaches. At night, we devoured steaks at Jesse's, and sipped drinks by the Travelodge pool or in the Green Room at Hotel Darwin. It was great to be back. I spent time with my old friend Ari. He took me for a ride in the Navajo Chieftain on the Maningrida run. All too soon it was time to return.

Adelaide felt especially cold after our time in the tropics. Our house was a simple design. It was now 'locked up' as the internal work neared completion. As July drew to its end, the builder walked us through. At the front door, he handed us the keys. I tacked sheets against the windows but, as we didn't have floor coverings, we immediately felt the cold. I asked the builders to leave any leftover materials. With the surplus bricks, I built a hearth in the family room. We bought a pot belly stove and this heated the entire house.

CHAPTER 9

No one had taken the Cup from the Americans in its 132-year history. Australia had contested many times, and I remembered the boat names of *Gretel, Dame Pattie, Southern Cross,* and *Australia*. In September 1983, Australia challenged once again. Alan Bond's syndicate was racing a 12-metre designed by Ben Lexcen and skippered by John Bertrand. As with previous entries, the yacht used a former name, and was designated 'II'.

The defender, *Liberty,* won the first two races, and it looked like an all-too-familiar pattern. But *Australia II* won the third race and, by the seventh and final race, each had won three. On the day of the decider, we watched as these racing craft tacked and battled their way through the course. Yacht racing wasn't something I'd taken much of an interest in, but on this Tuesday morning we were glued to the TV. Coming from behind, the boxing kangaroo bounded ahead on the final leg. As our nation held its breath, both boats inched towards the finish line. A puff of smoke blew as *Australia II* crossed. The Alan Bond and Royal Perth Yacht Club entry had won for Australia.

The Men at Work classic celebrating our '*Land Down Under*' became a pseudo national anthem, and the nation revelled as we ate our Vegemite sandwiches. In a Perth television studio, our Prime Minister shared a thought. Reflecting on his own words years later, he said:

> "I've got to say, of all the many brilliant things I said as Prime Minister, I think the one that is remembered the most is what I said then, that 'the employer who sacked a worker for being late that day was a bum!'"

The Australian keel design was revolutionary. After the winning race, the yacht was hoisted from the water, revealing a set of wings fanning from its base. Persistence, design innovation, and the crew's teamwork embodied our Australian psyche. It was as though our whole country was lifted, along with *Australia II*.

As October approached, however, so did clouds on our horizon. The new government made changes. Lump sum superannuation entitlements would be treated differently, with a substantial increase in tax. This not only affected us, but many others. Our occupation was unique in several ways. One such peculiarity was compulsory retirement. After 60, a pilot could no longer fly professionally. Our superannuation schemes were set up with this in mind; our aim to be self-sufficient. The tax increase could mean that retiring pilots no longer achieved this. Prior to the election, John Dawkins, Shadow Minister for Industry and Commerce, advised there were no plans to alter existing arrangements. Now in government, it was a different story.

To be honest, I hadn't thought all that much about superannuation. Retirement was something in the distant future. Even so, I did think that if more people self-provided, there'd be less need for government-funded pensions.

Flying with Keith, again he was worried. In the crew room, Lionel was worried too. These two, along with many others, would retire within the next few years. After his service in WWII, Lionel had trained as an accountant. If anyone was qualified to run the numbers, Lionel was. His entitlement would be reduced enough to make that all important difference. He lived in a modest house in typical suburbia and drove a common family sedan. He didn't aspire to waterside mansions, Mercedes-Benzes or other trappings of the high life. All he wanted was a comfortable retirement, relying on no one but himself.

Our Federation began asking questions and commenced a public campaign. The government responded and, with scant debate about policy, attacked us as a group. Apparently, I was now a "Highly paid, greedy elitist". This a mere sample of the many colourful terms directed at us pilots, perhaps, thought up over roast beef accompanied by a drop of red in the parliamentary dining room, or a beer or two at the Members' Bar. The charge was led by our PM. I thought of these privileged politicians. With so many perks, I wondered how many of them used old sheets to cover their windows.

The benefits of superannuation and advantages of more people covered were overshadowed by references to the size of our perceived pay packets. A backbencher did not earn a cabinet minister's income, yet this idea that 'pilots were overpaid' was pedalled when attacking us. Our pay scales had several components, but were basically calculated according to the 'speed/payload formula'. Most airlines used this factor in some form, so the highest paid pilot flew the fastest and largest jet. A career could span up to forty years, with only a portion spent in command of such aircraft. Even a jumbo skipper had to start at the bottom, maybe with a young family, living on bare concrete floors. The proportion of heavy jets in the Australian fleet was small and, despite the political ranting, average salaries were far less than those cherrypicked from the top.

We held meetings. The senior Captains grew even more nervous as the latest barrage hit. We voted to go on strike. I had never been on strike or participated in industrial action, but I understood the concerns of the senior pilots. I also felt strongly that goalposts should not be moved mid-game. It would be alright for me. I could adjust or make other arrangements, but those about to retire were out of time. Even though protecting our superannuation was such an important issue, I was wary. Two days on strike were not to be taken lightly. I was now labelled a 'Prima donna'. But what of those I often spied gliding towards parliament in chauffeur-driven limousines, while chugging to work in the old panel van? People would be inconvenienced. We gave enough notice so that plans could be adjusted, but strikes usually engendered anger among the wider public. I know how I felt when faced with this sort of disruption. There had been occasions, though, when I did sympathise.

Liz's sister also lived in Sydney and was a nurse. I saw firsthand the mountain of study and training her career involved. After qualifying, she worked odd hours and all-night shifts. More importantly, few did such lifesaving work. There were times when enough was enough, and they stood up for themselves. I would have gladly linked arms on their picket lines.

Back in 1979, Sydney was blockaded. I was at home at the time. Trucking companies were pushing drivers up to, and sometimes beyond, their physical limits. Inequitable taxes by governments and low rates paid by others sitting in plush offices sucking on Havana cigars squeezed owner-drivers. This, before even considering the oil crisis. As the truckies went on strike, Sydney came under siege, and supermarket shelves thinned. Even so, I thought these guys had a point. They weren't getting a fair go, and it seemed that no one cared. I drove up to Berowra in northern Sydney. Passing Ted 'Greendog' Stevens on the semitrailer-clogged highway, I pipped the horn with my left hand and hung my right out the window, thumb up.

The superannuation issue was important. Perhaps, people would see our point. This affected many, and I was initially surprised by the support. For me, however, it was another that angered. As I sat beside Jim, Keith, Lionel and many others, I learnt about leadership. Captains were leaders, and the best led by example. Always constructive, these professionals didn't raise their voices, rant, rave, or abuse. They did their jobs to the best of their ability and inspired others to do the same.

The Prime Minister, personally affronted, spewed a brilliant torrent of vindictive vitriol. While exhorting us to 'Do as I say, not as I do', it seemed that what was good for the goose, wasn't so good for the gander. When I went on strike in October of 1983, it wasn't only superannuation I was trying to highlight.

I wasn't angry — I was livid. This was not the way Australia was meant to be. Fairness and equity were values that should have defined us. Instead, they became a cheap, throwaway catchphrase.

There were elitists, particularly one group. The politicians' retirement benefit was an indexed pension, and unaffected. This group, who weren't subject to the new rules, must have searched the mirror when looking for new ways to insult. I wanted to shout, yell, scream. "Can you see this! Can you believe this?!"

Being on strike was an unusual feeling. It was not at all like taking a day off. Jim organised informal meetings. The days dragged on until the day came when it felt good to be back at work. After my Mount Gambier flight, while crossing the road, I saw Roger coming the other way. Roger and I had worked together in Darwin, and I hadn't seen him since leaving the 'Top End'. Roger had left the Territory about six months before and taken a job with a South Australian charter company. As we chatted, a gentleman walked past. Pointing to the ground, he said something directed towards me. I didn't hear, and asked Roger if he had.

"He said you dropped your superannuation."

I later heard that Roger, originally from Sweden, returned to his home country and picked up a job with a Scandi airline. He'd fly throughout the world in the DC-10, meet many people, and visit exotic countries. As a highly valued member of his former sporting organisation, the Darwin Rocksitters Club, he would also experience Saturday afternoon activities while sitting atop many international rocks.

Perhaps, it was the contrast between words and actions, but Lionel came to lose any trust he may have held in politicians. With the changes yet to take effect, he decided not to risk it. Aged around 57, Lionel still had a few years to go, and even at his age and with all of his experience, his love of flying hadn't waned. I remember a Lincoln–Moomba sequence when the Moomba trip was cancelled. Most would have been happy to go home early, but Lionel was disappointed. These were two sectors he'd now never fly. Giving up flying three years early must have been a hard decision, but it won out against Lionel's retirement plans being trashed. After 32 years at ASA and Guinea Airways, on top of his time in the RAAF, it was a sad day when Lionel hung up his hat and coat. Those additional three years were not only a loss for him, but for those who would have sat beside him. I would have benefited greatly from more time in this Captain's right seat.

Marcus flew with Lionel in his final month, and as was the tradition, a wheelchair met the aircraft after the last sector. I'm not sure where this tradition had originated or if any of the overseas airlines did the same, but in Australia, a Captain is wheeled from his final flight. Marcus pushed the wheelchair, helped on either side by flight attendants, Penny and Anne. Lionel sat graciously, with his usual beaming smile.

The superannuation strike had an effect. While inconveniencing people, it also mobilised many. We were joined by others with the same concerns, and after meetings in Canberra, we reached a compromise.

The tax would be reduced and only applied to the post-1983 portion. The Prime Minister, sitting Napoleon-like at the head of the table, conceded ground. It was noted, though, that indexed pensions were nowhere near this table. After further talks in Canberra, our representatives returned. During these difficult economic times, there was a need for restraint, especially in our industry. If we all pulled together and weathered the storm, then when times improved, everyone could share the gains.

At a high-level meeting in the capital, billed as 'The Summit', a resolution came. The aim was to bring people from all walks of life together to share ideas. This process was similar to how we resolved problems in the airline industry. We incorporated learnings into our training, often after the worst disasters in aviation history.

Over six years earlier, on the 27th of March 1977 at the Los Rodeos airport on the Canary Island of Tenerife, two laden 747s collided. One had attempted to take-off as the other was still taxiing down the runway. Foggy conditions obscured each from the other until it was too late. An unfamiliar airport, tarmac congestion, a missed taxi way, nonstandard ATC instructions and radio calls combined with misunderstandings and missed communications, all linked together to create the 'error chain' that led to this catastrophe. If one or two of the many errors had been 'trapped', the tragedy may have been averted. One last unchecked error led to the loss of 583 lives.

This tragedy changed forever how we worked on the flight deck. If, at any time, a crew member, no matter how senior or junior, is uncomfortable with a decision, course of action, or any other aspect of the operation, they are obliged to speak up. If a KLM crew member had queried the Captain, he may have sought to confirm their take-off clearance, and many lives would have been saved. What had for many years been viewed as 'the right stuff' — the omnipresent and domineering Captain — became 'the wrong stuff'. Instead, aviation sought to harness the strength of a team. When an emergency or non-normal situation arose, the entire crew became involved. The team focus continues today. Each crew member is assigned a specific task while encouraged to contribute ideas. With today's satellite communications, our information net has expanded. In certain circumstances, we can speak with engineers at home base or even the manufacturing specialists. A decision still has to be made, and this is the Captain's responsibility, but only after using all resources available. We call this Crew Resource Management (CRM).

Some innovative businesses have adopted the same principle. Modifying the first letter, they call it 'Corporate Resource Management'. With the door always open, anyone with an idea or something to say is welcome. This 'two heads are better than one', 'it's not who's right — it's what's right' approach has become as much a benefit to the companies utilising it as it is to flight safety.

The Prime Minister, ahead of his time, was applying this in the early '80s. Regrettably, the 'all walks of life' part translated to mainly representatives from government, the ACTU, and big business. Unfortunately, too, and throwing back to an earlier time, only one view appeared to be taken into account. As the Summit drew to a close, the PM returned to the chamber late. The ACTU secretary followed. Our Leader rose and stated that the agreement would be known as 'The Prices and Incomes Accord'.

While this sounded impressive, the accord barely glanced at prices. It focused on incomes. At the time, Australia was experiencing a period of high inflation coupled with high unemployment. The previous government was accused of tackling this 'stagflation' with the blunt and brutal instrument of unemployment. They denied this but, despite monetary and fiscal policies, they had made little headway. The Accord was an attempt to solve the problem by centrally fixing wages and salaries, and thereby reducing 'real unit labour costs'. If workers earned less, it was argued they would spend less, reducing inflationary pressures. The income foregone could then be used to increase business profits. Increasing profits at the expense of wages, it was theorised, would fuel investment. Business investment would thus create increased employment, which would spur economic activity, with the benefits 'dribbling down' to benefit everyone. Fine in theory, but the success of the plan depended very much on the windfall to the big end of town being used for its intended purpose.

Speaking to the House of Representatives on the 3rd of May 1983, the PM summarised the resolution:

> "Participants at the Summit conference recognised if restraint in incomes is to be exercised, then it should be exercised universally. In that spirit of equitable sharing of the burdens of recovery, the Summit also stressed the need for restraint in non-wage incomes such as dividends, professional fees and the like."

If the need for restraint in non-wage incomes was so important, however, why was it not incorporated into the Prices and Incomes Accord? The need for 'equitable sharing of burdens of recovery' seemed of at least equal importance to income restraint. Why was it not worthy of something more than 'should be' or 'in that spirit'?

The Prime Minister believed unflinchingly in the theory, but not everyone agreed the Accord was best practice. At least, he was in a position to set an example. Plans, commissions, and councils were established, aiming to achieve many social ideals. Few would argue with a safety net for the disadvantaged or assistance for those in need, but I felt these measures already fell within a government's guidelines.

I was sceptical. Why did the Accord only restrain wage and salary earners? Would the mere 'spirit of the agreement' ensure that burdens were shared equitably? Or would the rules be selective and apply to some but not others, as we saw with indexed pensions and superannuation? And what of the needs of different enterprises?

I'd experienced these inequities firsthand in the building industry. When interest rates were trending higher, people became reluctant to build a new house. Many preferred the less costly option of adding to or modifying their existing home. This benefited smaller builders like my father. As interest rates were trending lower, people were feeling more confident, and many more were deciding to embark on a new home. The benefits of this trend generally flowed to larger companies. Other industries were similar, in that different pockets performed differently at different times. The one-size-fits-all Accord didn't take into account these differences throughout our economy.

A struggling business may not be able to afford an increase imposed through the centralised Australian Industrial Relations Commission (IRC). Another business doing well could afford more. Where would the excess go? Supposedly, the excess went into investment and employment, but nothing in the Accord ensured this.

The Accord also bestowed a great deal of power upon peak union leaders. The ACTU secretary was the only delegate to accompany the Prime Minister back to the chamber, keeping all others, from business leaders to the federal treasurer, waiting. Under the current leadership, unions were 'rationalised' and 'restructured' (popular words in these times, as they are today). Many working people felt disaffected as they merged into fewer, bigger unions. We worked in transport, yet our working environment was markedly different from others who carried passengers, or delivered freight by road or rail. If pilots became part of the ACTU, maybe all transport industries would be dumped in together.

There was an opposing view. If employers and employees came together in a spirit of cooperation, they could make their own accords. With 'enterprise bargaining', the Industrial Relations Commission (IRC) would no longer be in the picture, which may even save taxpayers a few dollars. To me, this seemed like a possible option. Rather than losing my job, I would accept a pay cut to keep it. Conversely, during times of record profits, I would expect these to be shared.

During further talks in Canberra, our representatives were swayed by the Prime Minister's assurances, so agreed to abide by the Accord's guidelines. There was, however, a saving grace. The Accord was renewable, given a Roman numeral identifying the latest version, The Accord Mark I, II, III, and so on. We could consider our commitment at each renewal. I consoled myself with the thought that we could always opt out when the current version expired. We could then return to the tried and tested method of negotiating terms and conditions, through our representatives, directly with our employers.

CHAPTER 10

Sharon's birthday slipped by and Christmas approached. Rebecca was now 18 months old, so we took her to the city to see the window displays at John Martins. Strolling down Rundle Mall, exquisite scenes of European white Christmases abounded. We carried our wide-eyed little girl from one display to the next, ending at The Magic Cave. Each year the department store sponsored a Christmas pageant. Floats blooming in festive scenes and colours paraded through Adelaide streets. This massive event drew huge crowds, while still more watched it on TV at home.

Our quiet Christmas involved packing a picnic basket and heading into the Adelaide hills. Finding a spot, we unpacked and sat on an old blanket, eating our chicken and plum pudding. Rebecca was mobile now, and apart from the time spent eating, she romped and played in the field. She'd grown big enough for a car seat, and the seat joined her clothes, bassinette, pram, stroller and other necessities. It was all adding up. As usual, I had purchased the seat using my Bankcard. The lady slotted it into the imprint slide along with the docket, and after a back-and-forth motion, I signed the original firmly. As she returned the card, I feigned a frown.

> "Maybe I'll let it cool off before putting it back in my pocket."
> She looked at the card and then to me. "I really don't want to be the one to tell you this, but it only gets worse."

My panel van was built before the latest safety standards, and it lacked the anchor point needed to secure the new seat. On the way home, I dropped into the hardware shop. I took the bolt and, after checking the gauge, bought one twice as long, then added two nuts, stainless steel washers, and a heavy-duty spring washer. At home, I fitted the car seat and secured the lap sash seat belt around the base, as per instructions. Feeding the anchor belt to the back, I marked its position. I bored a hole in the tray. Fitting a stainless-steel washer, I slid the bolt through. Slithering under the car, I slipped the other washer, then the spring washer, over the bolt and tightened the first nut. Years before, Dad had taught me that if you wanted to be certain a nut wouldn't work loose, fit a second — a 'lock nut'. When finished, I felt the old car couldn't produce a head of steam capable of dislodging this handiwork.

Over time, I'd sensed a feeling. It was subtle; nothing was said, but, even with my dull male sensory abilities, I had picked up on it. When it came to the car, Sharon didn't share my enthusiasm. These days, the gears were a little loose and the hand brake was more for decoration. Changing down to first, on the odd occasion was a little crunchy, but I felt that such minor anomalies only added to its character. Any lack of enthusiasm from the queen of our castle, however, was more than made up by our little princess. She loved sitting in the seat beside us. We'd lift her in through the passenger side, and she'd raise her little arms so we could fasten the seat belt. Walking around to the driver's side, I'd take my seat. Immediately, a little elbow incessantly nudged my upper arm.

"Drive-a-car Daddy, drive-a-car Daddy."

It wasn't long before Rebecca noticed the gears. She pressed her little hand on mine as we manipulated the column shift. From this early age, she continued the family tradition of learning to drive far before the legal age.

On a day when Sharon was busy, Rebecca and I headed out. Down the hill with her ball in the back, we drove to the parklands. Starting by the river, we kicked and played in each of the four city surrounds. As I drove around, I explained the gears. Changing down, with the rev between, then dropping back into first — the double shuffle sometimes involved using heel and toe. Rebecca listened, her eyes wide with wonder. I did ponder, though, what she thought of her daddy's babbling. When my Dad had explained the ratio of engine revolutions delivered through gear box and drive train, I was much older. Even so, this had resulted in a certain amount of head scratching.

We discovered the Adelaide markets. On shopping days, we drove to the city and picked up fresh fruit and vegies, home-style bread and other delicacies. At our favourite stall, the Greek owner and his sons got to know us. Sometimes, we'd go straight to the markets after I returned from an early flight. To save time, I removed the tie, wings and epaulettes, and jumped back in the car. One day, as I added bananas, apples and potatoes to our basket, the green grocer asked if I worked for Australia Post. I guess it was the blue shirt. Thinking about it, I did carry the mail.

At work, the coming and going of pilots had ceased. Now the FO list, apart from Geoff and Dave, comprised the last two intakes only. We saw Coralee and Dave regularly, and Saturday afternoon BBQs were common, so we cemented our new friendships. Some were married, others single, some were around our age and others were younger — we formed a mixed but tight-knit group. Not only had pilots returned home to Adelaide, but some flight attendants too. Chrissie was one. Blond and with a fair complexion, Chrissie was the type of girl who, if she could, would gather the world's abandoned kittens and shower them with loving care. Chrissie's arrival hadn't gone unnoticed by Kim. Kim came from the south-east of the State where his family owned a dairy farm. Before Ansett, he'd flown out of Kununurra. Without knowing, we had probably crossed paths before Adelaide.

One BBQ was hosted by Chrissie and Kim. Following initial surprise, it became obvious as we cooked our steaks and sausages that they were now a couple. From our intake course, Dominic and Stephan were good mates, so were often out and about together, and Marcus was touched by Cupid's arrow and soon to be engaged to an Adelaide girl.

Lake Eyre filled with water. Water in a lake is usually nothing out of the ordinary, but this lake was normally dry. Like so many features of our country, Lake Eyre is immense. The basin covers over 1,000,000km2 and forms the largest drainage system in the world.

On the 25th of March 1984, I crewed an unusual charter. Flying with another of the young upgrade Captains, originally from Melbourne, we set out for Lake Eyre. Leigh Creek was our planned refuelling stop. Over the lake, usually covered by salt pans, all the inlets and bays were full. Water birds flew beneath and vegetation sprung up along the banks. Many passengers visited the cockpit and marvelled at the expanse of water and the wildlife populating it. Tourist charters popped up rarely, and John and I were lucky to fly this one. The image of so much water in inland Australia has remained with me until this day.

As winter approached, Sharon and I decided to do something about our floors. We couldn't afford carpets, but wanted to make our family room more comfortable. We decided on a floating wooden floor. There was a square section at the front door. We chose tiles, and with the aid of a tile cutter, glue and grout, the concrete entrance was transformed. I also tiled the kitchen, so half of our floors had coverings.

Business had started to pick up. Ansett Air Freight opened an F27 base in Brisbane. Dave submitted a bid. It worked out. They would leave for their new home in June. Dave would be junior and, as the base was smaller, promotion would be slower, but it meant a move to the city where they had decided to settle. Coralee and Dave's move to Brisbane made us think. While Adelaide was pleasant, it was a subsidiary base. Ansett promotion meant I'd eventually need to return to Mainline. Since starting to fly, I always seemed to be moving around. Sharon had lived a semi-nomadic life as well. We both felt the need to settle somewhere.

Avoiding the two biggest cities, our choice became the same as that of our friends. I submitted a bid for Brisbane. Checking the seniority list, there was little chance for the moment, but a bid stayed in the system until changed or withdrawn. At a BBQ, I spoke with Kris from the following intake. Both he and his wife Sherry were natives of Queensland. They wanted to return, so Kris also put in a bid. At subsequent BBQs, or whenever we bumped into each other, there was always discussion about company movement and estimates of how long it might be before we would rate a slot in the Sunshine State.

The Adelaide winter was just as freezing as the previous year. Sharon decided to spend time with her dad in Darwin. My block had days off at the month's end, so I could spend a few days up there as well. I dropped Sharon and Rebecca to the airport and went to work. Arriving home to the empty house, I lit the pot belly. The warmth was a poor substitute for that of the two ladies in my life. As my days off approached, I checked and listed on the Alice–Darwin service. Arriving in the afternoon, Sharon and Rebecca met me. The car seat was now in Sharon's dad's old Falcon.

Over the next few days, we visited all the old places. It was good to be back. I spent time with my friend Ari. He had decided to move closer to home and landed a job with Oxley Airlines. He'd shortly fly a Chieftain out of Port Macquarie.

We enjoyed an afternoon at Berry Springs, and another day at the Nightcliff swimming pool. John had free time, so took care of Rebecca while Sharon and I hired bikes. We rode from the city to Fanny Bay and dropped in at the gelati shop before continuing to Parap. Parap was the site of the old airport. Riding by, we noticed a former hangar with the side door open. Bits and pieces of old aircraft lay outside. Walking through the door, I saw more of the same inside. Noel, a former NTAC engineer I knew, was quietly working on an old engine. Somehow, he'd gathered all these old parts, the centrepiece being a Mirage fighter fuselage. Noel had a dream; he wanted to establish a Darwin aviation museum.

In what seemed like no time, I had to return for work. Back in Adelaide, the cold bit into my dry season skin. As I flew with Keith and then Jim, I looked forward to Sharon and Rebecca's return.

The weather warmed and my girls returned. We resumed our visits to the park, down the hill and then a right. The fun of our little girl running around was only tarnished by a common parenting problem — how much little ears could absorb. While the recreation area shared its official name with the adjoining suburb, Sharon and I had another name for it. Our little princess ran down the hall with a ball in her arms.

> "Mummy, Daddy, can we go to the dog poo park?"

We spent Christmas in Sydney. Rebecca sat wide-eyed by the Christmas tree as a mountain of wrapping paper grew beside her opened presents. We arrived back in Adelaide on New Year's Eve. 1985 would be our third in Adelaide. We had another problem. When Sharon needed the car, she dropped me at work and picked me up afterwards. The early flights and late finishes disrupted Rebecca's routine. There were now playgroup days and days Sharon needed to go to town or attend to the many features of life a little one added.

Greenhill was recovering. Encouraged by the January sun, lush growth sprouted everywhere. Although not likely for many years, the chance of another fire hung over us. If this happened, a car sitting at Adelaide airport would be of no use to Sharon and Rebecca at home.

On the 7th of January, I crewed the overnight freighter flight to Melbourne. At 5.30 am, my little family waited outside the freight shed. Rebecca was asleep in the car seat and Sharon sat bleary eyed. As we left, we drove past the same unmarked semi-trailer that seemed to always arrive around the same time as our flight.

> Sharon moved across to the passenger seat. "We really need another car."
> I bristled. "There's nothing wrong with the car we've got."
> "That's not what I meant."

Sharon was right. Had my job covered normal hours, I could use public transport (there was a bus stop out the front of our house).

Our current arrangement worked most of the time, albeit with inconvenience, but we really needed a second car. We couldn't afford one, and as we decided to install carpet for the winter, all of our savings were going towards this. If my bid for a jet in Brisbane came off, the problem would be solved. Unfortunately, as Kris and I regularly discussed, this change was years away. With no immediate solution, Sharon and I continued our many drives up and down the hill. I did promise, though, as soon as we could afford it, we would get a small car.

The Captain I was flying with was another from Melbourne. On the 18th of January, he swapped a flight and I flew with Keith on the Lincoln–Mount Gambier sequence. This would be my last flight with him, as he had news.

> "Mate, I've decided to retire early."
> I'd really miss flying with him.
> "It's because of the superannuation."
> "But that's all fixed."
> Most of his benefit would be treated as before.
> "Yes, mate, that's what they say, but remember what they said before the election."

After our flight, Keith invited me home. He was such a nice guy. Always helpful and generous, he shared his abundant knowledge, and rarely was there a flight I didn't learn something. I did feel a little sorry for him. In all the times we flew, there were stories of 'Mama'. It seemed that every time he wanted to do anything, Mama was a thorn in his side. "Mama wouldn't let me do this", and "Mama wouldn't hear of that." We'd flown together a lot, and I'd built an almost dragon-like mental picture.

Mrs McCoy met us at the door. She immediately made me feel at home. Guiding me to the sunroom, she asked after Sharon and Rebecca, and hoped we were enjoying life in Adelaide.

> "You've flown with Keith so often. I'm so pleased we could finally meet."

She made a pot of tea to which she added the homemade biscuits she had baked that morning. We chatted, with much banter between her and Keith. I could see she wasn't one to put up with any nonsense, but she had the same attributes and qualities I admired in her husband.

> Mrs McCoy offered another biscuit. "I hope he hasn't been telling stories, giving the wrong impression."
> "No," I lied.

Dominic flew with Keith in his final month. He gathered photos from past years and put together an album spanning Keith's career. It was a great effort and Dominic presented it to Keith at the farewell function at the Aviation Institute. At the end of the evening, Keith gave a thank you speech spiced with a few amusing anecdotes, with Mama and his daughter, Michelle, by his side.

It's hard to keep a good man down and Keith later went to Darwin and flew the Air North DC-3 part time. Some years after, a consortium built a replica of Sir Charles Kingsford Smith's Southern Cross. Keith flew this too, even crossing the Tasman. During Keith's final year, I flew four of the 12 months with him. Every flight was just as the first — professional, but relaxed, and most of the time with me flying. I would certainly miss him.

Towards the middle of March, my sister called. Bruce Springsteen was on his '*Born in the USA Tour*' and Maree was arranging tickets. She and her friends were planning for the concert on the 28th. Would I like to go? Would I what!

The Sydney Entertainment Centre darkened, and the crowd grew quiet. In one single burst, the chords and snare drum beat erupted. I hadn't been to the USA, so I couldn't have been born there, but this minor technicality failed to dampen my enthusiasm as I bellowed along with the band.

The beat pulsated through the stadium, and it wasn't long before everyone was standing on their seats clapping and dancing. Bruce and the E Street Band gave it their all. With just one 30-minute break, the concert lasted for around three and a half hours. It wasn't until the encore, but then it rang out, with drums pounding and guitars exploding. I loved every one of his songs, but this was the one I'd waited all night for. I stamped my feet and smashed my hands together in time with Max's snare drum beat. The stadium bulged with screaming tramps; as one with Bruce, we were *'Born to Run'*.

In April, the company held a staff meeting at the Ansett Gateway Hotel in Adelaide city. ASA had suffered a blow. The Moomba contract came up for renewal and one of our competitors, Lloyd Aviation, submitted a bid proposing to use an F28. Their submission was successful. ASA relied on that charter. Our regional routes were losing out to operators using smaller aircraft that had sprung up since intra-state routes were deregulated. Banderanties and Metroliners carried fewer people, but could offer greater frequency. In short, the F27 was now too big. Our managers wanted to share their plans for operating in this new environment.

The company opened a new tourist route to Yulara, the town servicing Ayers Rock and The Olgas (later, the Aboriginal names, Uluru and Kata Tjuta, were coupled to these). Jim and I crewed this flight in August but, unfortunately, passenger numbers were disappointing. It was the first time I'd seen 'The Rock'. The round trip took seven hours, the longest flight any of us had flown in the F27. On approach, we could see the huge mass in the distance. It sat alone, protruding from an otherwise flattened landscape.

Passengers visiting the cockpit marvelled at the sight, some more enthusiastic than others. Stephan had crewed the flight a week earlier. When they were in range, a couple of American tourists came up front. The husband asked questions as he searched the horizon for Uluru. He chatted, but his wife was quiet. Stephan, attempting to draw her into the conversation, pointed out this wonder of the world.

The woman looked disdainfully at her husband.

> "You dragged me all this way just to see a Goddamn rarck?"

The tourist flight was not popular. As the F27s plied the once lucrative routes, passenger numbers were down. Ansett linked up with Kendell Airlines and a few of their Captains rode our jumpseats for familiarisation. We planned to supplement our services with theirs, using the smaller Metroliner. At the start of October, while flying with Jim, he remarked that we were "route endorsing" these guys to "take our jobs". Our flights were reduced, replaced by this company. I agreed with him. It was an ominous sign.

Sharon needed the car, so she dropped me off. I'd return early evening and we arranged pickup for around six. After my flight, I waited outside the terminal. Kris finished around the same time, and we stopped to chat. With things finally starting to pick up, Kris hoped for a Brisbane slot the following year. I wasn't so sure. There was still slack to be taken up before then.

Sharon was a little late, but I guessed she was caught in traffic. About 10 minutes later, the blue car rounded the entrance road. Sharon slipped out of the driver's seat and I eased in. She could have driven us home, but seemed only to drive when she had to. On the road out of the airport, I turned the blinker on for the first turn. The sound and dashboard light were a fraction slower than usual. I asked Sharon if she'd noticed, but she felt everything seemed normal. It was probably nothing, but at the next turn I noticed it again. I'd spent a lot of time in this car, and even if small, this change was noticeable.

As we approached the base of the hill, we needed lights. When I turned them on, the dashboard dimmed. No other change, so I put it down to being overly sensitive. A car overtook us, as there'd be no chance once we started the climb. Another car stayed behind. Starting up the hill and under load, the car misfired. I jumped on the clutch and gave it revs, but I needed to change down a gear to keep it going. The headlights faded and I had to continually pump the clutch and accelerator to keep the car going. The vehicle ahead slowed down. The car behind switched to high beam. Aided by both, I could see where we were going, but I was worried that the engine would give out.

Greenhill Road wound its way up through the hills and was a single lane each way. With nowhere to pull off and many blind corners, this was no place to break down, especially at night. The car ahead and the one behind shepherded us along our way. Clutch continually in and out, and back in first gear, we crawled our way up. My heart raced, and a deathly quiet embraced both passengers. Our turn off came into sight. I stretched my arm out the window and waved our thanks to these two good Samaritans. Just around the corner, the engine quit. I tried turning it over, but no response.

Wrenching the handbrake, I left it in gear and got out. I grabbed a couple of rocks and chocked the back wheels. Sharon released Rebecca, scooped her into her arms, and marched off towards home. I got my flight bag from the back and caught up.

She turned to me with burning eyes.

> "That old bomb car of yours could've gotten us killed."

I was stung. The car had made a valiant effort, not giving up until we were safely off the main road. But what Sharon said was true. Stopping on Greenhill Road with minimal or no lights could have been deadly. There was blame, but not for the car. I shouldn't have started up the hill. My only defence was that I had no idea that the problem was so serious. With no doubt now about Sharon's feelings, we walked the rest of the way in silence.

My flight the next day was in the afternoon. Suspecting an electrical problem, I rang an auto electrician.

"That'd be the alternator, mate."

He advised that, after being left all night, it may start. Otherwise, I could have it towed. Allowing plenty of time, I changed for work.

"You're not going to drive it are you?"
"If it starts, going down the hill will be fine."
The auto electrician was on the edge of town, so if I got it down the hill, it'd be a short tow.
"But it's dangerous."

Assuring Sharon that I'd only drive it if the engine ran smoothly, I set out. If needs be, I could even 'coast' down the hill. It started first time. Turning around, it continued ticking over. Not under load and without lights, it ran evenly. At the shop, the mechanic quickly checked.

"The alternator's terminal, mate."

As I wouldn't be back before closing, he swiped the Bankcard and said he'd leave the car outside, key under the left mudguard. A taxi dropped me back after work. The engine burst into life with the usual purr. At home, I explained the alternator problem. With a new one installed, the car ran fine. This comment was met with a slight nod.

Joan called and asked us around for dinner. Since Lionel's retirement we'd kept in touch. Sometimes, after work I'd drop by, and this evening was one of many we'd spent with them. Marcus and Scott were also invited, along with another guest.

Flying with the senior Captains, I heard tales from the 'old days'. Keith often mentioned the integration disputes. Sometimes, I felt as though I'd attended these tumultuous meetings. When the various airlines were taken over or merged, the individual seniority lists were integrated. The story of how this was sorted took up several trips to Moomba and back.

Both Lionel and Keith spoke of another Captain, now also retired. Like many of the names, he was before our time. He was Irish and his name seemed to pop up more than most. A bachelor, he lived alone and had a dog. When flying the DC-3, he'd bring the dog to work. Sitting next to the baggage locker, the mutt quietly plied the skies alongside his master. It'd be interesting what Occupational Health and Safety may have to say these days, but the dog was generally well behaved. On one occasion, though, he broke loose and ran onto the tarmac. With Adelaide airport operations disrupted, the Chief Pilot put an end to these free canine flights. Over dinner, Captain Johnny O'Hagan entertained us with his Irish lilt. So many stories, but I liked the dog tale best. In thick brogue, he told us his dog's name.

"First Officer Barker."

CHAPTER 11

There was news with Qantas. Until now, they were an all 747 fleet, but certain routes needed smaller aircraft, so they were introducing the Boeing 767. The opposite of when the 747 replaced the 707 was happening, and the company needed more pilots. Two young guys from our intake applied and secured interviews. Shortly after, these two Ansett pilots moved to Qantas. Ari called. He also had an interview. I wished him well. A few weeks later, he called again. Following interviews, a psyche test and a simulator check, he'd received the call that afternoon — he was in. Great news.

Back when I went through flying school, among the 10 of us classmates, some of our names doubled up. As seemed often the case, there was another Paul, and two Steves. The younger Steve was from Sydney and had joined Ansett on an intake ahead of mine. The Aviation Academy at Cessnock was set up on a pseudo military basis. Each course was termed a 'Flight' and assigned a colour. In this series of Qantas interviews, our youngest classmate, Tim, was also accepted. Three of us from 'Green Flight 1977' were now working with the airlines.

Arriving to work, I checked the noticeboard. One newspaper cutting stood out. Bordered by red pencil and with added exclamation marks, the article detailed news of a semi-trailer that had overturned near the Victoria and South Australian border. On its regular overnight run, it had left Melbourne to arrive in Adelaide by 5:30 the next morning. It was unusual — neither the truck nor trailer had markings. The article concluded by observing that parcels and packages that were strewn across the road were labelled: 'Ansett Air Freight'.

Changes were afoot at Ansett. While not enough to open up Brisbane, vacancies emerged in other ports. Stephan picked up a slot back home in Perth, flying the F28. Dominic wanted to live at home, but a jet in Melbourne was still beyond his grasp, so he followed Stephan to Perth.

I loved the F27, but yearned to fly jets. I felt it would be years before I rated one in our preferred base, but the F28 was now an option. When flying in the Territory, I'd often seen this jet as it had routinely traversed the Top End. I stopped and stared with wishful eyes at its T-tailed fuselage and rear-mounted Rolls Royce Spey turbofans as it passed through Darwin and ports such as Kununurra, Tindal, Gove and Groote. Sharon and my eyes turned to the west. While waiting for Brisbane, I could fly a jet. The pay rise would allow us to take out a loan for a small car. The thought of living somewhere new was exciting. We decided that settling down could wait another couple of years. After all, Rebecca was still young.

In October, I took three weeks' leave. We spent the time with Sharon's dad in Darwin. But, this time, instead of heading straight to Darwin, my green ticket took a detour. As we might move to Perth, and neither Sharon nor I had been there before, I thought I should take a look. I called Stephan. He had a couple of flights, then a free day. The Perth flight arrived in the afternoon, and Stephan met me at the terminal. We set out for Scarborough. He was meeting friends, so we'd have dinner at a pub there.

Driving to this beachside suburb, I was taken by the white sandy beaches, one after the other. During my old school-day surfing trips back in Sydney, we'd often watch the sunrise over the Pacific. Looking out to the Indian Ocean, it was now setting.

On Stephan's flight the next day, I rode the jump seat. The performance of this machine was staggering. Flying beside Keith, with the F27 lightly loaded, he'd often remark, "Mate, she's going up like a homesick angel." Even fully loaded, the F28 was one 'homesick angel'.

Stephan had a day off. He'd recently taken up scuba diving and was going out on the boat. I was welcome to borrow his car after dropping him at Fremantle. I took him up on his kind offer, and used his street directory to explore. First, I drove to the city. Stephan made an early start, so it was well before the rush. About the same size as Adelaide, Perth sits on the Swan River. A pedestrian mall featured the usual shops and department stores. Driving through the nearby suburbs, older buildings contrasted with newer architecture.

Up on the hill overlooking the city at Kings Park, my eyes stretched upriver. Turning downstream, the waters meandered towards the port city of Fremantle, or 'Freo' as the locals call it.

There was someone I wanted to look up. Steve was the older of the two Steves from flying school. Back in 1977, he had driven his VW Beetle all the way from Perth to Cessnock. He joined the rest of us enrolled for 'Green Flight', our colour coded Commercial Licence course. Steve lived in East Fremantle and his number was listed in the White Pages. I had intended to call, but rather than find a phone box, I drove around. Under renovation, the house was an older, weatherboard type. Dad would have described it as a 'worker's cottage'. A new storey, partially complete, rose from the rear. Steve was working at the front door. I passed through the gate and he turned. Although we hadn't seen each other since our Cessnock days, more than seven years ago, Steve immediately smiled and offered his right hand.

> "Paul, how's it going?"
> "Not bad, Steve. How about you?"
> "Good. Come on in. I'll make a cuppa. What brings you to the West?"
> "I'm with Ansett. There's a chance of a basing here. What've you been up to?"

After graduating, Steve returned to Perth and, like several of us, he had completed an instructor rating. There was no work for a brand-new instructor, however. After numerous visits to flying schools in Perth and up and down the west coast, he grew despondent and gave up flying. He now restored old houses.

Walking to the door, he slipped his hammer through the belt of his nail bag. As I passed back through the front gate, I realised that at the same time that Steve became disillusioned and gave up on aviation, I had set out on my first road trip along Highway 1.

That afternoon, I picked Stephan up from Freo. Next morning, he dropped me at the airport, where I caught the flight to Darwin and was reunited with my family.

That October leave break was when I first met 'Poppy', Sharon's grandfather. He was up from Western Australia where he'd lived most of his life. Retired now, he was a diesel mechanic servicing power stations on the gold fields. A lifetime in close proximity to heavy machinery with no ear protection meant he now wore hearing aids. These curled around both ears and left barely enough room to secure his Coke-bottle glasses. Even when turned up to maximum volume, you still had to shout when talking with him. In turn, he shouted back.

When Rebecca thought Poppy wasn't looking, she repositioned his walking stick. He kept watch from the corner of his eye.

> Telling the story later, he yelled, "She's a little beauty, that one."

Sharon and her brother Lindsay had lost their mum when they were very young and, for a time, Poppy had looked after them. Their dad remarried, and John's new wife was English. When Poppy visited them, he'd discretely eat the children's Brussel sprouts, cabbage or kidney that little Australian tummies were not accustomed to. Also coinciding with Poppy's visits, small hands often found jellybeans in their dressing gown pockets or under their pillows.

After a hard life, Poppy was a bit rough around the edges, with patience being not one of his virtues. John once explained Poppy's concept of shopping.

> "Ned expects the shop assistant to meet him at the door and within seconds produce whatever he's looking for."

Poppy needed a few things, so I drove him to Casuarina. First stop, the chemist. The young lady took a few seconds to move from behind the counter to the aisle. The delay already started to irritate my companion. Greeting us halfway, she asked if she could help.

> "Got any pong?"
> She looked at him, as I did.
> He lifted his left arm, his right hand in a spraying gesture. "You know — BRUT."

Poppy rolled his own, and drank Emu Bitter, purchased by the carton. After consuming a few, tropical evenings became a magical return to the past as Poppy reminisced through a cloud of Douwe Egberts. Driving cars I thought of as vintage, he haunted sun-parched, one-horse towns as his gold fever had itched under faded grey and diesel-grease-stained overalls. Drinking in pubs perched on dry and thirsty gold fields, he'd pitched his tent on outback sand and rock, and resurrected stew that straddled a campfire.

Sharon and Rebecca stayed on in Darwin for another few days. As I boarded a jet south, the dry season was nearing its end. Remembering times flying through the wet, I was grateful for the radar and enhanced instrumentation on airline aircraft. Some types on our South Australian routes were the same as I'd flown around the Top End. To passengers, an aeroplane is an aeroplane. But for me, I'd much rather the enhanced engine-out performance, instrumentation, and more rigorous standards mandated by the category I now flew.

Back at work, Buck called out as I passed by his office. "So, you're going west, young man."

> I had no idea what he was talking about.
> To my blank look, he added, "You put in a bid for the F28, right?"
> I had, but it was only a short while ago.
> "You've got a slot in Perth starting in March."

My bid for a jet in Brisbane went nowhere but, on changing my request to Perth, approval had taken only a couple of weeks. It was exciting, but much needed doing in the meantime.

Arriving from Darwin the following evening, Sharon and Rebecca hopped off the Boeing. Sharon was always a little down when returning from the Territory. She assured me she was fine, but I sensed the usual low mood. I asked if she'd like a change. She said she wouldn't mind.

"We're going to Perth."

A real estate agent lived locally. He looked at our house. He knew a guy with a truck and bobcat. He suggested we level our dirt driveway and add white gravel. Gardens were minimal up there due to the lack of water, but a load of woodchips would look better than the clay and weeds of our front yard. He even lent me his whippersnapper. Not much could be done inside, but perhaps we could take down the sheets from the windows on open inspection days. He suggested entering the market after Christmas, so we planned a 'For Sale' sign in January. Christmas came and went. As I was working, we had a simple meal on Christmas evening, and a week later, 1986 began quietly. We placed the house on the market, and January slipped by.

On the weekends, we held open inspections, and the odd person made an appointment. After several weeks, however, there were no takers. The agent suggested we drop the price. Although unpalatable, this was the best course of action. In early February, I had a couple of days off. Sharon asked me to mind Rebecca. She needed to visit the doctor. I immediately asked if there was anything wrong.

"No, I'm fine, nothing to worry about."

Sharon took the car, and Rebecca and I rearranged woodchips and tidied up our woodpile out the back. An hour passed, and it was time for our morning snack. We were not yet finished our milk and biscuits when the blue van drove back up the driveway. Rushing to the door, I immediately asked if everything was alright.

> "Yes, just as I told you, there's nothing to worry about." She paused, "But come September, we're not all going to fit in that old bomb car of yours."

By mid-February, we were getting worried. The house was still not sold and my course was starting in the second week of March. Air New South Wales operated the same type, so ground school would take place in Sydney. After that, I'd undergo link trainer and then aircraft endorsement in Perth, followed by line training.

An open inspection was planned for the weekend. If no one was interested, the agent suggested we drop the price again. We had to sell the house, and we needed to make arrangements to move, so we reluctantly agreed. During inspections, we visited a park in the hills where Rebecca played on the swings and slides. We returned to find our agent on the phone, a document lying on the kitchen bench. I heard the words, "Just sold the one in Christopher Avenue." He put down the phone and turned to us.

When we had moved in, the house was a shell. It now boasted floor coverings and a smooth driveway and paths, not to mention the pot belly and several other additions courtesy of the hammer, nail bag and other tools.

> "A young couple came through. The wife loved the house and they made an offer on the spot."

With one problem solved, we turned to the logistics of moving. While on the course in Sydney, Sharon and Rebecca would stay in Darwin. Once in Perth, they'd join me.

What to do with our stuff? We still didn't have much, and Ansett allowed a few tea-chest-sized boxes as air freight. After this, there was even less to move. A removalist would be expensive, so I calculated that all of our possessions would fit in the car with a trailer. A small company at Parafield could build a trailer in a week.

The manager, an older guy, checked his specs. "The biggest, without going to double axels, is seven by five."

The size was ideal, and the price included a tow bar. Before leaving, I had one last question. I checked the chart and pointed.

> "Yeah, the blue's quite popular."

Years earlier, I would have driven across, but not now, and not loaded to the gunnels with a trailer on the back. The Indian Pacific, on its way from Sydney to Perth, stopped in Port Pirie. The train's flat top carriages transported vehicles. If I could get there, the car, trailer and myself could cross the continent this way.

A week later, the trailer was ready. After picking it up, I dropped by the bottle shop. At home, I unhitched the trailer and popped a bottle of champagne in the fridge.

In Sydney, Mum and Dad had remodelled my room around the time we had moved into our house in Adelaide. They no longer needed my bed, desk and bookshelves, so I had them sent to us, along with the stereo. The bed was now Rebecca's, and we had converted the second bedroom into a study. The desk went first in the back of the van. By mid-afternoon, the car was full. I attached the trailer and loaded the heavier items. By dinner, the only things left in the house were the bar fridge and Rebecca's and our mattresses and bedding. I could load those next morning.

Sharon and I were of a 'questioning' generation. We marched in the streets and challenged the powers that be. Just because a Prime Minister, President, Pope or anyone in a position of authority had said something, didn't necessarily mean it was right. This attitude got up Dad's nose.

> "Look, Son, if you spend your life going against the grain, then all you'll do is wear yourself out."

These days, I'd grown more mellow. Although still unconventional, I felt it silly to defy convention just because it was convention. This, I felt, was as stupid as going along with it for the same reason. There was something I'd been thinking about, and wondered if Sharon felt the same. There was only one way to find out. After tucking Rebecca into bed, we sat together, and I opened the champagne. With both glasses filled, I popped the question.

> Sharon's eyes held mine. "Will you look after us?"
> Ours was a case of each looking after the other, but this was a time for a simple answer. "Yes."
> Her reply was also simple. "Yes."

Throughout my preparations, I had one fear. Everything hinged on reaching Port Pirie in time. If I didn't make the train, our plans would fall in a heap. The car was getting old and a new mechanical problem could be waiting to happen. I consoled myself with the simplicity of the machine. It had an engine, gearbox, drive train and few other moving parts. With the major electrical component, the alternator, recently renewed, not much else could go wrong. My worry was the engine overheating with such a load. To counter this, I measured the distance. Under normal circumstances, the trip would take just under three hours. I calculated the time again, if travelling at 60 kilometres per hour. This would be annoying, not only for me but for other road users, but I felt it best to reduce the demand on the engine. I added another two hours. If it did overheat, I could stop, allow it to cool, and replenish the radiator from my plastic jerry can. Even with these buffers, I was anxious. In all the journeys and kilometres we'd travelled, I hadn't thought twice about the car's performance. This trip was far shorter, but the car had never carried such a load.

The alarm woke us. Tea and cereal, then the last of the load was tied down. Sharon and Rebecca would stay with friends that night, and fly to Darwin the following day. Sharon had baked a carrot cake. I added a thermos and slipped them into my small bag on the passenger side. With hugs and kisses, we said our goodbyes.

Behind the wheel, I turned the key. As I headed down the driveway, I could feel the weight. Up the small grade of our street, I stayed in first gear, already nursing. Down the hill that last time, the weight pushed the car and me along. Slowly and carefully, we manoeuvred through the Adelaide traffic, also for the last time. On the city outskirts, the road opened up. I kept the car at 60 as other traffic pushed past. Although my pace was slow and traffic behind built up between overtaking lanes, everything ran smoothly. The car was chugging along nicely, so I eased the accelerator a little more and sped up to 80. The trailer, evenly balanced, sat behind, barely noticeable.

I began to relax and, without realising, eased the accelerator a little more. When I looked again, I was doing 100. With not the slightest complaint, the old machine purred like the kitten it once was. Cars and trucks that had overtaken kilometres earlier came into view; I was now sitting on 110. I eased the wheel slightly to the right; they could eat our dust. The last time the pistons had pumped their canned heat like this was on the drive from Melbourne to Adelaide, just under four years earlier. My old car was like a thoroughbred stallion that had found the gate ajar and bolted. Champing at the bit, with me, the jockey, doing my best to hold back, we were on the road again.

This particular stretch brought back memories, but there was one slight mishap. As we ran, the wind rippled against the car's metallic body, and the cassette player ate my old, worn Bob Seger tape. Switching to the radio, I picked up a local station. The Scottish band, Big Country, were playing their hit, '*In a Big Country*'. Looking through the side window, I nodded. A few kilometres later, Icehouse belted out their 1982 classic, '*Great Southern Land*'. Looking out again, I nodded again.

I breezed into Pirie hours ahead of schedule. The lady at the station office remarked on my early arrival. She pointed to where

I could park the car and trailer for loading. I found a phone box and called Sharon.

> "Hi, it's me."
> "Oh, no! You've broken down. Where are you?"
> "I'm in Pirie."
> "Pirie? But you shouldn't be there for another couple of hours."
> I started to explain how well the car had run but, when venturing towards stallions champing at the bit, Sharon stopped me.
> "You and that old bomb ... Anyway, I'm glad you made it. What will you do now?"

That was a good question. I had hours to kill. The most nerve-wracking part of the journey was now over. If only I'd known — all that time fretting for nothing. Port Pirie had a small museum and a few other sights. After several hours wandering around and generally taking it easy, boarding was imminent. The ticket had a carriage and seat number, but before heading to the passenger section, I walked to the end of the train where the vehicles were mounted on flat top cars.

This crossing is one of the longest stretches of straight railway track in the world. A quick check confirmed that the tie downs on both car and trailer were secure. Years ago, I'd planned to cross the Nullarbor, but fate had intervened. I'd also planned to slot my favourite Bruce Springsteen tape into the stereo cassette player as we commenced the crossing. Finally, after all this time, and in the care of this wedge-tailed eagle, my van and I would cross the Nullarbor. The boarding announcement stuttered through the platform speakers. Reaching out, I gently patted the faded side panel of the car my Sydney friend, Liz, had christened 'Baby Blue', and mouthed the words I'd so long ago planned for this run.

CHAPTER 12

Until I started travelling around, I had no idea that so much in our country, both natural and man-made, qualified as the 'biggest' or 'longest', or was unique or so distinctive. Perth is one of the most isolated cities in the world, and this had been a long day. Perhaps, the mental strain of the last few days, not helped by needless worry, had taken their toll. I rested my head on the top of the bench seat as the sun set. The lady beside eased past on her way to the dining car. I'd been sneaking bites of Sharon's carrot cake (the best in the world), piece by piece, since arriving in Port Pirie. There wasn't much left.

I slept on and off through the night. We stopped at Cook, a fuel point and crossing loop, where the train remained for an hour. My fellow traveller had the window seat, but I could still see everything. Not that there was much to see. The flat expanse was populated by endless saltbush. After reading for an hour, I looked up to find that nothing much had changed. Finishing my book that evening, I returned it to my bag as we pulled into Kalgoorlie. Here the train changed locomotives and crew. It was 'time out'. Along with several passengers, I crossed the road to a pub and indulged in a counter meal. This long stopover allowed time for a quick city tour.

The morning broke as we powered through the wheat belt of the Avon and Swan valleys, and soon after, the sun rattled through the outer suburbs of the capital. We closed in on East Perth, and just after nine, rolled into the station. Stretching, I joined the other passengers on the platform. An announcement advised those with vehicles to wait, as these would take time to unload.

A guy in overalls was sitting on a bench. "It usually takes 40 minutes."

The mechanic was part of the maintenance crew. The train was to be shunted off for a thorough check, and in what I imagined to be a huge job, every brake pad on every wheel set would be changed.

My car and trailer were covered in dust, and the white drop sheets had turned to varying shades of red and brown. After washing the windscreen, I embarked on another difficult section of this journey, manoeuvring through an unfamiliar city. Before leaving Adelaide, I had copied a map of Perth's metropolitan area. I'd drive through the southern outskirts, cross the river, and pick up the Canning Highway.

My friend Dominic must've been happy with his decision to move here, as he'd bought a townhouse in Bicton on the way to Fremantle, which would see my journey's end. Dominic had a shed that was almost empty. I could store our larger items there, and our small amount of furniture would fit inside his spare room.

Dom heard the car and met me as I slid out. He put the kettle on and we talked for a while, but I didn't have long. In typical Ansett style, I would spend minimal time 'offline'. That night I was booked on the 'red eye' to Sydney. Dominic also had a five-day sequence and was leaving late afternoon for Alice Springs, and then 'up the Track' to Darwin. There's only one road in and out of Darwin, the Stuart Highway. The highway runs the whole way between Darwin and Port Augusta in South Australia. The stretch in the Territory is known as 'the Track'.

After unloading, I freshened up. It was time to leave again. At the airport, the Ansett WA offices were in an old hangar near the terminal. Recently, the business name had changed. Starting life in 1927, the airline was known for many years as MMA, MacRobertson Miller Airlines (the name was a combination of millionaire backer Sir Macpherson Robertson and entrepreneurial pilot Horrie Miller). In the West, everyone called it "Mickey Mouse Airlines". When taken over, the business kept the name, but changed to Ansett colours. In 1981, it had become Airlines of Western Australia, with new livery. In recent times, it has reverted to the Ansett colour scheme and has been rebranded Ansett WA.

The crewing officer handed me my Pax Travel Card for the evening flight. When positioning for duty, as I would tonight, the company blocked a seat. Some airlines called this 'deadheading' or 'positioning', but at Ansett we knew it as 'paxing' (or passengering). Rather than printed tickets for each segment, the company issued a travel card allowing multiple entries. Additional paperwork could wait until my return. The crewing officer then passed me the all-important staff carpark key. On my first visit, Stephan had demonstrated the procedure. After each entry and exit, it was imperative to confirm that the gate was closed, with the padlock secure. While I was on course in Sydney, the car and trailer would remain here.

After a short stay in my new city, early Sunday morning I was back in my old hometown of Sydney. Mum had made up my room, and I could use Dad's desk for my nightly study.

Sharon and I had not yet told anyone our news. At home with Mum, in the family room, which I thought apt, I told her. She was happy, but then frowned. The second piece of news fixed this. Reversing the sequence for Dad, he may have noted that we would shortly adjust our cart and horse.

On Monday morning, I became part of the peak hour and bought a weekly ticket to the city. The course was at the Koala Motor Inn, an Ansett hotel on Oxford Street. Two of my ASA colleagues, Scott and Robbo, joined several from the West and Air NSW as we entered the room for our conversion training. Greg, my classmate from our original intake, based in Melbourne, had decided to move up and consequently across. Those from other ports were upgrading. Like us, they would change base.

Just as with the F27 training, this was chalk and talk. Unlike our initial course, however, where Ansett procedures, philosophy and culture featured along with all the other induction requirements, teaching centred on aircraft knowledge. It would take two and a half weeks. This aircraft from the Fokker factory was much newer than my previous type, and had many advanced features. Each night I sat in Dad's office reviewing all I'd learnt that day. Exams came thick and fast. By Friday, we'd covered the electrical system. It was still a can of worms, but a more modern one.

The last time I'd seen Ari was just after he had joined Qantas. He rented a flat at Randwick to be close to the jet base while on course. Back then, it was just a quick visit, but things had changed. We sat on his two chairs and chatted. His flat didn't have a telephone, and after an hour, he needed to use the nearby phone box. He called a number in Port Macquarie. It was none of my business, but I was suspicious. After all we'd been through, there wasn't much we didn't share. Looking on from a discreet distance, I watched him, animated and constantly smiling while chatting. My two plus two calculation wasn't far out. While working with Oxley's, Ari had met someone.

Just back from a London trip, Ari was now checked out as a Second Officer on the 747. That Saturday night we met at a small restaurant. He was looking at an FO slot, probably on the 767, in two or at most three years. Command could be just a few years away. Quick promotion was a part of this new era for Qantas.

> "Why don't you come across?"
> A few domestic pilots had swapped, but then a couple of Qantas pilots left to join Ansett.
> "Ari, I'm more than happy in Ansett."
> "Still, you should think about it."

After finishing our beers and pizza, it was time to leave. Next time would be special, as I'd meet Roxanne.

We slogged on with another week of ground school. During lunch breaks, I wandered the city. I loved all the arcades, obscure alleyways and public areas. Sydney was a city I'd never tire of visiting. On the weekend, I visited Gemma and Paul. Chatting, Gemma wondered about our moving around.

> "Where will you go after Perth?"

"The plan's Brisbane, but that won't be for a while yet." I explained this depended on promotion, which in turn depended on seniority.

"And after that?"

"That should be our last move. Once we make it to Brisbane, we'll put down roots."

"Why isn't promotion on merit?" Paul's was a good question for someone not familiar with the airline system. "We all hold the same licence and adhere to standard operating procedures while complying with company operations manuals."

In an environment that stressed 'standard', there were no opportunities to stand out from the crowd. While spreading our metallic wings on the way to Melbourne, we didn't usually flip inverted over Mount Kosciusko or drop into the Australian Alps for the furious fire of a canyon run.

Years later, I read a post in an aviation forum putting it another way: "Our job is to not crash — how well we don't crash is a minor concern." Sitting next to Keith in ASA, and hearing of all the troubles before seniority, there seemed only one alternative. As imperfect as promotion by seniority was, it was better than the previous system. As Keith put it, "The suck system sucked."

After Computer Utilities, Paul attended Uni and completed his degree in Agricultural Science. Among other things, this qualified him to teach. Gemma went to Uni straight from school and also became a teacher. Paul also started a coaching business. After their school day, students dropped by and he helped those needing that little bit extra. The couple 'planned' a family, something I was starting to think a novel idea, and then Gemma would cut back or perhaps become a full-time mum. A couple of days later, we completed our final exams. It was time for those of us from the West to return to our base. For us, the endorsement would be in the aircraft, but the NSW crews had a lucky break. They'd complete their training in the Fokker simulator in Holland.

I enjoyed time with Mum and Dad, and the regular hours allowed me to develop a routine, as if working nine to five. Adding to this was the luxury of weekends off. My parents drove me to the airport where the crewing officer stamped my travel card. The service was direct to Perth and, on arrival, I proceeded to the staff carpark. After unhitching the trailer, I drove to Dominic's. He offered his spare room for as long as I needed it, but my priority was to find a place to live. With that sorted, Sharon and Rebecca could join me and our new life could begin.

As usual, my schedule was tight. After filling in paperwork, I reported to the Senior Regional Captain. The next phase was link trainer. This was a new generation version and nothing like the generic black box in Melbourne. Specific to the F28, while it didn't have motion or visuals, the controls and instruments behaved the same as in the aircraft. The first three sessions covered circuits, instrument approaches, and engine failures after take-off. The next two periods introduced engine failures during approaches. The final two sessions consolidated engine-out work. This certainly raised our levels of instrument scan, hand-eye coordination and perspiration. Even in this fixed base simulator, I noticed the increased speed of manoeuvres.

I spent my limited free time looking for somewhere to live. The America's Cup series was taking place later in the year, and Perth was already gearing up. In and out of real estate offices, I received the same old story. With two days off between link and commencing endorsement training, I checked in with another real estate agent. A house was available in East Fremantle. The catch — it was for sale. I could, however, take a three-month lease with the proviso that, if it sold, we'd move out.

The old house needed a lot of fixing up. It'd be a candidate for Steve-from-Green-Flight's handywork. The asking price seemed ridiculous. Set on a hill, it caught glimpses of the river from the front windows and veranda. I relaxed. Who would buy this old dump, and for such an outrageous price? Dominic helped move our stuff, and I collected our boxes from the freight shed and stored them in a back room. Such was my ease that I unpacked everything and even set up the stereo in the lounge.

Aircraft training commenced. Greg and I were sequenced together, and Elliott, a Check Captain, was rostered as our instructor. Scott and Robbo were crash buddies and programmed to follow. As Greg was senior, he was first in the seat. He raised the thrust levers and we catapulted down the runway. Nose up rotation for the F27 was around five degrees; this aircraft called for three times that. With just three on board and a light fuel load, we headed for the heavens. Out in the training area, Greg did some climbs and descents, followed by turns.

> Greg looked back to me in the jump seat. "You're going to love this."

After our session, Elliott parked the aircraft, scheduled for a later flight. The next day, we were out again, and it was my turn to blast off. Out in the training area, we each progressed through the syllabus. On the third day, we did circuits. Greg and I were both nervous. The cockpit was way higher than in the F27. Greg went first. From the jump seat, his flare looked too high, but then the wheels kissed the bitumen. On my turn, I'd learnt from watching Greg. Higher than normal, I eased back. The wheels touched and, after some roll out, around we went again.

The availability of endorsement aircraft depended on the airline schedule. After this last session, we had three free days. Weeks earlier, Sharon and I had planned this time for Darwin. My green ticket flew via Derby. There was only one spare seat, and the FO took his girlfriend, a flight attendant. They had tickets for the Dire Straits concert and she was in the jump seat. The last seat was mine, but on the stopover at Derby, our ground staff advised that the aircraft was full. The F28 only had one jump seat, and I couldn't imagine that the FO would leave his girlfriend behind. I called Sharon.

> "Can't you talk to the FO and tell him how important this is?"

If it came to it, I would tell him, but if acted upon, that would probably jeopardise the FO and his girlfriend's chances of progressing to what Sharon and I had planned for later that day in Darwin.

I sat waiting, stomach churning. Eventually, the traffic officer approached. I held my breath as he walked towards me.

> "There's been a no-show."
> My lungs expelled their incarcerated air.
> "The girl's sick of sitting up front. She'll take the seat, and you can join the pilots."

With a rush of relief, I thanked him. I would've sat in the toilet, if that was legal. Arriving in Darwin, I met Sharon's dad. John stood waiting on the tarmac. Arriving at his Nightcliff townhouse, I found Sharon had Rebecca ready and was getting ready herself. I needed a shower, and then dressed. John had recently remarried, and he and his wife, Gail, drove us. Our appointment was for six o'clock, and we pulled into the parking area five minutes early.

Still flouting convention, we both wanted simplicity. The dry season breeze gently fluffed Sharon's hair. At her side, Rebecca carried a small bunch of flowers. The light wind rippled my freshly-ironed shirt and lapped against my long pants — one of the few times I'd worn these in Darwin. Walking through the doors of St Paul's in Nightcliff, we approached the priest.

The Green Room at Hotel Darwin had a unique atmosphere. We stopped by for a drink and then on to a small restaurant. The 8th of April 1986 was a simple day, but it was just the way we wanted it. The day I was accepted into Ansett was relegated to the second-best of my life, after the cold June day in Adelaide when I first held our baby daughter. I now had another day to share first place. The following month, we sent a certified copy of our recently issued document to Adelaide. In due course, an updated certificate joined our growing family file.

With only a three-day break in training, this was a short, but momentous trip to Darwin. I had arrived on Tuesday afternoon. On Thursday the 10th of April, I caught the flight back to Perth. On the drive home from the airport, my pace slowed as I cut through a side street. People milled outside a church. A white limo waited, and a ribbon of the same colour was anchored from the centre of the bonnet, fanning out to the top of the windscreen on each side. The bride's white dress ruffled as she walked around the rear and slipped into the back seat. I stopped and made room for her as the chauffeur lifted the door handle.

Long brown hair flowed from under her white veil that was smattered with confetti. She glanced at the stationary blue van, then her eyes lifted and sparkled as she looked into mine. Her lips parted, and a huge smile lit up her face.

With my foot still planted on the brake, I nodded and smiled back, and although she couldn't hear, I said, "I know how you feel."

Our training continued. On the fifth and final day, our instructor Elliot taxied to the terminal. Back in the briefing room, he completed the paperwork. Greg and I were now endorsed on the F28 Fokker Fellowship. Shortly, we'd commence line training.

Greg hadn't wasted any time. Straight after ground school, he moved his family to Perth. They bought a house and shifted into their new home. To celebrate our first jet rating, Greg and Kerry invited me for dinner. They had a little girl, the same age as Rebecca, and Kerry was pregnant again. One year older, a few numbers senior, our careers weren't the only parts of our lives in step. Our licences needed five days with the Department. This was the longest of our free time so far. Sharon and Rebecca were due to arrive next week.

With our morning sessions complete, each afternoon I checked used car yards, without any luck. There was a Mazda in a dealership in the northern suburbs. Sharon liked the 323 and this one showed promise. The price was high, but I was prepared to pay for a good one. I could change oil and spark plugs, replace batteries, and undo nuts and bolts, but this was the extent of my abilities. I took Dominic along. With his greater experience, he took a simple check of the exhaust pipe. Black gunk covered his index finger.

"Don't buy this car."

On Sunday afternoon, both Dominic and Stephan were away. I decided to take a drive around Fremantle, as I had not explored it yet. On the main road, a Mazda dealership lay ahead. I pulled over and wandered through, checking the used cars. Without realising, I neared the 'new car' section. Two 323s were parked outside the office. Both were white, with black stripes on the lower doors and 'go fast' plastic venetians on the back hatch windows. On the windscreens, a sign read: END OF MODEL CLEARANCE. The one on the left had air conditioning. I found the black striping more appealing on the other, which lacked this unnecessary extra. I'd been all over Australia and, even in Darwin, I'd found that winding down windows was more than adequate. Admittedly, my van had an advantage. With the back clicked up, the air flowed through.

On Monday morning, I returned. Parking in the same spot, I pretended to look at the used cars. Next, I feigned accidently losing my way and ended up beside the two 323s. From the corner of my eye, I spied a salesman following my haphazard progress.

"Can I be of assistance?"
"Thanks, I'm looking for a used car."
"Do you have a particular model in mind?"
"A 323 with low K's"
He rubbed his chin thoughtfully. "Have you thought about a new one?"
"That'd be out of my price range."

> "For not that much more, you could trade up. We've got an end-of-model run out. There's only two left, and we've dropped the price to clear them."
> He pointed to the two cars I had inspected the day before. "Why don't you have a look?"
> I veered to the more expensive. "How much is this one?"
> He gave the figure, same as the newspaper ad I'd checked in the local paper that morning.
> I sighed. "There's no way I can afford that."
> He pointed to the other. "If you don't need air-conditioning, this one's cheaper."
> His price also matched the newspaper ad. I turned and pretended to walk away. "It's still too much."

With all this acting and pretence, he more than likely saw right through me. At least he went along with it.

> "Why don't we go inside where it's more comfortable? There may be room to shave a little more off."
> We settled in a small office. "Can I get you something to drink?"
> "It's OK. So, what's the bottom line, with registration, dealer's fees, all that sort of thing?"

Putting it together, the game continued. Like a Monty Python skit, we haggled. Back and forth, the number band narrowed. For effect, he drew out a blank piece of paper. Scribbling a figure, he inverted the page and slid it across.

One of the many advantages of being with Ansett was the credit union. They were happy to approve a loan, without all the rigmarole. All they needed was my ID. The figure that the salesman scribbled down was affordable. From the moment I had seen the little car, I had wanted it for Sharon. I looked up. He slowly lowered his head in a nod. Realising we'd reached the end, I mimicked his action. Two hands stretched across the table. The dealer needed three days for pre-delivery. That was fine by me, as Sharon and Rebecca weren't due until Thursday. If he picked me up around 10 and shuttled me back, I could drive away.

The little car shone in the sun. Even the chrome of the radio aerial glistened. A quick call fixed the cover note, and the salesman handed over the keys. Tracking beside the river, I reluctantly approached our driveway. The house had an inclined drive with a carport beside. I had parked the van there, the back wheel chocked with a brick. We had a lock-up garage underneath, but I hadn't bothered using it because the carport was conveniently close to the back door. I reversed in. Picking a pink rose from the garden, I placed it on the bonnet and locked the wooden doors.

I parked in the staff carpark and walked to the terminal. Their flight arrived on time, and three happy faces were reunited. We loaded bags in the van and I fitted Rebecca's car seat to its position on the bench seat. As we drove towards East Fremantle, I gave a running commentary. At home, I slowed and drove up the side driveway. Their day had been long so, once settled inside, I brought in their bags. Showing them around, we moved from room to room. Rebecca's bed was set up. I suggested a look outside, but Sharon wasn't keen.

> "We can do that tomorrow."
> "If we do it now then it's out of the way, and I have to go to the office in the morning."

Out the back door, a path led to the other side. From there we walked to the front yard. Sharon, not that interested, followed. Standing before the garage, I pointed to the garden.

> Sharon looked at the garage doors. "What's in here?"
> "I haven't bothered with it. It's easier to use the carport."
> I rummaged in my pocket. "I think I've got a key. If we have a look, then you've seen it all."

Unlocking the doors, I gently eased them open.
Rebecca rushed in. "Mummy, there's a car.." I clasped my hand over Rebecca's mouth. Sharon walked in. With her eyes wide, she turned to me, then back at the gleaming white paintwork. "It looks new."
Lifting the rose from the bonnet, I placed it in Sharon's hand. "It's yours."

After paxing to Sydney for ground school and back again for the endorsement, we positioned to Alice Springs to begin my 'line training'. My F28 Training Captain was John, and in typical Ansett fashion, he only answered to this. John and I met at the sign on desk. My safety FO was Geoff, my friend from Darwin and then ASA. He had moved to Perth on the course ahead of mine.

Our first flight was the shuttle between Alice Springs and Ayers Rock, three times. Easing me in, John flew the first sector, with Geoff in the right, as I observed from the jump seat. Back to Alice, it was my turn in the window seat, with John still at the yoke. Geoff helped with backup, and everything happened at lightning speed. On the jet, especially on these short sectors, John stressed the need to stay ahead.

"Always think of what's coming next."

If not, you found yourself behind the eight ball. This was flight management and, while the same as the F27, we were without the comfort of more time. This machine travelled so fast it took all my effort just to keep up, let alone stay ahead.

The last two sectors were mine. Each leg took around 45 minutes, and I worked at a ferocious pace. John talked me through, and Geoff added a gem or two from behind. By day's end, I was worn out. When I paxed home next evening, Rebecca was already in bed. Sharon had found a local playgroup and she was giving the little car a workout. They'd visited Fremantle markets and the city, and Sharon's knowledge of our local area now surpassed mine.

Dominic dropped by. He confided that everyone felt behind to begin with. He had felt the same, and Stephan before him.

> "Things will settle down. You just have to be organised."
> Once again, Mum's old adage came through. He could have added, "Travelling at seven tenths the speed of sound, even slight procrastination isn't an option."
> Over the coming days, Stephan shared more tips and, together with John's patience, training progressed.

Poppy returned to the west and he stayed with us for a couple of weeks. Sharon cooked stew, as it was easier for Poppy's ill-fitting false teeth. Sitting in the dining room, he'd often fade into a cloud of smoke. It was hard to ask an old man, a packet of Drum in top pocket most of his life, to refrain. We just opened the windows. In the evenings, with an Emu Bitter in his other hand, his stories resumed. As much as I wanted to stay and listen, I had to study.

> "There was this old geezer up Meekatharra way. Went out into the bush to stake a claim. He had a slab of beef hanging by the campfire, but when we found him, his number was up. He'd kicked the bucket." Closer to my study desk his voice trailed off. "Well, we couldn't waste a good piece a meat ..."

John had released Geoff from his Safety FO duties. John and I flew up and down the west coast, with multiple stops along the way, and then to Kalgoorlie and others to the centre of the state. Darwin lay further afield. Sometimes, we took the coastal route, or flew via Ayers Rock and the Alice.

It wasn't only the aircraft that was new to me. Flight planning was complex. As with most aircraft, maximum landing weight was set below that for take-off. On multiple sectors, the idea was to carry as much fuel as possible from Perth, as it was cheaper, while not exceeding the maximum landing weight at the first port. Another aspect was range. The aircraft was designed for short-haul European operations. Considering France, Germany, Spain, and the UK could fit within Western Australia (with room to spare), certain routes called for lateral thinking. Starting with our flight fuel, we added a variable reserve of 10 percent and a standard fixed reserve of 30 minutes. To reach some destinations, statutory requirements exceeded the size of the tanks. In these cases, we used an intermediate airport. We often flew via the mining town of Newman, planning the flight in two sections. Approaching Newman, if we met the reserve requirement for the next sector, we'd continue. If not, we'd drop in for a technical stop. My circular navigation computer, or 'prayer wheel' as we called it, a fixture in my top left pocket, had never been twirled so much.

We flew both inside and outside of controlled airspace. If outside, we'd arrange our own separation. Places like Yulara sported numerous light aircraft operators. 30 miles out we'd make a call, giving altitude and lateral position. If other aircraft were in the area, we'd each agree on an altitude or track that kept us clear of one another. This operation was like none I'd experienced. Somewhat like outback flying, as several airports had only basic facilities, it reminded me of the black hole approaches of South Australia.

As training progressed, I adjusted to the aircraft and operation. Just as with Jim in ASA, John was an excellent Training Captain. On overnights, he'd set aside time to work through the books. Like Jim, too, John invited me to his home where we spent the day engrossed in manuals.

By mid-June, I was ready for my check with the fleet manager. The usual butterflies fluttered in my stomach, and the car steering wheel felt as damp as on previous occasions. The check ride ran over two days, covering each variant of the type. Ansett WA operated the 1000 series (a 60-seater), and the 4000 (a 70-seater). Day one was Paraburdoo–Karratha–Port Hedland, and back to Perth. It was a long and nervous day. Next morning, the flight plan was for Kalgoorlie and back, twice. After chocking in on the final leg, we completed the shutdown checklist. Ken, the Check Captain, mentioned that my first landing was "a little firm". But that was normal for someone not used to the extra length of the 4000.

"You seem to know what you're doing."

I took this to mean a pass, which was confirmed shortly after in the briefing room. I spent the rest of the month on reserve, and was lucky enough to be home for the two birthdays. Mine, just before completing training, and Rebecca's, with far less stress, a few days after my check. Our little girl was now four.

There was a sad aspect to this month. Airlines of South Australia hadn't made it. Since the meeting at the Gateway, nothing had improved. The Moomba charters had essentially underwritten the regular routes. Without those and with continual pressure from third level operators, ASA couldn't compete.

Many years later, my former ASA Training Captain, Jim, and his friend, Nigel Daw, wrote the story of Airlines of South Australia in their book, *An Iconic Airline*:

> A last desperate attempt to change the decision to close ASA took place on Thursday, 6th March 1986 when Captains Peter Junner and Jim Evans, accompanied by two senior officers from the Australian Federation of Air Pilots, visited Sir Peter Abeles' office in Sydney. Discussion went on for quite some time; however regardless of which proposal was put forward, Sir Peter had a better idea — this was summed up in his final statement on the subject: "We can hand over the routes to someone else, and they will supply their own aircraft and staff to operate them, and we will receive 30 percent of any profit made."

The door had closed. After all these years, and the efforts of so many, the beginnings dating back to Guinea Airways' first flight on 1st December 1927, VH-FNP and VH-MMR operated the final ASA flights to Lincoln and Whyalla on the 27th of June 1986. ASA pilots were offered positions in other bases, and the flight attendants were transferred to Ansett Mainline, but were luckier, keeping their Adelaide basing. Melbourne was a popular choice for the pilots, given its proximity to Adelaide, while others moved to the remaining Ansett subsidiaries. My friend Kris, originally from Queensland, was finally granted his wish. He and wife Sherry headed to Brisbane, while several others joined us in the west.

CHAPTER 13

Our daughter Rebecca was full of life. We played in the yard and took outings to parks and playgrounds, many by the river, an integral part of this pretty city. In town, we ambled along the pedestrian mall, exploring shops and arcades. Up in Kings Park, we walked through the magical flora, and chased a ball for hours. The car seat had migrated to the Mazda but, occasionally, it returned to the Holden. A little hand then joined mine, ever ready to change gears. By and large, though, the small car transported our family, and my van drove me to work — a win-win that made both drivers happy.

I was more than surprised at interest from buyers in the house we were renting. One bloke returned several times, on the latest occasion with an architect. In Adelaide, this place would have been worth around half the asking price. I mentioned this to our agent.

> "It's the river, mate."
> To me, the river seemed a long way away; it wasn't as though you could cast a line from our front yard.
> "Doesn't matter. If you can see the Swan River, it's worth thousands."

The agent soon delivered the bad news. The guy had settled, and as per our agreement, we had to move out. The market was still tight when we started searching again. Sharon looked while I was away, but could only find a two-bedroom place in Applecross. The house was far from ideal. The bathroom hadn't been cleaned, and the stove sprouted remnants of someone's departed steak and sausages. In that market, little effort was needed. It made me angry. I felt this system of 'I'll rip you off or screw you because I can', otherwise called 'supply and demand', could do with tweaking.

The Applecross rental, with its unusual features, was also for sale. In the main bedroom, the bed sat on a platform with wall-to-wall mirrors behind. A wardrobe beside the bed housed a phone. The short cord meant you could only use it from inside the cupboard. This and other aspects were strange but, 'beggars can't be choosers', so we moved in.

This time, we only unpacked the essentials. I felt the house wasn't worth much; the value was in the land. In certain areas of Perth, homes are built on large blocks. At some stage, the ordinance must have changed, however, and two houses, with a common wall, were built on blocks this size. This dump would be a perfect candidate for a Caterpillar D9 renovation. A developer could then build a duplex, and make a tidy profit. We were wary. Tired of being shunted, we looked for a house of our own.

Applecross was highly sought-after, and we soon realised that it was out of our reach. Thoughts tended towards our Adelaide method. When I arrived home from work, Sharon and Rebecca had been out and about.

"There's land for sale at a place called Waterford."

My knowledge of Perth was still in its infancy. Sharon explained that it wasn't far. Living close to water was desirable, and while the Swan was usually first choice, it wasn't the only option. The Canning River flowed into the Swan at Applecross. Waterford was a new development a little further upstream.

Dr Barnardo's institution had released land. The cost of blocks closest to the water was astronomical, but those farthest from the river were reasonable. We found a corner block within our price range. Building methods were simple, and with timber scarce and land that was predominantly sand, a double brick house on a concrete raft footing with pitched hardwood roof was standard. Even Dad would approve.

In shirt, tie and black trousers, I drove to town and entered the agent's office. Once again, and not without the usual theatrics, haggling ended with a handshake. Money left over from our house sale in Adelaide had secured a block in Perth. We checked several builders' designs and found one we liked.

In shirt and tie, and with documents in hand, I entered the Commonwealth Bank.

> "Have you owned a home before?"
> "Yes, we recently sold our house in Adelaide."
> "What about land?"
> "We have a block."
> His quizzical eyes met mine. "You bought a block before checking with the bank?"
> I felt there were numerous things one could do in life without first consulting the Commonwealth Bank, but left my answer at the tried and tested, "Yes."
> "What do you do?"
> "I'm a pilot, with Ansett."
> After handing him my documents, he turned the pages. "This all looks good. If you and your wife would like to come back in a few days, we can finalise the paperwork."

Something had happened. Maybe it was my age now commencing with a three, or perhaps it was my years with a steady job, or even a history of mortgage repayments. Whatever the reasons, the cap in hand I'd previously carried when visiting a bank appeared not so important.

Building began in September. Sharon's tummy had grown, so, on our numerous visits to the block, we had to manoeuvre with care. Sitting on the sand of our future dining room, we ate our sandwiches. Our second baby seemed happy in its present domicile, despite being two weeks overdue. On the 9th of September, we were driving to the block. The concrete slab was being poured.

> At the turnoff, Sharon looked at me. "We need to go to the hospital."

I turned the car around. At home, Sharon gathered her things and her pre-packed bag. Shortly after, we arrived at the King Edward Memorial Hospital, Subiaco. Although we didn't know it at the time, Subiaco was a trendy suburb. Our baby could forever boast of being born in 'Subi'.

After the ASA shutdown, many of our friends had moved across to Perth. Kim was now on the F28, and Chrissie was an Ansett WA flight attendant. Several younger Captains were also here. We formed an ASA contingent. Jenny and Michael, the hosts of many ASA BBQs, were among the recent arrivals. We were good friends, so I called. Would they mind taking Rebecca for the night?

After settling Rebecca, night fell as I entered the hospital. I remembered the labour from last time, and the feelings of uselessness. Again, I couldn't do anything. As before, I held Sharon's hand and offered encouragement, but this time was different. Instead of pacing by a coffee machine, I stayed. Just before midnight, I experienced something that, although occurring every day in every country, seemed nothing short of a miracle.

Our son made good use of his less than hurried arrival. Checking in at nine pounds two ounces, by any measure, this was a big baby. I held him in my arms and looked into his eyes. All the feelings of just over four years ago returned. His gaze held mine and I could almost feel his question. Yes, I know. I stroked his few strands of pure blond hair and replied with my eyes. Things had changed in the last few hours. But don't worry, it'll be alright. We'll make sure of that.

Now we had two little people to care for. We were the quintessential Australian family: two children, a girl and a boy. The difference this time was that we hadn't agreed on a name. Sharon's suggestions had older English origins. To this, I countered, "What will happen when shortened to something less elegant in the playground?" My contribution was one I'd always liked and, by coincidence, it was shared with a well-known book and movie character. While appreciating the suave sophistication of a triple digit secret agent, Sharon preferred to continue our search.

A week passed and, with our brand-new infant capsule fitted in the Mazda, it was time to bring our newborn home. We were getting better at baby stuff. The problem was, as subtly reminded by the hospital's administration, 'baby boy', although correct, was not sufficient for a birth certificate. My sister Maree arrived to stay with us for a couple of days. Inheriting the strong will of both our parents, she became insistent.

> We were feasting on hamburgers down in Freo. "If you two don't make up your minds, I'll take charge."

Maree suggested that our little boy, asleep in his capsule, be named after our father and uncle. Dad was born while his father was away droving. My Grandma chose his first name, but he didn't take to it and went by his second name, Joe. It may have been a nod to the pilot founder of my current airline, but the thought of a child named Horace Bede spurred us into action.

We gravitated towards the biblical. When Sharon said it, I instantly agreed. With all effort expended on the first name, I managed to slip my suggestion into second place. It's a timeless name, and who knows, perhaps it could find its way to another generation, even if the same as someone who preferred their martini shaken, not stirred.

The next couple of months continued with reserve. Even so, I picked up some good flying, and the more time I spent in the seat, the more I loved this aircraft. Rear-fitted, clamshell speed brakes allowed us to slow down when mixing with light aircraft, and in primary control zones, we could speed up. As Dominic and Stephan had noted, handling and flight management became second nature. Layovers, however, were another experience. I'd been an airline pilot for over four years, yet only recently had packed an overnight bag. At many night stops, other crews also laid over. This enabled us to get together and chat.

There was disquiet amongst the older pilots and those who'd joined before the takeover. Some had friends who were engineers. Not long after taking control, the new Managing Director adopted an on-demand approach. He also sold engineering's stockpile of spare parts. This meant a short-term gain on accounting sheets. Aircraft stuck on the ground waiting for parts, however, became a significant cost, not to mention an inconvenience, with the potential to snowball.

Another unusual decision was apparent every day on our routes. The F28 had proven itself over many years. It handled short hops up and down the coast, longer routes to remote areas, and inter-city runs. Despite this, while at an air show, Peter Abeles signed for another type. It was in the same category and a similar size, with equivalent passenger load, range and speed. It wasn't a replacement, and the two types now operated side by side in the West. The result, however, was as though a taxi operator had split the fleet — half Holden, and half Ford. While both aircraft performed the same task with similar characteristics, the advantages of commonality for pilots and other staff were lost. Instead of single crew schedules, there were now two. Different engines and systems also increased maintenance costs. Not only were specific parts required for each aircraft type, but engineers, just like pilots, had to be rated, adding another encumbrance.

The new aircraft were a redesign of an older concept, and they had four engines. The BAe 146 was a good machine but, as with almost every new type, it had teething problems. Most glitches involved the engines, which evolved from a helicopter turbine. Over time, the problems were solved, but we were often called off reserve to ferry the F28, picking up passengers stranded when the 146 broke down. BAe stood for British Aerospace, but we thought of it as, 'Bring Another engine'. Management's thinking seemed back to front. If new owners inherited a mixed fleet, they could take steps to rationalise. Why create not only extra costs, but complexities that spanned from rosters to engineering?

Since arriving, I'd noticed terms unique to this part of the world. They were so common, they slipped into my speech. From my time in Darwin, I knew that there were two places in Australia — The Territory, and South. In Western Australia, however, the outlook differed. Everywhere east of Kalgoorlie (with the exception of a few towns still in the state) was 'over East', or more formally, 'The Eastern States'. South Australia may have had its slight accent but, in WA, tone was a feature. Whenever these three words were uttered, an incremental change in tone accompanied. Facial expression, also subtle, could change as well, with corners of the mouth lowered, forming an inverted crescent moon.

Sharon and I kept in touch with Coralee and Dave. Their move to Brisbane was initially short-lived. An economic hiccup hit demand for air freight and resulted in fewer pilots required. Dave was bumped, forcing a move to Sydney. After a year with Air New South Wales, business recovered enough to regain his former position. Not long after our good news, prior to leaving Adelaide, Coralee and Dave had some to match. A recent cigar-sharing phone call announced a baby boy born in Brisbane.

Another two birthdays came and went, and with Sharon's in November. With two children, the effort didn't double, it quadrupled. We developed routines, and planned trips to the clinic and outings based around feeding and sleeping times.

Ansett resumed recruiting. As positions were filled, I clawed my way up the seniority list. Enough First Officers had moved over east by December to rate a block. Geoff, the young Captain I had met on that first ASA Melbourne freighter, moved to Perth. We spent the month together and flew as far north as Darwin, did the Alice and Yulara shuttle, and then across to Cairns. We dropped in to Geraldton, Derby, Newman and others, with charters to Barrow Island and the diamond mine at Argyle.

The agent called. Our dump of a house had been sold. Now we had to find somewhere to live, again, and just before Christmas. In two months, our house would be built and ready to move in. To add insult to injury, the real estate company withheld a portion of our bond. After moving in, we had disinfected, vacuumed, swept and tidied. Handed back in a far cleaner state than we had received it, the agents complained about the yard.

> I climbed the stairs to the office. Rows of glassed cubicles ran the length of the back wall where power-suited men barked at secretaries or into constantly ringing phones.
> "He's busy, wait over there."
> I sat in a black vinyl chair outside his door.
> He barely looked up. "The grass wasn't cut."
> "I don't have a mower. I hire one from the service station across the road and was leaving it until the day before we moved out."

His dismissive hand waved as if backhanding an annoying insect, and his eyes returned to the file on his desk.

> "The place was filthy when we moved in. We've left it spotless."
> "Yeah, well, no one twisted your arm when you rented it."

The feeble strength of my one voice had all the power of a tack hammer as I belted against the steel of this real estate consortium. They kept our money.

CHAPTER 14

While I was on a trip, Sharon found a two-bedroom townhouse closer to the airport. Furnished, it was available for short-term lease. We moved in two weeks before Christmas, not even bothering to connect the phone. After stacking most of our gear in the lounge, the place looked like a storeroom. We set Rebecca up in the second bedroom, with Matthew in the bassinette by our bed. Christmas was hot and we spent a quiet, simple family day. I was rostered for an overnight on New Year, so saw in 1987 at the Argyle diamond mine.

Falling short of a block, I spent January on reserve. Even so, I did quite a bit of flying with several different Captains, and on the 16th of January, as soon as he walked in, I thought of a night years ago in Darwin. I felt like saying, "Mudguard, how the hell are ya?" Tom and I set out inland: Newman and Paraburdoo, then across to the coast for Port Hedland and Karratha. The F28 had a thick wing, giving high-lift performance. This resulted in a steep descent. During training, John had used a distance-to-run formula. Coming from the F27, I was used to thinking in terms of height. John's worked, but Tom had another method.

> "With average landing weight, if you double the height to descend and add eight miles to slow down, you'll be on the money."

This tip became one of many passed from an experienced professional, and I used Tom's descent calculation from that day on.

February saw another month on reserve, but with almost the same flying as a block. Towards mid-month, I did a 'Track Trip'. Starting in Darwin, we routed via Tindal to Alice. Over the next three days, we shuttled to the Rock. When I returned to Perth, our newly built house was ready.

Dominic was available, so he helped us move in. We were back to concrete floors and I again tacked sheets to our windows. The house had a carport but, while driving in across the sand, the van bogged, so we parked the cars in the street. Although basic, this house was ours — well, more accurately it was the CBA's, but without landlords to turf us out. It would take time, but we started to plan. Our first priority was floor coverings. As winter approached, we installed parquetry in the family room.

On the last two days of February, I flew with another young Captain. After a couple of stops along the coast, we overnighted at Derby. An outdoors type, the next morning, Gary suggested a trip to the town wharf. Borrowing a couple of bikes, we cycled down. King Sound has huge tides, and my Captain suggested that the afternoon would be a good time for mud crabs. We dropped the pots over the side. If lucky, we could take the spoils back to the hotel kitchen. The chef had a recipe and we could share our bounty with the crew. Gary managed to trap a few.

We chatted. At Ansett before the takeover, Gary explained how things had changed. He thought the new owners regarded Ansett as a cash cow for their other businesses. Disillusioned, he'd applied to another airline. Cathay Pacific was recruiting and was targeting Australian pilots. They operated the Lockheed L-1011 TriStar, a three-engine wide body, and the Boeing 747. Promotion was quick, and although starting as an FO, a left seat could be only a few years away.

Gary was accepted. Others left too. The younger Steve from Green Flight in our Cessnock days, was among them. He'd shortly fly the big Boeing out of its vibrant hub of Hong Kong. Huey, the young guy who'd helped bring in our washing machine back in Adelaide followed Steve to Cathay Pacific.

Back home, we both had a free day, so Gary invited my little family around to his unit. Rebecca sat on the open steps drawing while Matthew slept in his car capsule. We studied company material and Sharon flipped through pictures of a dazzling, modern city. She pointed to a photo featuring Star ferries shunting their way to Kowloon across a sparkling-blue Victoria Harbour.

Cathay wanted experienced pilots, which was reflected in their pay and conditions. Sharon and I talked it over. We liked Perth. It was a beautiful city and a great place to bring up kids. Even so, it had the same problem as Adelaide. It was a subsidiary base, and with two children, we wanted somewhere permanent. Kris, in Brisbane, was still flying the F27. For our generation, a jet slot in that port remained out of reach. Hong Kong sounded exciting, and it was Cathay Pacific's only base.

We decided to test the waters. I wrote, giving qualifications and experience. Two weeks later, a letter arrived. I was surprised. They quoted my last correspondence, giving the date I'd written when in flying school. It seemed I already had a file. My jet time now met their requirements, and they were pleased to forward an application form. Dreaming about an exotic place and far-off destinations was completely different to taking pen to paper. Leaving Australia would be a huge decision. All I'd ever wanted was to be an Ansett pilot. Holding the form, I realised nothing had changed. I consigned Cathay Pacific's application to my file.

Enough FOs had moved for me to continue rating blocks. March saw me fly with another pilot from the west. He'd joined MMA. Progressing through the types, he flew the F27 initially and, when it was replaced, the F28 — right, then left seat. He was one of the few with a beard, and his was grey.

The bean counters may have thought of us as 'non-crashing units of labour', but we strived to work to the best of our ability. On our first day together, Phil announced, "The landing competition's on." Most passengers judge a flight by the landing. This isn't always fair. Short runways require a firm arrival followed by immediate braking. In holding off for that soft touchdown, valuable runway is wasted. Chances are, passengers would remember the bumpy bit when the aircraft departed the bitumen, rather than a 'smooth as a baby's bottom' landing. Wet runways are another concern. Tyres can aquaplane, with no braking or lack of directional control. With heat build-up, tyres can also burst. I imagined an invitation for tea and bickies extended by the Fleet Manager: "Everything was going fine — until you ran off the runway." Weather in the West was usually good, and most runways had length to spare. The goal was 'a greaser'. I watched as Phil gently raised the nose while smoothly retarding the thrust levers. The wheels rolled on. I wasn't aware we'd landed until Phil's hand moved to the extra lever on his set, backing up the lift dumpers.

Sometimes, we flew up the coast, waited for a couple of hours, then returned via the same route. On these turnarounds, we had time to check the paper and rest in the cabin. Phil read the local rag while I usually chose a national edition. Looking across, he'd comment on such a 'highbrow' choice, not uncommon for "a wise man from the East." A few seconds passed before his serious face broke into a big smile.

On an all-night stint, we flew the coastal route to Darwin. We arrived tired after our many stops. This day's aircraft was a 4000 series, carrying an extra flight attendant. The hotel had unfortunately only planned on four rooms. It would take an hour before another was ready, so the junior FA had to wait in the lobby.

> "Surely, somewhere in this hotel you must have one spare room."
> Apparently not. Reception issued keys for us and the two senior flight attendants. Phil spoke again. "Give my room to the young girl, and I'll wait."

The guy behind the desk hesitated; even without the four gold bars on his shoulders, Phil had the presence of command. Quick phone calls followed. Regrettably, there'd been a mistake. He was terribly sorry. There was now a room available.

We ascended in the lift together. On check in, Phil always waited until last. Some Captains rushed forward, collected room keys, and disappeared. Phil's method allowed him to sort any problems, as on this occasion. Being a good Captain not only meant caring for passengers, colleagues and a multimillion-dollar aircraft. Phil's care extended to when he was off-duty.

Over the following months, I flew with several older Captains, a few with origins in the Eastern States, and my experience was helped by much good advice, many take-offs and landings, and tips generously passed on.

The month of the two birthdays rolled around. On a day off, Sharon asked if I could mind the children. She had a doctor's appointment. I looked at her and she at me, but with nothing said she rummaged for her car keys in the kitchen drawer. Rugged up, Matthew crawled about the wooden floor with his toys, while Rebecca played in her room.

I heard the Mazda as it returned. I opened the door and Sharon returned my inquisitive look with a smile and a nod. We'd now fulfil a saying common for our big but sparsely populated continent. Dad was fond of it, "One to replace each parent, and one for the country."

With this good news, we headed east for July. The grandparents hadn't met Matthew and my annual leave was a good opportunity to head across. Sydney was cold. We caught up with friends and spent another day in the city — trains, ferries, and walks by the Opera House and then through the Botanical Gardens across to Mrs Macquarie's Chair. By the end of our day, big and little feet alike were all sore. Nana prepared a belated birthday dinner for Rebecca. The highlight was a chocolate cake, and our youngest family member displayed a keen appreciation. As always, the days passed quickly, and it was time to leave for Darwin.

Arriving in the northern capital, the weather was typical for 'the Dry'. We caught the bus and visited familiar places. As friends had moved on, we wandered the Darwin mall and pushed the stroller along the wharf. We swam at Berry Springs and ambled along both Casuarina and Mindil beaches. We bumped into my old ASA Captain, Keith. Up from Adelaide, he was on a stint with Air North, flying the DC-3. He was an affiliate member of the yacht club, and suggested dinner.

Keith's wife Mama was also up from the south. Since our first meeting, there had been several more. Each time, she had asked after Sharon and the children; breathing anything but fire, and I couldn't help but feel a tad guilty when thinking of my image of her before we met. We ate our meals under the tropical sky, and chatted and sipped drinks while glancing over darkened waters that led to the Timor and Arafura seas.

Back in Perth, I looked after the children on a day off while Sharon went for her usual check-up. Our newest little one was doing fine, as could be noted by Sharon's broadening tummy. September approached, and our little boy turned one. Rebecca hadn't slept through the night until this age and, despite our clinic sister's advice, Matthew was showing signs of bettering this record. Sharon prepared a birthday dinner with a solitary candle atop the chocolate cake. Little hands reached out, conveying cake to mouth, both at the same time.

On the 25th of September, I flew to Karratha and back. I hadn't flown with this Captain before. Quiet and considerate, Mike flew with precision. Levelling out, he was bang on — not 10 feet high, nor 10 feet low. Using the autopilot minimally, his speed control was equally impressive. I could learn a lot from this Captain, and resolved to bid for a block with him.

Although nowhere near my first choice, I picked up blocks every month. I spent October with another who'd transferred from Melbourne, and on the 17th, I used my passport for the first time. Qantas, as designated international carrier, couldn't service all the routes at its disposal. One, too thin for a wide body, was to Bali. They chartered our F28 to run across to Denpasar from Port Hedland. Instead of our usual phonetic call sign, we used a QF flight number. This required extra attention, as sometimes over the Timor Sea, Ansett pilots wondered why a certain Qantas aircraft wasn't answering its radio calls.

We approached over what looked like an industrial area, with oil storage tanks, and landed on the westerly runway. We parked, disembarked our passengers, refuelled, boarded, and shortly after, took off for Australia. Back in Hedland that night, the Captain cracked his duty-free scotch as I sipped my beer with satisfaction. I could now say I'd been overseas, if just for an hour.

On Sharon's birthday, we indulged in the usual roast dinner and the usual chocolate cake with the now usual enthusiasm of both children.

In December, I picked up a supervisors' block. One Check Captain was well known for his sour moods. For more than half of this month, I had shared his flight deck. He rarely spoke, and when he did, he was grumpy. Gloomy by nature, this had become his nickname. Luckily, I was not rostered over Christmas, and I had enough leave saved to take January off.

CHAPTER 15

1988 marked Australia's bicentenary. The Queen visited, and tall ships graced Sydney Harbour. The re-enactment of the First Fleet was just part of celebrations, with festivities continuing throughout the year. Special coins were minted and our new Parliament House opened. Most Australians who lived through this time will probably never forget it. Our family had another reason to hold this year as special.

We made plans, not a usual feature of this part of our lives, and I delivered Sharon to the Subi hospital at late morning on New Year's Day. We asked Chrissie and Kim to look after Rebecca and Matthew. Getting organised wasn't easy. The children, caught up in the excitement, were difficult to manage. I organised their meals, and Chrissie and Kim settled in.

By three that afternoon, I was ready to return to the hospital. Snatching car keys, I was just through the door when the phone rang. Rushing back inside, I grabbed it. It was Sharon. I was too late; our little one had arrived. With renewed vigour, I rushed to the hospital. This one had taken less time than the others. I raced through the entrance, went up in the lift, and dashed to the room. Sharon sat on the bed, alone, except for the bundle in her arms. Moving to her, she offered this to me.

With the barest hint of fair hair atop a 'Snow White' complexion, I saw serenity in those light blue eyes. Although prepared, I was once again engulfed by feelings. Without a cry or movement, she lay in my arms, and her brand-new eyes looked into mine. I sat on the bed beside Sharon. Two sets of arms held our youngest princess.

This time, a name wasn't a problem. Just as with the previous two, my gut feeling was correct. We hadn't agreed on a boy's name, but Sharon had suggested one for a girl. This came with the usual discussions. I thought of a touching Fleetwood Mac song that Stevie Nicks wrote several years earlier.

> "Yes, it's a pretty name and a pretty song, but we probably wouldn't be the only ones to think so."

Years later, our youngest daughter shared the schoolyard with several Rhiannons. Just like her big sister, we had wanted her name to be special, one just for her. Sharon's choice wasn't common, but one I thought pretty. It even had an aviation flavour. A week later, we left the hospital. Across the backseat sat one booster, one car seat and one capsule, complete with its second occupant. A new birth certificate would shortly be issued, noting Amelia was on her way home to Waterford.

Outings became a feat of organisation. It would be handy if, at least, we could park the little car in the empty carport. A concrete drive would be functional, too. One day we'd sell this house, so it would present better if, like most others in the area, the entry was paved. We chose bricks, and the paver provided a quote. As well as the driveway, we planned a path to our front door. Another path out the back joined a glass sliding door to a rectangular section that we could bill as an entertainment area. It was a tight fit, but both cars squeezed in. What a luxury to drive in and walk to our door without trudging through sand. As in Adelaide, I asked the builders to leave any left-over materials. A pile of hardwood off-cuts stood beside a stack of bricks. I had a plan for the rectangular 'entertainment area'. Measuring off an oblong section, I laid a small concrete slab. Bringing back old memories, I mixed mortar, and attempted something I hadn't turned my hand to since our pot-belly hearth and small front porch in Adelaide. The brickies made it look easy, but even with trowel in hand and level and plumb lines at the ready, it was nothing of the sort.

Brick by brick the structure grew. My inspiration was Dad's work, and at the end of a long day, two storage boxes were positioned either side of the firebox. The chimney was bigger than Dad's, a result of surplus bricks, and I structured two small planter boxes where Sharon later grew herbs at the rear. At the sheet metal plant, they cut a 13mm steel plate, which, when fitted, finalised the project.

Johnno had left Darwin a year after us. He took a job with a commuter airline in Sydney, and after accruing more hours, was accepted by East-West Airlines. Linked with Skywest, Johnno transferred and was now based in Port Hedland. He and his wife often dropped down to Perth. A day after I'd completed my project, using hardwood as fuel, it took a while to heat the plate, but we all enjoyed the BBQ.

Ari, another visitor, dropped in several times. The 747 had a route to South Africa that staged through Perth. Ari spent time on his layovers with us. Although a favourite sequence, he wasn't with one of his favourite Captains.

> "We call him Captain Crime."
> My curious eyes held his. "Crime?"
> "Yep, I've flown with him before." He frowned and shook his head. "Whenever the crew goes out, he always manages to be on the tail end of the shout. By the time it gets to him, everyone's usually had enough."
> "Yeah?"
> "Yeah. Crime doesn't pay."

Mum and Dad, very pleased to be grandparents again, planned a trip across. They hadn't been to the West, and for something different, caught the Indian Pacific. Waiting on the platform reminded me of my last time here. Looking to the carpark where I'd picked up the van and trailer, I reflected on our current, settled state.

They'd booked a holiday unit, so we dropped them off to unpack, then all drove on home. Amelia was still asleep in our bedroom. Mum was so excited she couldn't wait, so we showed her our slumbering beauty. Shortly after, it was feeding time, so both Mum and Dad nursed their newest grandchild. We needed both cars to get us all around. The city first, then up to Kings Park. Throughout the parents' stay, we took many river walks. We made our way with the cars in tandem across the Swan to the mansions of Nedlands, Peppermint Grove and Dalkeith. Somewhere amongst these, Alan Bond had his residence.

Rebecca had started pre-school, so our visits to this area coincided with drop-offs and pick-ups. Up the coastal highway, we stopped at many bleached, white, sandy beaches. Visitors were a good opportunity to do things not usually part of everyday routines.

One night, I took Dad to a pub in Freo, one of a handful that brewed beer onsite. Stephan had introduced me to The Sail and Anchor, and Dad agreed that they brewed a nice drop. We also fired up the BBQ several times on many happy days and nights but, as usual, the time passed quickly.

Several pilots had moved to Mainline, so I moved up the list. My FO friend, Geoff, picked up a 737 slot in Melbourne and would shortly move across. In March, I crewed with an older Captain, another originally from MMA. With greying hair, he was quiet, and appeared conservative. Several FOs bought former police cars when they came up for auction. In the staff carpark, Lindsay held the keys to a pale blue Commodore. The tyres were wider than standard, but it looked innocent enough. Calling me over, he lifted the bonnet to reveal a monstrous V8. Had my quiet and conservative Captain so desired, he could have chased down the speediest of criminals.

On the 24th, Lindsay signed on first. A new recruit was scheduled for a familiarisation flight. Lindsay was surprised at his level of experience. He'd recently left the Air Force where he'd flown the Boeing 707 in VIP Squadron. Blond-haired and sporting a Biggles moustache, I noted an extra kilo or two around the midriff, but he wasn't the only one guilty of that. We made our way to the briefing office and worked through our flight plan. As he'd train as an FO, it was up to me to show him the ropes. Lindsay gave me the first sector, which was to Geraldton, providing a practical demonstration. He'd do the next to Carnarvon, and the third back to Perth was mine again.

Lindsay was keen to learn the reason our new FO had left the RAAF. After a certain number of years, promotion was to a desk. Many former service pilots, like our new colleague, chose this time to leave.

> Walking to the aircraft, I turned to him. "We've met before."
>
> I could see the cogs turning.
>
> "You flew the Caribou out of Darwin."
>
> His eyebrows raised in surprise.
>
> "I flew GA up there, and remember meeting you one night at the Aero Club." He was sorry, but couldn't remember me. That's okay. I probably wouldn't have remembered him either, if it wasn't for a mutual acquaintance. But that was none of his business.

It seemed not only did Dave's and my career parallel, but so did our lives. Shortly after Amelia's arrival, Coralee and Dave were also blessed with a baby girl. We often talked on the phone. Our friendship had started in Darwin and became cemented over the years. Assessing the seniority list, Dave felt he'd soon rate a jet in Brisbane. I was one intake later, so wouldn't be far behind.

Chrissie and Kim planned a party. Social events with our ASA throng had continued and expanded, with new friends from the West. The party, though, seemed to involve more planning than normal. Sharon accompanied Chrissie on an expedition and came home suspicious.

> "I think this is going to be more than just a party."

Thereafter, whenever 'the party' was mentioned, Sharon inserted visual quotation marks. We found an older lady through a babysitting service. We'd take Amelia, as she could sleep in the capsule. Our middle-aged babysitter arrived.

"Where's your furniture?"

Our two cane chairs, bought in Adelaide to sit by the Pot Belly, now sat in the lounge, and our card table and fold-up chairs were next to the kitchen in the 'meals' area.

"Can I watch TV?"
"Sure."

I pointed to the portable 10-inch black and white I had bought in Darwin that was sitting on the bench. We had cake for her and a snack in the fridge, and her mood brightened.

Chrissie and Kim's preparations had apparently extended to checking rosters. This was the biggest gathering to date. They had bought an old house on a big block in Applecross. Kim, an accomplished handyman, ripped up carpets to expose jarrah floorboards. He polished these and renovated the kitchen and bathroom. A marquee was erected on the back lawn, along with chairs and catering. This was a lavish departure from our casual get togethers.

Sharon looked at me. "See."

Chrissie and Kim moved around, chatting. A few hours passed. They disappeared, and an older lady who no one knew turned up.

The back door was open when we arrived, but had been closed for a time. Now it opened again. Kim emerged in a light grey tuxedo. Sharon turned to me; the look said it all. Chrissie followed, in her wedding dress. We all moved under the marquee, joining the older lady and the happy couple. Swapping rings, the bride and groom kissed. Chrissie's flight attendant friends rushed forward showering them with confetti. The look on the bride's face: priceless.

The months passed and Rebecca turned five. I clicked over another year too, but my enthusiasm for birthdays was waning. Matthew was approaching two, and our littlest one was six months; Sharon would face a new decade come November.

I was moving up the slippery pole and my block was my first choice. It was with Mike, the Captain originally from Adelaide who'd flown so precisely when we last shared the fight deck. Throughout the month, we flew our vast network. Mike's precision in flying was an inspiration. Every time that I handled the controls provided an opportunity to sharpen up. With practice, my aim was to match Mike's accuracy, not to mention his cool and calm demeanour. In the control zones, ATC managed traffic. Sometimes, to fit the sequence, they requested high speed. This was Mike's forte. He executed his high-speed descents (commenced later with greater distance to slow down) meticulously, as I'd come to expect. As the month progressed, this was one of many techniques he passed on to me.

Each year the company projected the following year's requirements. Some ports catered to business travellers, others to recreational, and many more were a mix. Yield management governed which aircraft were deployed. A smaller aircraft could be substituted with a larger type, and vice versa, at different times of the day, week or year. Flight and duty time limits and curfews at certain airports added to the equation, which was factored and calculated. With the numbers crunched, requirements for pilots and bases were fed into the computer. Vacancies were published, bids submitted, and then slots awarded in line with seniority. Casual vacancies were filled as needed.

While resting in my hotel room in Alice Springs, the phone rang. It was Sharon. Stephan had called. The annual equipment assignments were out. He picked up a 737 slot in Brisbane. Dave also scored the 737, and Dominic was off home to Melbourne, with several of our vintage split between the two main bases. It didn't take much to figure the reason for the call; I was senior to Stephan.

"We're going to Brisbane."

My last month of flying in the West was set for September 1988. Ground school was rostered for October, followed by simulator in November, both in Melbourne.

At home, we laid carpets for the winter and lino in the kitchen and laundry. Outside I built a pergola between the entrance and carport, and spread topsoil over the sand, with grass runners. We had a brush fence, reminiscent of Adelaide, erected along the boundary next to the road. The house was ready for market. With a practical design, in a good location, and less than two years old, it didn't take long for an offer. After the requisite haggling, we signed. The catch — the buyers wanted a quick settlement.

Allowing for my tight training schedule, we decided to stay in Perth while I was in ground school, with me commuting back on weekends. With simulator straight after, there'd be time to move before commencing line training. We found an old house in Applecross and took a short-term lease. We'd become fond of Perth. I had loved the flying and challenges of the route network. Ansett WA was a bigger operation than ASA, but it still had its own friendly atmosphere. With more aircraft, and two types, it was extended but still a branch of the Ansett family.

Matthew turned two, and at the end of the month, I did my last flight with Lindsay, the conservative V8 Commodore driver. After an overnight in Derby, we returned to Perth via Broome, then a Geraldton turnaround. He offered me the last two sectors. We flew in VH-FKI, one of the two 4000 series. On my final landing, we taxied in, and after descending the steps, I looked up at the graceful lines of this F28 — the finest aircraft I'd yet flown.

CHAPTER 16

Sharon's dad was on long service leave, and he came down from Darwin to stay with her and the children. I left for Melbourne, and on Monday morning, my course began, including several younger guys from the Fokker 50. Fokker had updated the F27 to this new type with the latest engines, propellers, cockpit instrumentation and airframe and cabin enhancement. Ansett operated these together with Air New South Wales.

Several older pilots were upgrading to command and a few others were around my age. However, I was the only Brisbane-based pilot, with the rest from Melbourne or in the process of moving there. The 737-300 was the latest variant fitted with upgraded engines and the new generation 'glass cockpit' flight deck. Replacing the old analog mechanical instruments, computer-generated information was presented on glass panel screens. We called it the 'glass cockpit', or 'glass' for short. As always, there was an acronym, EFIS (Electronic Flight Instrument System).

As with previous ground schools, training was intense. Exams were scheduled every second day, if not every day. We studied the systems, with an emphasis on the new computer technology. When flying the Fokkers, we'd time the number of miles per minute using the DME. Multiplying by 60 gave groundspeed. We could also calculate the wind, but this was complex, using the ground and airspeed and difference between heading and track over the ground. Twirling the prayer wheel, it could take several minutes to figure out. The new Inertial Reference System (IRS) threw this up on the EFIS panels, with continual updates.

On Friday, as I had a few hours before my Perth flight, Chrissie and Kim chatted as they showed me around. They had moved to Melbourne the month before and were renting at Mount Macedon while house hunting. The time with these friends wasn't nearly enough and, all too soon, I had to catch my flight.

When I arrived home in the late evening, the children were already in bed. Our house wasn't far from the river, so the next day our family wandered down to the grassed foreshore. Pristine white extended out to form a sandbar. The sun shone on our bare arms, and reinforced how much I'd miss this city.

Back in ground school, the pace continued. The Flight Management Computer System (FMCS, or FMC) integrated with EFIS, and interacted with the auto flight and other computer systems to provide all the information presented on our old round dials (now somewhat haughtily referred to as 'steam driven'), and much more. This reduced pilot workload, but only after understanding the system and how to operate it.

Even though the interface to operate the FMC, called the Control and Display Unit (CDU), had a screen, side prompts and alpha/numeric keyboard, it also had electronic 'pages'.

> "You'll find the distance to run on the progress page, or if you're looking for optimum altitude, it's on the CRZ page," said our instructor.

Delving inside, the new system had many layers, and finding the one needed was an exercise in itself. With all these pages and all this information, I reminisced about the simplicity of the past. The Flight Management System sat between the pilots' shoulders. It seemed to require 10 times the mental effort to work these airborne computers.

Our instructors understood the frustrations.

> "It's all new, but you'll get used to it. People in the days of horse and buggies probably found the new technology of the automobile complex."

I thought of the F28 as more of a flying racing car than a horse and buggy, but the new technology was here to stay, so the sooner I got used to it the better.

Final exams approached. I had time at home between ground school and simulator. The night before returning, we celebrated Sharon's birthday, a few days early, with the standard roast dinner and chocolate cake.

When I fronted up for simulator on the 1st of November, I partnered with an upgrade Captain from Melbourne. The simulator was the latest technology, and our endorsement would be solely based on this. Designated as 'Level D', the first time we'd operate the actual aircraft would be on our first 'line training' flight.

After loading the FMC, we taxied for take-off. The initial sessions concentrated on the FMC and related systems. After this, we moved to handling. I held the column and felt the solid feel. After several normal circuits, the instructor introduced engine failures. The machine lurched to the left. I stepped on the right rudder while instinctively rotating the control wheel. He stopped the simulator using the freeze function.

> "See how much aileron you've used?" He pointed to the slip indicator. "You need more rudder."

The F28's rear engines were close to centreline, while the 737's fanjets were wing-mounted. A failure needed more footwork. The instructor positioned us back to the threshold, and next time, I gave the rudder pedal a boot full. With the ailerons close to neutral, we tracked the extended runway centreline. We moved on to instrument approaches. EFIS screens were positioned in front of each pilot. The Primary Flight Display (PFD) on top combined several of the old flight instruments, with the Navigation Display (ND) beneath. The ND was a moving map, with the track presented in magenta. We could check course bar or needles, but the map gave present position, relegating these to back up. As the sessions progressed, we became more familiar.

The tenth session was our check. To cover the syllabus, each pilot would take two hours. The simulator ran 24/7, with sessions usually blocked for four hours, signing on an hour before to allow for briefing. Our session ran from 8pm to midnight. I'd come to hate the midnight to four, but not as much as the bleary eyed four till eight. Four hours passed. Back in the briefing room, our Check Captain asked us to wait. On his return, he plonked two green cans on our side of the table and one on his.

"Have a Vee Bee, you deserve it."

Next day, I caught the flight home. We had ten days before the 'In Operational Experience' phase, or line training, commenced.

Sharon and I hadn't added much to our possessions, and we'd discarded some. Once again, everything fitted into the back of the van and trailer, with the boot of the Mazda taking the overflow. Sharon and I loaded the cars and trailer, and drove to the trucking yard. A little over two and a half years had passed. We had many memories, had met fine people, and, for me, had done some great flying. We felt as we had when leaving Adelaide. Just as we'd had one little reminder of our time there, we had two to remind us of our stay here. That night we caught the red eye to Sydney. We would stay with Mum and Dad until the cars arrived in Brisbane.

I took a morning flight up to our new city, hired a car, found a place to rent, and returned that night. Not having any idea where to start, Sharon had checked the directory and suggested the western suburbs. She found Greenhill and Waterford, and I was more than happy to go with her gut feeling.

The truck was delayed, so the cars arrived on the last day of November. I caught the morning flight up the next day. Arriving in our new home, we'd once again live in the same city as our good friends. Coralee made arrangements, and we took a taxi to the trucking yard. Coralee drove the Mazda with their two children in the back, and I followed.

Coralee and Dave lived to the north, in a semi-rural area. Dave teamed up with Coralee's dad, and they had built the house. She hoped I wouldn't mind the concrete floors. They still had work to do, and planned floor coverings for winter. I parked the van at the end of the house, and we transferred the contents of the Mazda's boot to their storeroom. Next morning, I drove to Brisbane airport and reported for my first duty.

One of the crewing officers passed me a key to the staff carpark. Howard was my Training Captain. Rob, my safety FO, arrived shortly after. Rob had been on leave, so Howard offered him the first sector to Sydney. I observed from the jump seat. For Sydney to Melbourne, I moved to the right, with Howard flying. The last leg, to Hobart, was mine. These two relaxed professionals programmed our 737 and tracked the magenta line. Each explained what they were doing as we flew south. The new technology varied little with the old, requiring constant monitoring and updating. Coupled with ATC communication, this kept them busy.

Out of Melbourne, it was my turn at the controls. It was bigger, heavier, and higher off the ground than the F28, but similar in that it had a nice feel. Hobart had a crosswind. Flaring higher than normal, I dropped the right wing a touch while kicking a bit of left rudder to deliver our passengers, crew and aircraft to our southern island's capital. This wasn't just my first flight in the 737, but my first time to this city. The shuttle bus drove us to the hotel and I looked wide eyed out the window. Howard and Rob planned to meet later, and I was welcome to join them. I rushed to the room, changed, and was out the door. I walked the short distance to the city. The harbour held fishing boats and other craft tied to wharves. Open markets fronted a large, paved pedestrian walkway. The weather was cooler than Brisbane, and the ambience, I felt, tended towards an English feel.

One day, I hoped to visit London, the city my great grandfather had departed. Found guilty of pickpocketing, he was offered complimentary travel to the colony, and after arriving in his new homeland, he started the ball rolling on the Australian branch of our family (it, and chain, later discarded).

The following day was a big one. Hobart–Launceston–Coolangatta–Brisbane, then back to Launceston and Hobart for another overnight.

The day after, we'd pax back. If Sharon and the children caught the flight up, I'd meet them at Brisbane airport. The technology was a big leap, but the aircraft itself was less of a jump. Slightly faster than the F28, it handled well, and by the end of our second day, I felt more comfortable.

Back in Brisbane, Sharon and the children were waiting at the terminal. I brought the car around, fitted the car seats, and drove us to Coralee and Dave's. Dave was back from a trip, so we sat and talked until it was time to leave. I drove the van, with Sharon following.

The real estate office was in Kenmore Village, a shopping centre in this western suburb. After collecting the keys, we continued to our new house. With a double garage, it had a small room beside with steps that led to a fairly standard three-bedroom layout. We unloaded the beds and cot, and left the rest for the morning. The house was built on a sloping block, with a small flat space out the back door, before the incline continued.

We settled in, and my training progressed. Stephan had arrived the previous month, and Sherry and Kris from Adelaide were well entrenched, with Kris also flying the 737. Jenny and Michael were due next month. Ari dropped in. As anticipated, he had upgraded to First Officer, scoring a window seat on the 767. Brisbane was a frequent port of call, so we'd see him more often.

Just as with the previous types, things fell into place. The downstairs room became my study, and I spent time between flights slogging through the books. I was still getting used to the 'glass cockpit' but, with Howard's patience, I made headway. Howard was scheduled for leave in January, and as the end of December approached, he recommended me for check. After a subdued Christmas, we flew our last training flight on the 31st, with my check scheduled for the 5th and 6th of January.

Our trip was Perth via Melbourne, and on New Year's Day, we positioned back. I arrived home from her birthplace on her special day. Amelia was one year old. After settling the children, Sharon and I moved to the lounge room. There was a small balcony with a sliding door, so we shifted our chairs there. Last New Year, the significance of the day had forever changed. Sitting outside, Sharon and I soaked up the warmth of the Queensland night. It was a time for reflection.

After years of moving around, we were finally home, despite not having lived here before. I was flying Ansett Mainline, and while promotion and that coveted left seat would take longer than for my Melbourne classmates, it was a price I was prepared to pay. Sharon planned to pursue an interest put on hold for years. She wanted to learn another language and enrolled at TAFE.

Joining Ansett, I reconciled not being able to fly the one aircraft every pilot dreamed of, the Queen of the Skies — the Boeing 747. I could have applied to Qantas when Ari and my two former classmates had, and I could have filled in and returned my Cathay Pacific application. At either, a jumbo slot would have been within my grasp. But this would have meant leaving Ansett — a price far too high to pay.

The subtropical lifestyle of this vibrant river city, with the rush and tear left behind when two young hopefuls headed north in an old blue panel van, was now ours. Our children could grow in our adopted city and state — beautiful one day, perfect the next. We popped the cork of our sparkling white wine. The clock ticked towards midnight. With one little Croweater and two little Sandgropers snug in their Sunshine State beds, we clinked our glasses. Our future looked bright — the year, 1989.

CHAPTER 17

Mum and Dad had lived through a Depression and a World War. These times left an indelible mark, and they shaped the way my parents approached life. My latter years of school and then entering the workforce were a period Dad called 'the good times'. Dad had plenty of work, so I walked into a job with him. A slot in the public service followed an application and later I had easily gained a position in the fledgling computer industry. In the seventies, I had bought a car and decked it out with a few extras. I had a drum kit that could have served as Mick Fleetwood's office. I'd never felt the icy chill of ill winds, and thought all this was normal.

As the '80s wound down, an ominous warning from those earlier times surfaced. The day came, amid the glare of a shiny blue panel van, sparkling gold drums, and shoulder length blondish-brown hair, when Dad took me aside.

"Son, it's not always going to be like this."

While politics sat in the background as more of a general rather than specific concern, changes would soon impact our lives. Events would re-shape our political landscape, revealing differing destinies, not only for the political players, but for those caught in the fray.

On that first trip to Canberra in 1966, the political landscape was relatively stable. Taking power in 1949, Robert Menzies, who had helped found the Liberal Party, started a run that lasted until 1972. The Party's aim was to represent ordinary people. Menzies termed this group 'The Forgotten People':

> "We have realised that men and women are not just ciphers in a calculation, but are individual human

> beings whose individual welfare and development must be the main concern of government."

When the FX Holden rolled off the assembly line in 1948, it was Prime Minister Ben Chifley of the Australian Labor Party who welcomed it. The Labor Party aimed to broadly represent working people. Their philosophy was encapsulated in one phrase, 'The light on the hill,' as coined by the man who warmly greeted the first 'FX'.

If the welfare of ordinary people was the concern, then rhetoric suggested that both major parties held this at heart. Differing in approach, however, the Liberals were thought of as 'Centre Right', while Labor was 'Centre Left'. How far off-centre depended on the pendulum of the times. The Liberal's long run ended in December 1972 when William McMahon left office. Too young to vote in '72, politics wasn't an activity I followed closely. It was noted, though, that the Prime Minister had an attractive wife who, on a visit to the White House the previous year, wore a dress with a somewhat revealing split up the side. Sonia McMahon's graceful entrance lent an airy atmosphere to what could have otherwise been a stuffy occasion.

Mr McMahon, known as 'Billy' and later knighted, inherited some difficult issues; one of the most prominent was the war in Vietnam. Without thought to the devastation and tragedy, not to mention catastrophic human cost on all sides, Australian forces expanded their role during Harold Holt's term, in the spirit of 'All the way with LBJ'. Local protests and anti-war demonstrations highlighted how the conflict was as divisive as it was difficult. Prime Minister McMahon maintained our commitment to the war, although diminished. However, by the time of the 1972 election, it appeared that Australians wished to terminate our role. The party that promised an end to our involvement in Vietnam, along with many new policies, was elected.

It was time. The new Prime Minister, Gough Whitlam, headed the first Labor government in 23 years. As promised, our troops were brought home. Many had been conscripted as 'Nashos', as, at the time, national service was compulsory for males aged 20 years and older. They were subjected to a 'conscription lottery'. Whether a just cause, political expediency or folly, it was their blood that was spilled. This was a low point in Australia's history, as those who returned were neither honoured nor given their due respect until many years later; there was no flag waving or ticker tape parades in 1973.

The new administration made many changes, and the pace was brisk. Conscription was abolished, and universal health care and free tertiary education were established. The government, however, wasn't without controversy. Several large natural resource, energy and infrastructure projects needed funding. Loans were sought, but the method used was unorthodox, as it was independent of the treasury. The Minister for Minerals and Energy contacted Tirath Khemlani who worked for a commodities firm based in London. He then liaised with Middle Eastern financers, and brokered the loan.

The intent was pure — the objective was to renew and update vital infrastructure along with a radical concept: ensuring the benefits that flowed from the national resources of Australia were shared with the people of Australia. The end, however, cannot justify the means, and to cut a long story short, it didn't work out. The whole deal turned pear-shaped, leaving the government with a serious amount of egg on its face.

The government was seen as vulnerable, and the opposition put the boot in. Led by Malcolm Fraser, they blocked 'Supply' (budget finances) in the Senate where they had the numbers. The whole process of government ground to a halt.

Australia is a Constitutional Monarchy, which is to say that the head of state is the Queen of Australia. A long-distance relationship, she lives in Buckingham Palace, London, England. The Queen does, however, have a local rep, the Governor General. At that time — Sir John Kerr.

In the Governor General's office, a few options were explored, but in the end, maybe Sir John sat down, and appreciating their subtly, rifled through a few recent Palace Letters. Perhaps, he dropped a couple of ice cubes into his scotch and read some limited news.

Possibly thinking that whoever was responsible for such writing had a point, Sir John tended towards a new broom approach.

On the 11th of November 1975, our Remembrance Day, the Governor General of Australia dismissed the Government of Australia. The opposition were instated as caretakers while public servants arranged for those who, perhaps, could have been asked in the first place to decide.

In his now infamous impromptu press conference, PM Whitlam said, "Well may we say 'God save the Queen', because nothing will save the Governor General." Even under such personally and constitutionally stressful and damaging circumstances, Gough Whitlam could put together a concise statement, not only demonstrating rage, but touching on the essence of our heritage versus our future (which we still haven't got around to sorting out).

Malcolm Fraser became our new PM. Fraser held the Liberal Party together at a time it could have easily fractured, but it's Fraser's human rights and humanitarian convictions that I remember. Malcolm Fraser remained Prime Minister until 1983. On the day that he called that year's election, a startling development occurred across the parliamentary aisle. In what could best be described as a deft piece of political wet work, the leader of the opposition suffered a fatal wound when the political knife wielded.

Bill Hayden seemed a decent chap. From Brisbane, he had served with the Queensland Police Force and held a degree in economics. After Gough Whitlam retired, Hayden took over to lead the opposition. Coming close to winning the 1980 election, Hayden was in place when another who obviously felt more suited to the job turned up.

The leader of the ACTU had reluctantly given up the care of those in 'the movement' and entered parliament. He seemed to feel all could benefit from his vast talents. He was also physically appealing, but modesty would only allow his use of the words, "good looking". A little blood on the hands was a small price to pay, and maybe it helped that it wasn't his.

The 1983 election resulted in the defeat of Malcolm Fraser's Liberals and installed a new Labor Government. I first saw him through the plate glass, while working in the Sussex Street computer room all those years ago. He strode with such gravity through the foyer of the Labor Council Building. In March 1983, he vaulted towards The Lodge. Prime Minister Robert James Lee Hawke took up his position to the right of the Speaker. Andrew Peacock led the opposition.

The Liberal Party leadership slipped from Andrew Peacock to John Howard in 1985. Mr Howard faced Mr Hawke at the 1987 election, and the Labor Government was returned. Tussles continued, and Mr Peacock reclaimed his former position in May of 1989. Our next general election was due by July of 1990.

I'd been with Ansett for seven years. On the 5th of January 1989, I wore my senior First Officer's three-bar epaulettes for the first time. It was the first day of my check ride as we positioned to Sydney, then flew to Canberra and back. The next day was up the coast. I had done this run once before with Howard: Brisbane to Townsville and Cairns, with a return in opposite sequence.

That trip was my first glimpse of the Great Barrier Reef. I looked down, mesmerised. Before then, I wouldn't have thought so many shades of blue were possible. Almost clear turquoise waters ran to the depths of this favourite colour, and blended with the whites of coral. The coral also had varying shades and colours but, from altitude, the white and blue dominated as it laced its way up 3,000 kilometres of the Queensland coastline. Stan, the Check Captain, noticed my downward glance.

"Magnificent, isn't it?"

This was another beauty on our list — the largest coral reef in the world. We arrived back to Brisbane. It would take time to feel completely comfortable with the glass cockpit, but all in all, the two days were deemed satisfactory. I spent the rest of the month on reserve, as my seniority in the base was only a few numbers from the bottom.

Cleared to the line and in our new hometown, we were impatient to settle. Suburban Brisbane where we hoped to buy a home provided a pleasant area, convenient to shops and schools, and with busses to the city. For over a week, the real estate agent showed us through several houses. By Friday, we were growing tired and impatient. With one more that afternoon, we parked outside. In the adjoining suburb of Chapel Hill, the elevation provided a light breeze on this warm day.

The block wasn't all that big, but a fence enclosed the front yard. Children could play safely, protected from the road. The entrance was through a gate to the side of the double garage. The lounge/dining room was to the right of the front door, with a family room to the left and kitchen at the rear. The three bedrooms and bathroom were upstairs, and the backyard gate led to a nature reserve.

Back at the agent's office, we finalised our offer, subject to finance, as usual. After the standard haggling, our offer was accepted, and we made an appointment with the Commonwealth Bank. This visit proved to be in the same spirit as the last, and the agent arranged a quick settlement. We would move in February. Next on the list, Sharon found a school for Rebecca in the next suburb. Holy Family had the same name as the school I first attended. Things were falling into place.

Peter Abeles was at it again. Another type bloated the fleet; this time an Airbus, the A320. It was as though Abeles had heard a heavenly voice warning of a coming catastrophe and was building Ansett into a sheltering vessel for every kind of airliner, containing everything with wings.

Reg Ansett was meticulous with aircraft. He had fought for the L-188 Electra, and when I joined, the fleet was from his time. The F27 operated regional services, the longer of these in the West with the F28. Mainline ran two types. The DC-9 flew the shorter and thinner routes, and the longer range B727 the rest. The

Electras were converted to freighters, which expanded air freight and extended their life.

The B737 took over from the DC-9, and the fleet was lean and economical. The newly added A320 was around the same size and carried a similar load to the 737. Not a replacement but a variant, the two types operated side by side. The extra costs of engineering, rostering, training and complexities experienced in the West were now experienced by Mainline. Reg Ansett's lean operation had become a Sir Peter Abeles' hotchpotch.

February meant my consolidation block. As befitted my seniority, mine was the last block allocated. My Captain, Frank, had an Eastern European accent, and he sometimes reverted to the grammar of his mother tongue. We met at flight planning where he barely spoke, only to say he'd fly the first sector. Although shorter than me, it was as though he'd started off taller. As if a weight bore down on him, every feature was squat. Squinty eyes sat in a face that seemed to spread out towards his ears. Even his caterpillar moustache looked to be trying to escape from under his pudgy nose in both directions. Whatever the weight applied, it was when wearing his uniform cap that our Ansett emblem stood tall and proud. Frank's emblem, however, sat compacted, along with his hat, on his squat head above his squat body.

As we prepared for departure, our purser asked if we'd like something to drink. Cockpit setup in the new aircraft was more involved than the older types. The flight attendants were also busy; it was a courtesy for her to ask. Without looking up he grunted, "Coffee, black." As she left, he barked at me, "Do the walk around."

Always in a hurry, once airborne, Frank plugged the automatics in early. We had a Sydney overnight. I elected to stay with Mum and Dad rather than at the crew hotel.

"Tell them we want high speed."

I passed the message to ATC, followed by our descent clearance. The FMC computed a descent profile and, like all computers, it operated on the GIGO principle. Frank, in such a hurry, forgot to input the new speed.

During training, Howard had demonstrated descents using the old method. For the old hands, the computed path was just a backup. Each time I flew, I multiplied height to descend, and added the slowdown. Using this formula, we looked to be descending too soon. A quick check confirmed the standard speed was still in the FMC. If you didn't update the system, then the original input was garbage, and true to the operating principle, the output could be termed the same. It was my job, so I reminded Frank. He ignored me. We levelled off miles too early, with thrust levers up burning kerosene like dollar bills out the back of our CFM56s.

There was nothing unsafe in the way Frank flew. It was just the lack of finesse that I'd grown used to after sitting beside people like Mike in the West. At the terminal, we completed our shut down.

> "That stupid woman. She keeps waving at me."
> I looked up. "Frank, that's my Mum. She's waving to *me*. I'll see you tomorrow."

On a flight up the coast, we had an overnight in Cairns. We waited in the crew bus as a flight attendant was yet to come. Frank became annoyed and turned to me.

> "Where is that flight attendant?"

By this stage, I'd had enough. Without thinking, I replied, "Frank, I have no idea. If it's such a big deal to wait a few minutes for a colleague, then why don't you go look for him yourself?"

As soon as the words were out, I thought, oops. Frank simply turned and sat looking out the front window. A few minutes later, our workmate arrived, with apologies. His bag was last out on the carousel. At the hotel, Frank rushed forward, grabbed his key, and headed to his room before the last of our flight attendants were through the entrance.

On the way back to Brisbane, Frank changed. He started to use my first name (before this, I'd been addressed by differing versions of "hey, you"). Frank began to speak as if we were friends. Maybe, he thought our previous day's exchange was normal verbal discourse.

> "My wife, she crazy. She does some course at night school."

He also informed me they had no children. This, as with other personal details, was not a result of my inquiry. If his wife chose to improve her qualifications, then I thought this was her business.

> Frank continued, "All she needs to do is cook and clean."

The month dragged on. Leaving after that last flight, a thought struck. The reason I'd flown with Frank was because no one else wanted to. With my seniority, on the occasions I may rate a block that would be the least desirable or, in other words, Frank's block.

After moving house in early February, we began to settle in. With the security of living in our own home, and the stability of an Ansett Mainline base, we began making plans. During my years in the subsidiaries, I had rarely taken my allotted leave. Our holidays were to Sydney and Darwin. We enjoyed these shorter trips, but my leave had built up. With several months in credit, we decided to take a month off later in the year. As Matthew would turn three in September, I requested this off, which was granted.

In addition to two little mementoes from our time in Perth, we'd arranged another. Chrissie and Kim found a small business. The owner employed a handful of tradesmen who crafted Jarrah furniture. We ordered a dining table and chairs, our first piece of real furniture. Not long after moving in, these arrived. The delivery guys struggled with the heavy hardwood. Taking pride of place in our dining room, evening meals were now from a table without folding legs.

CHAPTER 18

The 'Prices and Incomes Accord' had been in place for several years. It was hard to remember what mark numeral they were up to. Each year the treasurer, Paul Keating, found a backroom, and negotiated with the ACTU secretary, Bill Kelty. The latest version was then presented to the IRC for their rubber stamp. From its beginnings, I thought the whole process stupid. I didn't know Bill Kelty from a bar of soap, as was his knowledge of me. He knew little about our work environment, or that of many others. We pilots weren't part of the ACTU, and we had no input in the process, yet the system saw him decide our terms

Years ago a former ACTU leader made an overture to the Pilots' Federation. Pilots wished to retain their independence, and declined the invitation. This caused resentment and a carte blanche attitude towards us which appears to have been handed down as if from master to apprentice. I'd seen Bill Kelty on TV. Beneath an explosion of curly locks gushed a torrent of flowery waffle. I did not wish him to perform any task on my behalf. Voting in accordance with our democratic processes, we, as a group, chose our representatives.

When the Accord was first instigated, our association's president was from Ansett. His term expired and another was elected. From Trans Australia Airlines (TAA), he was a senior A300 Captain. His term came to an end, and it was time to vote again. Although I knew little about the candidates, there was one I did relate to. I liked his profile, and we had something in common. He was from Australian Airlines (TAA changed its name in 1986). I filled in my ballot paper with a vote for First Officer Brian McCarthy.

Back in 1983, we had all needed to pull together. I felt there were better ways than the Accord, but believed in the principle. Drought was ravaging our country, adding to the economic pain, and sharing the burden with fairness and equity was an honourable ideal. In these times, when wage and salary earners weren't even keeping pace with inflation, another group showed no such restraint. On Christmas Eve 1988, Justice Barry Maddern, the president of the IRC, released a statement endorsing a pay rise for federal politicians. As if wheeling a bin to the political curb, the timing generated little public comment. With wage and salary earners carrying the load, politicians were awarded an increase of 36 percent. 'Fairness and equity'; we must have dreamed it. While the Accord may have obscured the light from the hill's distant beacon, it illuminated the path to the farmhouse.

The increase would be paid in increments, perhaps to mask the total, and at the Prime Minister and treasurer's urging, it was reduced slightly as a token gesture. These weren't the only ones making a mockery of the system — an 80 percent salary increase was determined for judges. It was argued this was needed to dissuade them from moving to more lucrative positions and to attract others to the bench.

I thought of all our pilots now working overseas. Cathay Pacific was bursting with Australians. Shortly after completing initial training on the F27, my instructor Derek transferred to the 727. Becoming disillusioned, he took a job in the Middle East. He later moved back to his former home, filling a position with a small European airline that operated regular services and 'charter runs' to the Caribbean and Far East. Howard, my 737 Training Captain, must have felt the same. He left for Malaysia.

Other professions surged ahead and this soon hit home in our industry. Our joint managing director and head of TNT nabbed a pay rise. His percentage increase was even greater than that of the politicians! Company heads, often under pressure, made decisions affecting peoples' lives and were responsible for plant and equipment worth millions of dollars. While this was reflected in their salaries, Abeles outstripped what I thought were the bounds of common decency. His income was now more than a hundred times my salary. He was the chief of a transport conglomerate, but was his responsibility greater than his close friend? The transport sector is vital to any economy, but only a part. Sir Peter Abeles was now paid more than 30 times that of the Prime Minister (even after the recent hike). As Captain Brian McCarthy later remarked (the First Officer I voted for had earned a promotion), "Those who did well out of the Accord were those who weren't in it."

It wasn't the money. It was the principle. The restraint of regular wage and salary earners had merely filled the trough. Public servants granted six percent watched on as the ones preaching moderation seized a multiple five times greater. The private sector was the same. Any time this disparity was raised, however, a bogey man emerged — wages breakout. I couldn't see any logic in this. Where was the difference in 100 Ansett employees each spending a dollar to Abeles flipping a hundred into the economy? At a time when 'restraint' had become a rant, and fairness and equity was hammered into us, the darkness of the skull and crossbones unfurled defiantly into the industrial wind. Sir Peter Abeles' remuneration was upped by a staggering 40 percent as he grabbed a nothing less than obscene, $5.1 million.

FRIEND: Sir Robert Askin

FRIEND: Bob Hawke

In April, TNT opened a $30 million computer centre in England to control its integrated road and air express transport operations in Europe in anticipation of an expanded market with full economic integration in 1992.

The group has also targeted the huge new aircraft market in eastern and central Europe which is estimated to be worth $US18 billion over the next decade.

In April, it announced it had ordered a further $149 million worth of aircraft engines for its fleet of Boeing 757s to prepare for this new market through Ansett Worldwide Aviation Services (AWAS).

AWAS is a leasing specialist company based in Hong Kong which is jointly owned by TNT and News Corp. It is now the third largest aircraft-leasing operation in the world.

AWAS has an option to buy 72 freight jet aircraft of the 146-QT (Quiet Trader) series for $2.25 billion from British Aerospace, equal to five years' production.

The group has been operating in South America since 1973 when it acquired the Transpampa road transport company. Now there are more than 4,000 employees and more than 50 transport terminals linking the country.

TNT's stay in another South American country, Chile, has been less smooth and in May this year TNT offices were one of the targets of a bombing campaign which included the US consulate.

This followed a protest in the capital, Santiago, last November by 400 truck drivers against TNT's presence in Chile.

They complained that Chile's locally-owned transport companies had investments of only $US1.5 billion which could not compete against TNT's multi-billion-dollar international assets.

TNT's expansion is not confined to Europe and South America. In October last year it announced a further $70 million investment in the US and Canada to strengthen its foothold in the fiercely competitive North American freight industry.

It acquired two further regional trucking companies giving it five operations in diverse markets. Now 20pc of TNT's assets are in the US where it employs 6,000 workers across the country.

Also in the US, TNT has a 20pc equity in a regional airline, America West, the 10th largest in North America. (It also owns 21pc of the tiny Oslo-based carrier Norway Airlines.)

Phoenix-based America West has just joined the major league of US carriers after being reclassified as a major airline by the Department of Transportation. A major airline in the US is defined as an operator with an annual operating revenue of more than $1 billion.

The Asia and Pacific Rim is the next target. TNT has operated infrequent freight charter flights between Australia and Asia using a Boeing 707 and in June revealed plans for an Asia-Pacific air freight network based in Manila.

It is planned to have connections to countries such as New Zealand, China, Hong Kong and South Korea. In 1987, TNT won a licence to operate out of Hong Kong as Transcorp Airways. But it is still the Australian operation which contributed about 40pc of total earnings in the 1989-90 financial year despite a 13pc to 15pc drop in revenue in the past three months.

The controversial pilots' dispute cost TNT $53 million which helped cause a drop in return on shareholders' funds from 24.2pc to 13.4pc and a 25.6pc drop in pre-tax profit to $223.4 million.

Despite this downturn, Sir Peter picked up $5.1 million last year as part of his "performance package".

This provoked a bitter protest at last Wednesday's heated annual general meeting from Jack Tilburn, a director of the Australian Shareholders' Association, who said the total remuneration of $28.3 million to directors was unjustified given the company's performance.

Although he is regarded with suspicion for the stealth and effectiveness of his political lobbying, Abeles is not an entrepreneur of the Alan Bond type. Nor does he go in for asset-stripping operations or share manipulations.

He is a practical industrialist, a tycoon blessed with mystical powers to sway politicians and a man for whom power and influence hold the same importance as wealth.

Above: Excerpt from 'The Wide World of Sir Peter Abeles', by Keith Gosman, *The Sun Herald*, November 4, 1990.

If our company and parent company could afford to pay one individual so much and increase executive salaries to the same tune, then why not share the fruits of everyone's labour? The Accord delivered few advantages to ordinary Australians and failed on its heralded 'economic development'. Reverse 'Robin Hooding' appeared to be the pact's major achievement, as illustrated in pay rises for politicians, judges and airline executives, not to mention others with pockets sewn by the same tailor.

Disquiet swelled within our ranks and filtered up to our executive. Our commitment to the Accord was conditional on sharing the rewards promised (but undelivered) to wage and salary earners, at every renewal. Little had changed since we had renewed the previous September. Our Federation called a series of 'stop-work' meetings, for the 20th of February. I felt the same trepidation as I had during the superannuation strike. I believed it was wrong for politicians to behave this way. But, with a young family, I was also wary of anything that may disrupt our lives.

Bob Hawke was the 'Captain' of our country. He could have led by example but, instead, he urged wage and salary earners to tighten their belts, while at the same time loosening his.

We knew that aircraft on the ground for 24 hours would inconvenience people. Once again, passengers would need to alter their plans, and once again this weighed heavily on me. If it was a Prices and Incomes Accord, and incomes (well some anyway) were controlled, then why not control prices? I knew this was simplistic, but so was trying to squeeze workers from differing fields, industries and circumstances into a single-sized, fiscal straitjacket.

Australian Airlines had made a record profit the previous year and our company was obviously doing well, as were many others. Between 1983 and 1988, company profits increased by 25 percent each year. In those years, however, real wages fell. It was time that ordinary peoples' welfare and development were considered, and shown the respect they deserved.

Our stop-work meetings were to consider future salary positions. Surely, it would be a simple matter to let our commitment expire. We could then return to enterprise bargaining. Not only us, but all Ansett staff, if they wished, could negotiate to benefit from the good fortune of our company. After all was said and done, the Accord was an agreement. Our commitment would expire on the 30th of June. Did we really need to stop work to decide this?

As at other times in my life, my view proved naïve. It may have been a renewable agreement, but the shimmering light of the Accord had become our hotel on a desolate Californian highway. Imprisoned by our welcome; now that we'd checked in — we couldn't check out.

I spent March on reserve but with good flying up the coast, down the coast, and across the country. There was even another overnight in Sydney. The irony was that Mum and Dad were up for a visit in Brisbane. The more I flew the machine, the more I liked it, which proved the case almost every time I changed types. I did miss the F28, though. Inside controlled airspace, then outside, black hole approaches and bush flying were now replaced by the workload of capital city to capital city, with big regional centres in between.

Towards the end of the month, the Captains' bids were out. Several of the senior First Officers took leave and, if lucky, I may just rate the last block. It wouldn't be first choice, or anywhere near it, but any block was better than being stuck on reserve. Life provides a certain balance, maybe as per the ancient Chinese philosophy of yin and yang. To the light that was my block, the shadow was my Captain. I spent April with Frank.

On our first trip, Frank was his normal obnoxious self, yet more friendly, which wasn't saying much. Maybe, he thought I had bid for him. We flew our trips and did our overnights, with Frank just as rude to the flight attendants as he was to me. My skin grew thick. When he was rude, I returned the courtesy. It was odd, but he seemed to think of this as normal human interaction. So much so, he started talking again of his personal problems. His wife was progressing with her course, much to Frank's annoyance, and she planned to finish in June. I hadn't met her, but wished her well.

On a return from up the coast, Frank requested the short runway. Usually, we landed on the longer one, leaving the short strip for GA aircraft. We could do it, but why? It would require the 'short field' landing technique and then hard braking. A few extra minutes and we could position for the normal approach, giving our passengers a more comfortable arrival. I voiced my concerns, but Frank insisted. It was my sector, so I plonked the 737 on. The spoilers deployed and the brakes grabbed, with thrust reverses out. Frank took over, adding his heavy boots to the pedals. I hoped our first-class passengers were strapped in tightly, otherwise they'd join us. Frank seemed in even more of a hurry than usual. He taxied fast and was out of the cockpit before I could stow my charts.

Our next trip was another up the coast to Townsville and Cairns, and then back again. It was great to have a flying block, but the feeling was dampened a tad by my Captain. This was one more thing going for composite blocks. There were senior guys who bid reserve and ran a business on the side, but these were few and far between. The company didn't care as long as they had the coverage but, by and large, it was us younger ones who were saddled with reserve, and we hated it. If the flying and reserve patterns were compounded into all the blocks, then not only would it share the flying and standby, but the crew could rotate as well. Composite blocks would mix in the good guys with the Franks. If ever it happened, it'd certainly be a welcome change for us on the tail end of seniority. Some overseas airlines scheduled this way, and with a good rostering system, it could prove even more efficient.

Driving to work along Coronation Drive (or 'Coro Drive', as it's known) the river reflected the sun from its brown-flushed blue. On the left stood a row of terrace houses, the last of them backing on to Park Road. This was a trendy area with street-front coffee shops and eating places. The end terrace housed a stylish seafood restaurant. Diners could look out through the plate glass windows on both floors and glance across the river. Maybe, one day, I dreamed. A meal at Ryans Riverfront wasn't for us, but over the road, the riverside footpath was. On many occasions, we took the children's pushers and bikes with trainer wheels to stroll by the water's edge.

As I tootled by in the old van, past the Mercedes-Benzes and BMWs that shuttled through this area, I thought of our recent newsletters. Anger with the system was growing. A couple of Ansett First Officers, brothers, wrote several open letters. They detailed the failings of the Accord, as so graphically demonstrated by those parliamentary pay rises which snuck through at Christmas. If the Accord was vital to our economic recovery, the letters posed, why were the guidelines elastic for politicians but rigid for ordinary working people?

Our employment contracts were renewed every two years, and the Australian Airlines agreement was due midyear. Peter Abeles expressed a desire to harmonise ours and theirs so, however this panned out, it seemed that 1989 was the deadline. Our executive began a series of newsletters entitled 'Deadline '89'. These newsletters, I thought, were part of the process. If nothing else, they provided light relief. One suggested starting a lawn mowing business if times turned tough. Another added other ideas for a NIP (Non-Income Period). One of my neighbours owned a lawn mowing concern. A typical small business, it had all the usual headaches of time management, weather, machine maintenance and such. I knew I'd have as much success at this as he would at the controls of a jet.

I bumped into a senior First Officer the day I had plucked that particular 'Deadline '89' from my mailbox.

> "See this," he said, holding his copy.
> "Yeah."
> "May as well send it straight to Wally."

I thought the same. What pilot would take that seriously? There's always a certain amount of posturing. My first move when buying the small car now sheltered in our garage was to feign walking away. Sir Peter's girth had spawned some unkind nicknames — 'Wally' (the whale) was one, 'the Fatman' another.

The month finally ended, with one fervent wish. I would have given almost anything to be one number higher on the seniority list. I spent a quiet month in May on reserve. I hated waiting around to go flying. Rebecca settled in and was doing well at school. A bright and happy little girl, she had many friends. Parents helped with reading and Sharon was a regular, sitting with the children as they worked through their books. On my standby days, I joined in as well, beeper in pocket. Beyond our back gate, heavy machinery worked on the reserve. Wondering what was going on, I chatted with the bulldozer driver. The area was being converted into a park.

June was another on reserve, but I was called out often. I was away for mine but home for Rebecca's birthday. It was hard to believe that I was the father of a seven-year-old. When away for special occasions, we had a system. We celebrated when I returned home. As the children grew, they became used to this. They often had birthdays or Christmas twice, as Sharon always made a fuss on the day.

Arriving back from a trip, I bumped into another 737 FO.

> "Did you hear about Frank?"
> "No."
> "His wife left him."
> I hadn't seen Frank since our last flight in April.
> "Apparently, she did some course at night school then got a job. Frank came home and she'd cleared the place out."
> "Yeah?"
> "Clean as a whistle. She didn't even leave a teaspoon in the cutlery draw."

I recalled Frank's bravado as he talked of his 'crazy wife', sporadically inserted between his general inconsideration. The reality must have differed as he rushed home to an empty house.

The Australian Airlines pilot agreement came up for renewal. Talks began at Lorne in Victoria from June the 26th and ran up to the

30th, the day our commitment to the Accord expired. Productivity changes were discussed, and a log of claims presented.

In 1987, Australian Airlines had experienced difficult times. To help the company's position, pilots decided to stick with the 1985 conditions. They had also worked extended overtime with no salary benefit after the company underestimated crewing levels when the B737 was introduced (the company scheduled training after, not before, the aircraft arrived). The latest financial period saw a bumper year — a record profit. On the 18th of July 1989, however, Australian Airlines advised no value could be placed on the proposals discussed at Lorne. Apparently, Peter Abeles was insisting on "industry acceptance". Whatever that implied, it meant one thing — no negotiation, so the pilots' log of claims was withdrawn.

July saw yet another month of me on reserve. One morning, we dropped Rebecca at school before I looked after the little ones. Sharon needed to go out for a while.

> "How long will you be?"
> "Not long. I just need to see the doctor."
> "Is everything OK?"
> "Yes, I'm fine. Nothing to worry about."

I had the feeling we'd had this conversation before, more than once.

The Mazda slotted back into its position in the garage, and the three of us met Sharon as she stepped through the hallway door. Her radiant smile said it all.

I'd seen Peter Abeles on TV, but only once in the flesh. Now he wanted to talk with the pilots. Meetings were scheduled at each base to discuss future plans for Ansett. My opinion of Peter Abeles had changed through the years. Watching his business dealings and interests, the people he dealt with and how he operated, my thinking was more in line with the wizened Brisbane Captain I had met many years prior in the Adelaide crew room. Why was Abeles calling meetings like this now?

The venue was a city hotel. I sat with Kris, Dave and Stephan as the conference room filled. Abeles arrived and made his way to the elevated platform. General Manager Graeme McMahon and Personnel Manager Ian Oldmeadow followed. At the end of the procession, Len Coysh slinked into a chair at the rear.

Len Coysh was the previous Executive Director of the Australian Federation of Air Pilots. For years, he had worked with our pilot volunteers on the executive. Now in Abeles' employ, Coysh had no apparent function. A pilot who knew him from past times shook hands and inquired as to his health. Coysh looked less than comfortable.

Sir Peter adjusted to his chair, serving to emphasise a couple of his more uncharitable nicknames. A sedentary lifestyle and constant Havanas probably hadn't helped. A hotel employee leaned across and flicked on the microphone. The room reverberated with a tortured intake and expulsion of gasped air. It was as though we were part of a cartoon, the walls expanding and contracting in concert with Sir Peter's raspy in and out. Abeles spoke of general plans. If he thought to rationalise the fleet, he didn't mention it. Others at the table added a snippet or two but, after an hour, they'd said nothing we didn't already know.

Sir Peter left the podium. He wished to speak personally with each of us. Did we have any ideas or suggestions? When my turn came, I looked into his steely eyes, his dead fish handshake as cold as ice. Pat stood beside me. We had both joined on the same intake back in '82, flew together in Perth, and moved to Brisbane around the same time. Pat had an idea to improve rostering. Sir Peter turned to Graeme McMahon, positioned like a small pampered dog waiting behind.

"Graeme, write zis down."

Len Coysh lurked in the background. Many senior pilots knew him, but he made no effort to mingle. On leaving, each of us wore a frown. What was that all about? Nothing new, no real plans, just a general rehash of old news.

CHAPTER 19

Our attempts to negotiate went nowhere. In the AFAP's head office, someone with a very sharp pencil worked through the figures. Professional salary rates (which I understood to be income) powered ahead. These were factored, along with past productivity and inflation. Examining the financial years 1984/85 to June I989, pilot salaries had trailed the cost of living by an average of 22 percent. Inflation was estimated at seven percent, compounded to cover 1989/90. The calculation was precise, extending to two decimal places.

Our accountant's estimate must have been in the ballpark because, although less than the politicians' 36 percent, it was similar. Perhaps the politicians' pencil was sharper, or then again, maybe more blunt. Under the Accord, we had slipped behind by 29.47 percent. Similarly, paddling against the tide in the same boat, *all* wage and salary earners had fallen behind.

AFAP's claim, based on this figure, was presented to the airlines, with a meeting set for the 1st of August. To say this was not well received is an understatement. The response came that the companies required us to formally commit to the Accord's wage-fixing guidelines. Justice Coldham of the IRC called the AFAP's claim "outrageous". What he thought of 80 percent for his fellow judges, not imparted. Around the same time, the full bench of the IRC handed down the latest guidelines. Apparently, in these times, income had more than one meaning. A maximum of six percent was granted, but only after productivity trade-offs. Justice Coldham directed the AFAP to hold meetings with its membership. The threat — "submit or else".

Already angry, I became furious. Australia was a free country. If I didn't want to renew an agreement I thought stupid, unfair and inequitable, why was a gun being held to my head?

In accordance with Justice Coldham's order, meetings were arranged. The AFAP represented pilots from the two major domestics, plus East-West Airlines (integrated into Ansett in 1988), and the freight airline, Ipec. Each base met on a different day in August. To allow attendance, duty was restricted between 3.00 am and 3.00 pm.

Feeling uneasy, Sharon and I discussed how I'd vote. We believed in the freedoms of our country. Australians had gone to war defending these. An agreement was an agreement, not associated with threats. Balanced against these thoughts, we considered our expanding family. Any disruption would make life difficult. Also influencing our thinking was my upbringing. Politically, we strayed slightly to the right of centreline, but not enough to depart the runway.

Dad had owned a small business. In the building industry, a notorious union stood out. The Builders Labourers' Federation had a history of militancy. In the past and led by Jack Mundey, they had fought hard and long. Many majestic buildings in Sydney owe their continued existence to Green Bans instigated by the BLF. Strolling through 'The Rocks', Sydneysiders may be unaware that the current elegance of many old buildings was something bequeathed by Mundey and his labourers. While many didn't believe in Mundey's actions, he did. Whenever workers were on strike, he, as an official, had stopped his own pay. Although in a position to benefit financially, not a penny slipped into Mundey's pocket.

The story differed in later years. With Norm Gallagher leading, strikes gave way to guerrilla tactics. Workers were directed to "down tools" during concrete pours. Not only the cost of the concrete was lost, but when left as a solid glob instead of building structure, this was a nightmare to jackhammer and remove. Corruption was rife, as revealed by a Royal Commission, and the BLF was eventually deregistered.

Unlike this union, our history was not one of industrial action, losing only 14 days in the previous 37 years. Even if only mild, industrial action was industrial action. My unease, dating back to the superannuation strike and stop-work meetings, returned. I believed the blatant elitism emerging in our society should be challenged. One group was subjected to rigid controls, while those administering the system and cohorts wallowed in the spoils. I rationalised. If a gun was levelled at our heads, why not point one back? To be honest, I still felt uneasy. The wage-and-salary earner's arsenal was limited to one weapon but, in our case, if either side pulled the trigger, many innocent people would be caught in the fray.

Cracks were forming in the Accord. How could they not? There was only so much blood in a stone. The rewards of restraint that were meant to be shared equitably, as so passionately proclaimed, had instead been funnelled to the top. Rather than investing in our country's future, there came a splurge, now known as 'the excesses of the 80s'. Dubious transactions, company raids, real estate and stock market speculation joined obscene executive pay rates, similar to Peter Abeles'. Of no benefit to employment or our economy, highly geared businessmen ploughed money into assets, inflating prices to ridiculous levels, and pushing the cash rate to 18 percent. Such excesses fuelled an asset bubble that drove us headlong towards recession.

I hadn't been to a mass meeting before. Occasionally, I had attended branch meetings. This was different. How would the meeting be structured, and what specifically would be put to the vote? It wasn't the money. We'd fallen behind, but as Dad had said years ago, we were making ends meet.

Back in '83 when our Federation officials returned after the superannuation problems, I disagreed with their decision to join the Accord. I know our then president believed he was doing the right thing, but in hindsight, I felt he was influenced by the trust and respect fostered during Reg Ansett's days.

If the choice was to resist the pressures and not renew the agreement, pursuing our right to negotiate, then I would vote for this. If the vote was a simple yes or no, go on strike for more money, I'd vote against. I felt that keeping both sides at the table was always the better solution and, practically, any period without an income would make things, at the very least, difficult.

If the meeting offered a return to the Accord with a pay rise fudged through the IRC, then a ballot paper the size of a house would be too small to accommodate my 'NO' vote. If Justice Maddern decreed that a 36 percent rise fitted within the guidelines for politicians, then why did these same guidelines allow only a six percent rise for wage and salary earning Australians? If six percent was cancelled from both sides, it'd be a case of "give them 30 percent but give everybody else nothing". If we accepted a pay grab under a similar formula, which fitted 'magic-pudding-like' within the guidelines, then we would become part of a system that I thought was rotten to the core.

Later that evening, the phone rang. An FO had called in sick. My duty was a Sydney run. Away from Brisbane, I missed my chance to vote. I returned that night. The news, when all the bases correlated, was an overwhelming result, 95 percent. Our leaders were directed to approach the companies once again, leaving the option for future industrial action open.

Justice Coldham called us back. I despised this institution. Sitting aloft, rubber stamps fobbed off as determinations, the IRC was just part of the club. Our intransience, however, was not a mark of disrespect for the man. Coldham was 70 years old and a former bomber pilot. He had served with distinction. Flying Lancaster bombers in World War II on the Pathfinder missions, he was twice decorated. Awarded the Distinguished Flying Cross, his service to country reminded me of a few of the older pilots I'd had the pleasure to fly with. With his retirement looming, Coldham made little effort to hide the fact that we were getting up his nose.

On the 15th of August 1989, the Prime Minister invited several people to meet in his office.

Bob Hawke hosted Sir Peter Abeles (in his position of Joint Managing Director of Ansett Transport Industries), Ted Harris (Chairman of Australian Airlines), Graeme McMahon (General Manager of Ansett), Peter Morris (Minister for Industrial Relations), and Ralph Willis (Minister for Transport and Communications). Bill Kelty (Secretary of the ACTU) joined the discussion by telephone.

Afterwards, this meeting between the airlines, Government and ACTU was initially denied. When it became evident that the meeting had occurred, those involved further denied that any minutes existed.

Dr D.S. Harrison was a public servant in the Prime Minister's department in 1989. He was subpoenaed in a later court case when pilots challenged government changes to Australia's immigration regulations. Dr Harrison recorded the minutes of the 15th August meeting, and on the 21st of February 1992, he tendered these minutes as evidence in the federal court:

> Australian Airlines Chair, Mr Harris, was the first noted speaker: "widespread disruption. A & A not tolerate. Should cancel agreement. Kelty thought Coleman should end agreement — put pressure, loss of seniority."

This slight misspelling was a reference to Justice Peter 'Coldham' of the Australian Industrial Relations Commission. Cancelling awards is not only a rare and drastic step, but one used solely in the direst of circumstances. The meeting minutes continued:

> Sir Peter Abeles: "agreement should be cancelled but once they are outside industrial agreement then government should have strong presence"

Abeles, Harris and Industrial Relations Minister Morris continued with ideas of how they could apply pressure, with Abeles stressing government backing. Next, the question of compensation arose:

> Chairman Harris: "If they tie us up — Australians costs are $14 million a week. Government ought to compensate by not paying charges to FAA & CAA. 3 million per week for each week not flying, don't pay charges for X weeks."

Would the owners of the Federal Airports Authority and Civil Aviation Authority have a say in this?

> Ansett Director Abeles readily agreed: "government should compensate. Wouldn't stand anyone down, isolates the pilots. Pilots split down the middle. If let them do it their way, rolling strikes, disruptive over a long period and they will get more than they should. No sympathy for them. Don't compare themselves with others in airline industry."

Slipping a few taxpayer dollars Abeles' way wouldn't hurt the cause and, obviously, he and the boys in the office were beyond reproach. This line of discussion continued until Transport Minister Willis raised the spectre of 45D. Section 45D of the Trade Practices Act covered secondary boycotts. A trademark of a former Liberal government, 45D was hated by the Labour Movement. In 1984, Mr Willis had introduced legislation attempting to repeal the most arcane aspects, including, oddly enough, what he was just about to propose:

> "go for 45D or common. They want to be outside the system."
> Bob Hawke, the Prime Minister of Australia, had a thought: "will Kelty cop 45D or Crimes Act? If so, go for 45D, etc."
> Sir Peter Abeles, now in his element: "sign them up on individual contracts fast. Eliminate everything we want to eliminate. Same contract for all. Lose superannuation if they leave/ don't sign."

A nice bit of standover, but what did they wish to eliminate?

> Australian Airlines Chairman Harris: "Kelty [sic] as vigorous in his views as we are."

That was a relief, but something this important should be confirmed.

Sir Peter Abeles of Ansett, IR Minister Morris and Australian Airlines Chair Harris discussed various ways of applying pressure.

> Morris asked, "how poisonous do you want this to be? Will pick one at a time."
> Abeles: "government shows support through charge waivers. If one airline off ground then 25 percent of revenue goes to other airline."

An interesting trade practice.

> Ted Harris noted: "have to do this through government."

Back to that important matter.

> PM to ACTU Secretary Kelty by phone: "what [sic] your attitude to suspension of agreements, then move 45D, common law."
> Bill Kelty had a stipulation: "Has to be on basis of award suspended."

Could an ACTU leader do this? Did a Prime Minister even have the power to do this?

> Union Secretary Kelty warned: "... it is no soft option to be out of the system ..."

This would certainly teach us a lesson, but were the dubious lack of work choices dictated by individual contracts something an ACTU leader should embed in an Australian workplace?

> Abeles: "If there is aftermath, subsidise each other."

A little collusion never hurt anybody but, as most things do in situations such as this, it came down to tactics and money.

> PM: "tactic. Government be in court with airline — we want to be in the system but if not, then government will support airlines in any

> punitive action. DIR/9 trade practices. DIR/6 — cancel agreement if you go for this, Coleman [sic] will move quickly won't he." To which he added: "horrendous proportions."

Again, note the slight misspelling: 'Coleman's' real name was Coldham, and he was an impartial commissioner of a statutory institution.

Australian Airlines' Chair Harris, Ansett's Sir Peter Abeles and PM Hawke discussed various aspects of suspending agreements and punitive action, with the PM's thoughts turning to compensating the airlines: "Have a talk to Walsh/Keating re waiver of charges." Noting that Abeles was losing $11 million and Harris $14 million, the Prime Minister, no slouch when it came to mathematics, did the sums: "say $12 million each."

> Abeles: "will get goodwill of ACTU. Shows what happens to those outside the system."

Thank God for that. And, of course, he wasn't talking about politicians, executives, judges and others slurping from the same trickle-up trough.

> But Abeles was still fretting about the money: "subsidy will strengthen airlines."
> The leader of our country needed information: "on financial grounds you would stand down."

If all this resulted in stand downs, especially involving a government airline, then it was probably best if Sir Peter told the PM about it now. Further discussion on tactics ensued, with the Prime Minister promising to look at the question of compensation, while it perhaps slipped his mind just who this money belonged to.

> Before finishing up, Ted Harris wanted the record put straight: "make it clear we have had no direction from Government."

Abeles stressed that the airlines "should stick together". He then expanded on how he had dealt with 400 transport workers using his method of implementing individual contracts:

> "24 hours to come back and sign or they lose employer contribution superannuation."
> Then, the man who cultivated a public persona of 'Bringing Australia together' and preached, "Confrontation never solves disputes — only negotiation and compromise offer solutions" proffered his final advice: "use judgment. Use instruments which hit hard. Hit as hard as you can, quick as you can, carte blanche from me."

IR Minister Morris did mention Qantas, but that could wait for the next meet. With planning for the Airline Dispute of 1989-90 more or less attended to, the meeting adjourned.

"Come into my parlour," said the spider to the fly.

CHAPTER 20

After six days of working nine to five, Abeles, flanked by Hawke and Kelty, levelled his stony glare — if you think your pathetic effort ranks as industrial action, then watch this.

That night they grounded aircraft, shut down operations, and locked the doors. In the furore, and despite Abeles' decree to shut down the airline, several journalists failed to recognise who held the keys to these locked doors. Abeles shoved the keyring back into his overstuffed pocket as PM Hawke removed any doubt as to who was gripping the industrial baton, "If it means shutting down the system for 'x' number of weeks, then it will be shut down."

Locked out and with our awards cancelled, they launched into the next phase. The following morning, on the 24th of August, the airlines commenced serving their writs.

The AFAP representatives rushed to the airline companies. The phone rang. Tom on the line. Tom ("Mudguard, how the hell are ya?") had moved to Brisbane shortly after us, and he also flew the 737.

> "Hey, you know that piece of paper you signed last night?"
>
> I silently nodded to the phone.
>
> "It was submitted today."

I breathed the greatest sigh of relief I ever have (which still holds true to this day). No matter what happened from now on, Abeles and Murdoch could not place one grubby finger on my family.

I was lucky enough not to be one of those served this vile document. Other pilots weren't as fortunate. Their writs were served before the torrent was stopped by our resignations. Airlines could sue pilots for breach of contract. Several of these writs failed the legal test, while others relied on coordinating witnesses in different parts of the country. While more than half were discarded, 67 remained.

The majority of pilots resigned on the 24th of August 1989, but a handful didn't. It's difficult to estimate the exact number who resigned from each airline. Ansett's numbers were complicated by their inclusion of only the 'Mainline' pilots, excluding the subsidiaries and East-West Airlines, which, by this time, had merged with Ansett. I have the Ansett seniority list that was current before our resignations, and there are 1,195 pilots on it.

Following the resignations, we ceased to be Ansett/Australian/East-West and Ipec pilots, and thought of ourselves as 'Federation' pilots. The hard figure is that 1,647 pilots resigned from all of the airlines and this combined figure became the total we used.

One journalist expanded on a comment by the Minister for Transport and Communications about 'Kamikaze Pilots'. The thinking was that resigning wasn't a smart industrial move. He had no argument there. The problem with this logic was that ours was not an industrial move. Through one eye, this IR specialist viewed with precision who said what, where and when, at some IRC hearing. But when it came to common law, it was as if an eye patch covered his other eye.

A young family huddled together under the William Jolly Bridge, a solitary blanket secreted away, as the Abeles-Murdoch forces possessed their family home and everything in it: "Good thing we didn't resign. That would've been a silly thing to do."

It's hard to say what the airlines planned to achieve with their writs. Abeles' intimidating "if they leave/don't sign" threat was probably the primary aim. A psychological king hit, he could say, to each of us: "In my right hand I hold everything you own, and in my left I have a Kelty Contract." Just as with Barry Jones on *Pick a Box*, it was our choice. Select the left and the right is released. But elect not to sign, then the right hand crushes its contents, clenched into a fist.

There was one sweetener though. Bill Kelty tweaked the contracts, giving a bigger pay rise than the pilot Federation's claim. It involved one small catch. As is traditional in transactions such as this — you had to come alone.

Abeles had previously used strong arm tactics to crush a group of tarmac workers. If we didn't acquiesce, then he could see us in court, seize our belongings, and bankrupt every one of us. A knock on the door and everything would be swept away. One writ was even pegged to a clothesline. Journalists who expounded on industrial matters and decried the stupidity of taking this threat seriously had obviously never stared down the twin barrels of Sir Peter Abeles' loaded shotgun.

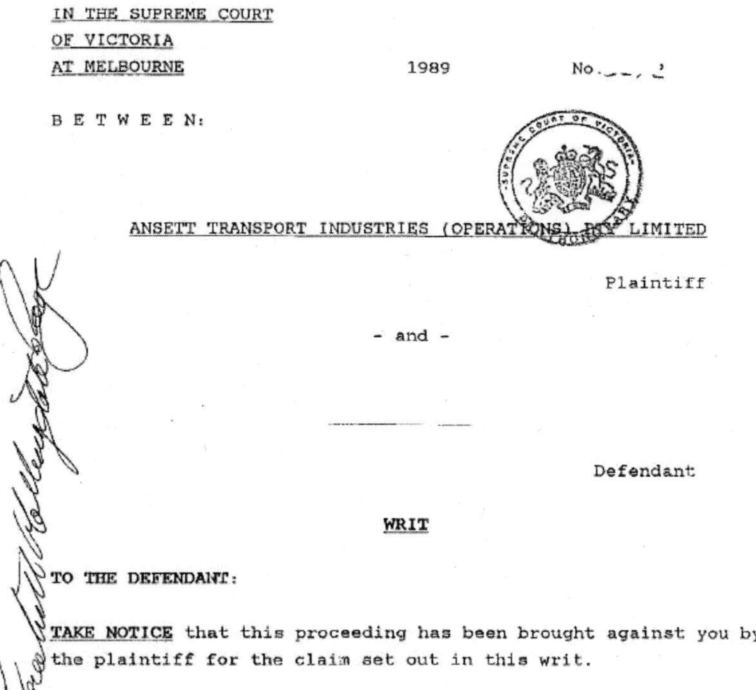

IN THE SUPREME COURT
OF VICTORIA
AT MELBOURNE 1989 No.

B E T W E E N:

ANSETT TRANSPORT INDUSTRIES (OPERATIONS) PTY LIMITED

Plaintiff

\- and -

Defendant

WRIT

TO THE DEFENDANT:

TAKE NOTICE that this proceeding has been brought against you by the plaintiff for the claim set out in this writ.

Above: Excerpt from the writ served to an Ansett pilot in August 1989. 1,647 pilots resigned en masse from Ansett, Australian Airlines, East-West, and Ipec. The resignations stopped the planned torrent of writs, however, an estimated 140 were served before AFAP officials reached the airline offices. Approximately half of the served writs were legally invalid, but 67 unfortunate pilots received valid writs prior to submitting their resignations. They faced legal action seeking damages for breach of contract.

On the other hand, maybe they were having two bob each way. They had lawyers too. The resignations allowed them to restructure, sweeping aside the industrial protections in our collective agreement. Again, from the Brad Norington book:

> Much later, Graeme McMahon gloated: "I'll be perfectly honest. I couldn't believe my luck. Christ! Who would do that? Resign from what one of their own members described as the best contract any pilot in the world had."

Until that day, I had thought that Ansett was the best airline in the world. Working with Ansett, I believed I had the best job in the world. On meeting Graeme McMahon, sadly, my impression was of a thug in a suit. Despite my low opinion, I found it hard to imagine he would not strive to protect his family if placed in the same situation. As an Ansett executive, he probably couldn't believe his luck. Christ! Who wouldn't do that? Use tax payers' money to restructure a private company.

In one of the many ironies, Bob Hawke and Bill Kelty, in cahoots with Peter Abeles, offended another group. When it came to industrial relations, these people were diametrically opposed to intrinsic Labor values. Hawke and Kelty made them look like a bunch of left-wing radicals:

> 'Mr Hawke's zeal in all these matters thus went even further than our own. The H.R. Nicholls Society had never argued that a body of employees should not have the right to be represented by a union (or association) of their own free choosing — a basic right which Mr Hawke and Sir Peter [Abeles] were determined to deny to the pilots.'

The PM likened us to bus drivers. My next-door neighbour at the time drove interstate coaches. Our jobs were so different, with the only common ground that we both carried passengers. By the tone of delivery, Hawke's comment was meant as an insult. Maybe, attempting the Whitlamish double slight, he wasn't fond of bus drivers either. Without the style or grace of Gough, or the sharp-tongued skill of his treasurer, Bob Hawke's stampeding rhetoric was more akin to "a bull in a china shop" (as Dad may have said).

On the 19th of July 1989, just a short time before Mr Hawke's taunt United Airlines Flight 232, a DC-10, suffered catastrophic failure of the tail-mounted, number two engine. Shrapnel was flung from the disintegrating engine, which punctured skin and severed the hydraulic lines of all three systems, knocking out flight controls. The remaining wing-mounted engines became the only means to alter the flight path. Captain Al Haynes, First Officer William Records, Second Officer Dudley Dvorak and Captain Dennis Fitch (who was travelling as a passenger and offered to join the crew) nursed this wide-body back to Sioux City. Barely controllable, they managed to crash-land the aircraft. 111 people were killed, but 185 survived. Before this unparalleled feat, an overwhelming failure of this magnitude assumed no survivors. Glorified bus driving, such as this, if mishandled, could result in the deaths of all on board, including the glorified bus drivers, and the loss of millions of dollars' worth of capital equipment.

Bob Hawke spoke with a voice of authority, backed by knowledge and experience. He did some flying when studying at Oxford. Of the 1,000 hours minimum required for an Airline Transport Pilot Licence, he had flown two thirds of that necessary for a Restricted Private Licence. Yet, he regarded flying as "not something flash — it's a relatively easy thing to do."

Several management pilots did not resign. Henry Theunissen stayed on at Ansett but refused to fly. For a company to hold an Air Operator's Certificate, it needed a Chief Pilot. Threatening to sue someone fulfilling such a legal requirement could be counterproductive, however, and Abeles became annoyed. He issued an ultimatum to Captain Theunissen. I heard that Henry calmly packed his briefcase. Having dedicated decades of his life to this company, he walked out the door.

The airlines engaged psychologists. I'm told that the initial group believed that their job was to help with the psychological damage the dispute was causing. When they became aware that their brief was to create harm, several refused. But, unfortunately, there were others who heeded their master's voice. The king hit of the writs was nullified by our resignations, so the psychological tactics shifted.

While Sharon drove Rebecca to school, the postman dropped a letter in our box.

The white envelope bore the blue Ansett logo.

I climbed the stairs and pulled an old suitcase from the cupboard.

> "What are you doing?"
> "The company ordered me to return my uniform."

I remembered the pride I felt when wearing it. The one I had dreamed of, above all others. One gold stripe, another added two years later, and now three; my heart sank as I placed the jackets in the bag.

We drove to the airport and parked in the public car park. Carrying the suitcase, we approached a counter. Escorted through a door that my ID card had once allowed me free passage, we were guided to the crew room. A manager sat at the other side of a desk. We remained standing. I held Matthew in my arms; Sharon nursed Amelia. The manager looked up.

> "You can sit down."
> "We'd rather stand. It's in the bag; where do you want it?"
> "Look, I have to tick off each item, and the quantity. How about you take a seat. I'll get your wife a chair."
> Sharon and I said nothing as we settled opposite my former colleague.

"Shirts first."
I handed these across, silently.
Counted and ticked, he continued. "Three pairs of trousers."
With these handed over, he placed them in a black plastic garbage bag. He continued filling the form, which he later stuck to the outside.
"What are you going to do with it?"
He pointed to a back room three-quarters full with garbage bags that, until now, was a briefing office. "We'll keep it here. When you come back, you can pick it up."

I stared straight through him. We ticked off my cap, ties and epaulettes, and then the two jackets. The list complete, I passed him my freighter jacket.
"What's this?"
"It's my freighter jacket. Look, it's got Ansett written on it."

When operating the Melbourne freighter from Adelaide, we were issued freighter jackets. They were warm and comfortable, a Godsend in the cold F27 cockpit on winter nights. When I transferred to Perth, we crewed night freighters up the west coast. Reporting for my first flight, the Captain asked why I wasn't wearing my uniform. I told him the jacket was company issue, pointing to the Ansett emblem above the pocket. He was from the old MMA days.

"That's not part of the uniform over here."
Apparently, this was the case in Brisbane too.
"It's not on the list."
"I don't want it, so how about you shove it in the bag with the rest."

He seemed hesitant, so I grabbed the bag and stuffed the jacket inside. There was one last item. Only weeks before, the company had issued each of us a small metal tag meant for our flight bags. It read 'Ansett', in blue stylised font on one side and had a slogan on the reverse: *You can't have the best airline in the world without the best people*.

Reflecting on the people who now frequented this room, I handed it to him. Picking up on my belligerent attitude, he left it on the desk, and said he didn't want it.

"Well, I sure as hell don't want it."

I plucked the badge from the wooden desktop and hurled it into the metal waste basket. Not realising the tension and my anger, I flung it so hard it hit the bottom, bounced to the top, then rattled around the sides. Everyone looked on as it settled, 'best people' side up.

"Can we go now?"

I shouldn't have been so rude. He was only doing his job. But the anger and hurt overwhelmed what I hope were usually better manners. Handing me a copy of the form, he opened the door. Nursing our children, we walked out, neither looking back.

CHAPTER 21

Everything had happened so quickly. It was like being hit with a one-two-three every few days. At night, I lay awake, sick with worry. Some days, I couldn't eat, and others no matter how much I stuffed in, nothing seemed to fill the void.

The media raged. 30 percent! How could we think ourselves so precious? I raged back, "Why don't they ask those who *took* it?" It may have been a subtle difference, but this was important to us. I understood the calculation, showing just how far we'd slipped behind under the Accord and its clinical accuracy, but we weren't the only ones disadvantaged by the system. The amount wasn't important; the principle was. I wanted our right to negotiate, with our requested figure used as the starting point.

My phone group leader called. The Federation execs were flying up from Melbourne, with John Raby at the controls of a loaned Piper Navajo.

> "The meeting's being held at Valleys."
> "Valleys? What's Valleys?"

I was still getting my bearings. On the night I had signed my resignation letter, there was at least one stop along the way to check the street directory.

> "Valleys Football Club. You know, the Fortitude Valley Diehards."

I apologised, but I hadn't heard of them and explained that we'd not long arrived from the West.

> "It's at Neumann Oval, Albion. Not far from the Fed office."

I wrote it down. This was the first of our Brisbane meetings. Sometimes, they would be held at Valleys or at the Brothers Rugby Club. When consulting the street directory, I didn't recognise the suburbs and studiously mapped out the differing routes to each.

The hall filled. Journalists and TV camera crews lined the entrance. We allowed them in to record the attendance, but asked them to leave as the meeting began. It was a good feeling just being here. Our families all formed one big family.

Brian McCarthy, John Raby and Noel Holt, the pilot members of the executive, sat behind a rectangular table. Terry O'Connell, our executive director, along with Tony Fitzsimons who was on the negotiating committee, sat with them. Up on the podium, they looked over the gathering.

Our Federation used secret ballots to elect officials. A bottom to top organisation, the membership directed the leaders, voting on issues and actions. I felt sorry for those on the dais. They were copping a lot of heat, on our behalf. ACTU officials must have thought it ludicrous — pilots working as representatives for nothing.

Tony Fitzsimons was the AFAP president when I had joined. I remembered him from my first Annual General Meeting all those years ago. Later that evening, we had chatted while sitting at a BBQ table outside the Darwin Aero Club. A former Navy jet pilot, Fitzsimons commanded the DC-9, later transferring to the 727. Active in the branch, Fitzsimons added a local presence.

In his book, Brad Norington not only offered his opinions, but descriptions. I'll borrow a few in describing the other AFAP executives:

> "Although he was not a pilot, O'Connell loosely fitted the stereotype with a black moustache, dark hair, hard-set eyes and a lived-in face. He was 38 years old, short, nuggetty, worked hard and was rarely far from a telephone. He was an amiable person but was also intensely private and wary of others.
>
> Raby was a former Ansett management pilot who had returned to pilot ranks in 1986 to

become a senior Check Captain after becoming disillusioned and wanting a change. During 10 years in management, he had been Ansett's assistant flight standards manager with responsibility for recruiting and training pilots. He also introduced an innovative human factors program into Australia's aviation industry.

Raby had joined Ansett at 21, immediately after flying school. Now 45, he lived in the Melbourne suburb of Kew with his wife, Deidre, and two children. He was a highly intelligent, articulate fellow, tall, red-faced with wavy white hair and a moustache.

McCarthy looked and sounded the way an old-time pilot should: 41 years old, moustache, craggy features, sad, piercing blue eyes and the kind of deep baritone that wafts easily through the intercom of a Boeing 727. He had the bearing of a military man, a relic from his days in the Army, but he was relaxed among those who knew him well. McCarthy portrayed himself as the voice of calm reason and principle, the man you can trust.

Noel Holt was a Boeing 727 Captain at Australian Airlines who led early negotiations with his own management in June 1989 before the pilots' dispute blew up to involve all Airlines. Holt had worked for the airline for almost 20 years, starting as a First Officer on Fokker F27s in 1970, qualifying as a DC9 Captain in 1987 and then moving to Boeing 727s a year later. He was 46, shortish, bearded, balding and regarded as a pugnacious acerbic character with a dry sense of humour."

Brian McCarthy moved to the lectern. He gave an update of events and options for future directions, before handing over to John Raby. Again, my memories were stoked; that silken baritone on the end of the phone had announced my Ansett interview was successful, and later, it had filled my evenings after F27 training in Launceston. Each of these pilots had a speciality. After John Raby, Noel Holt spoke, followed by Terry O'Connell.

Several microphones would be passed around the hall to anyone who had something to say. A theme had emerged in the media reporting: 'pilots led by the nose by a rigid leadership'. Journalists reporting in this manner shared one thing: they'd never attended one of our meetings.

An Ansett First Officer from the intake ahead of mine spoke. His suggestion related to a common concern among the Ansett group. The person whose company owned half the airline also owned the lion's share of Australian media. Very few issues we had tried to highlight were making it through. Warwick suggested we approach a public relations specialist. This was noted, and with frustration mounting, the AFAP hired a PR firm a few weeks later.

Underlying the meeting was our commitment. It was simple; all that each asked of the other was to do nothing. Some volunteered to answer the office phones, while others ran errands or generally helped out. None of this was expected — all we asked of our colleagues and their families was to stand in line.

The meeting moved along. Questions and suggestions crossed from the floor to the dais and back. Families sat with young children and older family members with greying hair lined the walls on extra chairs. All of these people were us.

An older guy across the aisle raised his hand. I hadn't seen him before. He knew Brian McCarthy and addressed his concern to him.

> "Brian, we have one big problem." He paused. "We have a weak link in our chain, and that weak link could bring us all down."
>
> Obviously a senior pilot, all eyes fell on this man as he talked his talk.
>
> "The young First Officers have the greatest pressure. If they buckle, they'll rush back, sign the contracts,

> pick up Kelty's silver, and jump over everyone else's seniority."

I was affronted, as was every other young pilot. Hell would freeze over before my family abandoned this person or anyone else in this room. Following more questions and discussion, the meeting drew to a close. As we left, cameras followed us. I caught up with Dave and asked if he knew the older guy. He did, a former Ansett 767 Captain. He was one of the most senior in the base, which meant the company.

The IRC showed its colours again, not that it needed to. Off its own bat, the Commission proposed setting aside the GA pilots' awards. Although many were represented by the Federation, they had nothing to do with this and had a hard enough time as it was. I couldn't make up my mind — loath or despise? In the end, I settled for both, with 'and' in between.

The press ramped up their coverage. Determined journalists probed and questioned. Democratic rights, inequality and much of what we attempted to showcase began to be discussed. I admired these journalists who showed no fear. We weren't immune from the odd tongue lashing, but we had limited our working hours for almost a week. What I found impressive was when journos did their best to present both sides in a fair and balanced manner. Unfortunately, these reporters seemed few and far between.

In *The Australian,* a headline squealed, '13 hours' flying a week for $128,000'. The article by Stuart Rintoul commenced: "A typical domestic airline pilot earning $128,000 a year flies about 13 hours a week." Rintoul's article, for me, was in a class of its own. I kept it, along with several others from this time, in a box that originally bore Sao biscuits. Even after so many years, my chest and arm muscles tense when I hold this yellow-brown paper, with nibbles around the edges from long-departed silverfish, and read again the fading black ink.

THE PILOTS' DISPUTE

13 hours' flying a week for $128,000

By STUART RINTOUL

A TYPICAL domestic airline pilot earning $128,000 a year flies about 13 hours a week.

When he stays a night interstate, it is in a five-star hotel to which he is taken in a stretch limousine.

There are "grey days" on his roster block — those days when, according to an airline official, "they could be assigned but usually they're not and they don't have to hang around at home".

Depending on seniority, a pilot can choose to fly as much or as little as he wants.

Rosters vary enormously, from days where a pilot does five sectors of flying with half-hour turnarounds, to days where he might make a single flight. He is contractually limited to five landings a day.

A typical week might be:

Monday: Beginning at 6am for pre-flight planning, then round trip Melbourne-Sydney-Brisbane-Sydney-Melbourne, ending at 3pm.

Tuesday: Off.

Wednesday: Melbourne-Adelaide-Perth overnight.

Thursday: Perth-Sydney-Melbourne.

Friday: Off.

Saturday: Off

Sunday: Off.

A typical eight-hour day might include an hour of pre-flight planning, including weather checks and fuel calculations as well as checks of the aircraft, four hours of flying with two hours of turnarounds in between, when a pilot would normally just wait around, and 15 minutes to sign off.

"Just like war," a besieged official said. "A lot of the time is spent waiting."

While Civil Aviation Orders impose a safety limit of eight hours of flying time a day, 30 hours a week, 100 a month, or 900 a year, domestic pilots never fly that much.

They average 350 to 400 hours' actual flying or "stick time" a year — less than half the 900 hours limit laid down in the orders.

A domestic pilot averages nine nights interstate a month. At these times, he is driven to a five star hotel in a stretch limousine — either a Mercedes Benz or a stretch LTD.

The hotels which are used include the Hilton and the Regent in Sydney, the Hyatt on Collins, Menzies at Rialto, Hilton and Regent in Melbourne, the Hilton in Adelaide and the Sheraton in Perth.

Accommodation in these hotels — which are used by many companies, including *The Australian* — costs $110 a night. When he is away, the pilot receives a daily travelling allowance of $2.58 an hour, but pays for his own meals. If he returns when not on duty he flies home first class.

He earns between $42,000 and $130,000, and has six weeks' annual leave. When he retires at 60, he receives an average superannuation payout of $700,000.

THE Coalition plans to re-introduce to Federal Parliament next week a Bill aimed at strengthening the powers of the Industrial Relations Commission.

The Opposition introduced the legislation — which contains some elements dropped from the Government's original 1987 industrial relations legislation — into the Senate last week, but it was rejected by the Government.

The legislation would empower the commission to give directions to stop or prevent a dispute. If the directive was not followed, the Federal Court would intervene.

Foreign carrier

By BARRY LOWE

INTERNATIONAL airlines are earning a windfall in revenue as they step in to plug the gaps in Australia's strike-crippled transport system and move domestic passengers around the country.

Several thousand passengers were flown between State capitals yesterday as the international carriers responded to the Government's invitation to fill their empty seats with stranded travellers.

With restrictions lifted on carriers backloading with domestic passengers on the Australian legs of their journeys, the foreign airlines were able to fill planes that normally fly half empty.

British Airways gained an extra 600 passengers this way yesterday, divided among three flights: Sydney to Brisbane, Brisbane to Sydney and Sydney to Melbourne.

A single Malaysian Airline System flight from Sydney to Melbourne took 277 extra passengers while two Singapore Airlines flights — Adelaide to Melbourne and Melbourne to Adelaide — each carried 100 domestic passengers.

A Cathay Pacific flight from Brisbane to Sydney had only 43 spare seats in its business class and first class

Captain McCarthy (left) with Mr Terry O'Connell in

Captain fair fist a 'hard l

By EWIN HANNAN

THE president of the Australian Federation of Air Pilots (AFAP), Captain Brian McCarthy, did an amazing thing during a 45-minute press conference in Melbourne yesterday.

He made everyone feel that, as far as workers go, the pilots really were pretty

Above: '13 hours' flying a week for $128,000' by Stuart Rintoul, *The Australian*, 25th of August, 1989.

Perhaps, I should have left the tattered piece of newspaper in the dusty old box. Several articles in there stood out, but for opposite reasons. This article encapsulated the distortions and misinformation others regurgitated onto newssheets and through the airwaves, but unlike most of those, this effort incorporated them all in one sitting. Even so, I felt a grudging admiration for this journalist's masterful play on words.

The craftiness of this piece was to quote the salary of a small group while confusing their job function. A typical domestic airline pilot did not earn $128,000 a year. A handful of senior Captains earnt this figure, but these were management pilots. Management pilots ran departments, managed fleets or performed check and training duties. While management pilots typically flew a few flights each week to maintain currency, this was not their primary function. If a typical management pilot earned $128,000 this was for the responsibilities of their supervisory position, and not the 13 hours they may have flown in addition to their administrative duties.

The article moved to rosters, focussing on 'grey days'. Monthly rosters were known as 'blocks', and grey days were incorporated into the flying blocks. These added a standby buffer in times of high callouts. If pilots on reserve had been allocated duty, the companies could utilise pilots on grey days to maintain the schedule. Grey days were additional to rostered flying, so a pilot still achieved the productivity the airlines built into the blocks, even if not assigned duty on a grey day.

The airlines built the monthly blocks with approximately the same amount of hours. Blocks were awarded on seniority. Pilots could bid for preferences such as trips, days off or morning or afternoon flights, while those who lacked the seniority were usually stuck with the reserve blocks. But you either flew a block or suffered standby duty on reserve — a pilot could not 'choose to fly as much or as little he wants'.

The journalist noted that flight sectors could 'vary enormously'. If Australian cities were positioned equally apart then rosters could be homogeneous. As our cities are not equidistant, some days could be filled with short hops and others could have less but longer legs. Allowing for differing sectors on differing days, the companies produced rosters with the monthly flying hours they required.

Citing an example of what 'a typical week might be', the reporter's sequence began on a Monday and worked through. The pattern of Rintoul's words appeared to form a journalistic scowl. Out of these seven days, four were marked as days off. Our rosters covered a calendar month. Selectively plucking a week, then fobbing this off as '*typical*' seemed to be Rintoul's MO. After feeding in a month's flying, *might* a 'Crew Roster and Tracking System' spit out rosters with four days out of every seven off? *Might* an airline (or any company) be satisfied with a scheduling system that allocated just three working days each week? Airlines had dedicated departments responsible for planning and producing rosters. Their productivity calculations covered monthly totals, not those in a selective week.

The article alluded to what a 'typical' eight-hour day might include. A pilot didn't just slide into the seat, turn the key, drop the clutch, and zap the Boeing off to Alice Springs. If this journalist thought that flight planning, take-off calculations, loading route and performance data into the Flight Management Computer System, setting flight and navigation instruments for departure, organising ground staff and performing an external inspection, was *just waiting around*, it illustrated how little Stuart Rintoul knew about airline operations.

Subtly confusing 'flying hours' and 'working hours', the article moved to statutory limits. Pilots were limited to 900 stick hours (at the controls) a year. The reporter suggested we averaged less than half this. Just as we didn't fly aircraft to their limits, our scheduling allowed a margin. Averaging flying hours in an operation that relied on standby coverage is a pitfall and this article's calculation was less than a perfect match for the flying blocks recorded in my logbook. When focussing on scheduling, why did this journalist fail to mention the menagerie of aircraft types that swelled the airlines' fleets? As the companies chased the maximum yield, they pursued an active policy of cancelling one type of aircraft and substituting it with another. This policy created mayhem with rostering efficiency.

With no journalistic stone left unturned, the article progressed to transport and layovers. Apparently, the drive from the airport to our overnight accommodation was in a Mercedes Benz or LTD stretched limousine. In the major centres, the companies opted for hire cars, as 'on time pickup' was essential. With bulk bookings, they could also be cheaper. It was up to the hire car firm as to which vehicle they dispatched, but the airline companies ordered sedans. Away from the big cities I travelled in minibuses and taxis.

Stuart Rintoul named several of the capital city hotels the airlines scheduled for overnights and the costs (did they all charge the same $110 a night?). These hotels were the same as his company used (and probably at the corporate rate, just as with the airlines). Did I detect another journalistic scowl? Was '*accommodation in these hotels*' acceptable for a resting businessperson or journalist, but not the pilots responsible for their safety the next day?

When covering an assignment interstate, a journalist staying in, say, the Hilton, could claim 'away from home' expenses. Most businesses attended to these, as I imagine was the case with a news corporation. Airlines did the same using a daily travel allowance. Maybe, when discussing ours, Rintoul could have explained how his expenses were calculated.

There was more confused reporting when it came to duty travel. If this journalist covered an interstate assignment, the return to head office would form part of his duty. This was no different to pilots and when positioning on duty the company blocked a seat. When not on duty, I sat wherever a spare seat was available — and then only if one *was* available.

In the final paragraph, the reporter noted standard annual leave. However, when it came to superannuation, he reverted to his opening technique. If discussing politicians, would he offer the Prime Minister's salary and benefits as typical? Would he link this to only the hours spent on parliamentary benches? Trotting to its close, the article quoted our salary range as between $42,000 and $130,000. An image flashed in my mind's eye. A Jack Russel terrier with head slightly cocked listened to an old-fashioned gramophone. Instead of playing with words, punching 42 + 130 into a calculator and then dividing by two might have given readers a more balanced idea as to what was typical. A colleague interviewed Brian McCarthy, a typical B727 Captain, who was good enough to give his salary,

$85,000 per annum. Without the need for annoying calculations, Stuart Rintoul could have checked with his colleague or, better still, asked his boss. After all, he was the other Managing Director of Ansett.

The initial weeks of industrial action passed. The stresses of a simulator check proved a walk in the park compared with this gut-wrenching time. We offered to resume flying between 9:00 and 5:00, if genuine negotiations commenced. Australian Airlines countered, offering its pilots re-employment with full seniority, if they signed a Kelty contract. Ansett did the same, with the same cut-off date. We then offered to resume full services, if negotiations commenced. Offers and counter offers lobbed back and forth. Bob Hawke became emotional and, perhaps overplaying his role, he put his reputation on the line.

The airlines kept their aircraft locked in their hangars while 14 international airlines with foreign pilots picked up passengers on domestic sectors. The government also commissioned the Royal Australian Air Force. Minister for Transport, Mr Willis, announced that the RAAF would begin carrying domestic passengers between larger cities, despite a decision by the Transport Workers Union to refuse to refuel them.

Even those within the ACTU thought this was going too far. 10 years earlier, air traffic controllers had walked off the job. The Liberal government had proposed engaging RAAF controllers. This was opposed and thwarted by the ACTU leader. Wearing a younger man's clothes and worried by such a precedent, he had knocked it on the head.

The Liberals, now in opposition, felt it improper to use our defence forces in such a questionable civilian role. The former ACTU leader snarled from his Prime Ministerial chair. The Minister for Defence considered this 'hogwash', as the rapidly rotating gale force winds formed by intentionally shutting down the airline system threatened his stance — the air force evacuated civilians from Darwin after Cyclone Tracy.

The idea was to hire out defence force aircraft at standard charter rates. Australian Airlines agreed. Abeles scowled. This was a business arrangement and so subject to negotiation. He drove a hard bargain. The PM intervened, resulting in aircraft leased below the market rate (while passengers were charged full fares), leaving the Australian people short-changed by around $800,000. At least, he was allowed to negotiate. In the overall scheme, this cost was spare change, as Bob Hawke started slipping $15 million to the airlines every week.

The trick was for no money to change hands. To recompense, or subsidise the airlines, the government decided it politically expedient to waive certain charges. Just as if the electricity company, for some reason (although I can't think of one), decided to waive my bill. That month, I'd be better off by the amount not collected. Airlines were charged fees to use navigation and airport facilities, as levied by the Civil Aviation Authority and Federal Airports Corporation. This money owed to the Australian people was, in Ansett's case, shunted to a private company (and incidentally, exactly as Peter Abeles and Ted Harris suggested at the meeting on the 15th of August).

The tourist sector was haemorrhaging as the dispute, anticipated to be short and sharp, dragged on. Airlines chartered foreign aircraft and recruited foreign pilots. Steps were taken to alter our immigration laws, allowing these workers more permanence.

The reasoning for such measures swayed towards a sort of national emergency. I thought it was a long bow to draw, but if tending that way, then it was a manufactured emergency. Our campaign meant services ran at around 50 percent. It wasn't good, but did six days of office hours constitute a national emergency? The airlines reduced this to zero by shutting down on the 23rd of August 1989.

The Labor Party used Rod Cameron as its pollster. Again, the Brad Norington book noted events:

> "Cameron also found that shutting the air-ways would be a non-issue for most voters because only about 5 percent used the domestic airlines with any regularity."

Although the lockout was formulated at the 20th of August meeting, it was on the table before the Dispute began. Until the minutes from the gathering in the PM's office on the 15th of August were unearthed, no one knew (except those present) the extent of connivance planned. This only became public knowledge much later, when the Federation challenged changes to the Immigration Act. These changes allowed foreign pilots to replace qualified Australians.

On the 21st of February 1992, Dr D.S. Harrison, a public servant of the Prime Minister's department, was subpoenaed in the Federal Court. Having taken the 15th of August's meeting minutes, on the stand, he read them. The Immigration case ran for several years but in its early stages Justice John Keely granted an injunction in April 1990, and another in May. These injunctions halted the entry of foreign pilots and stopped those already here from converting their temporary visas to permanent residency.

In the spring of 1989, students gathered in Tiananmen Square, Beijing, China. In a crackdown on 3rd and 4th of June, the military opened fire with rifles and tanks against unarmed civilians. No one knows the extent of casualties, but estimates run in the thousands. In a humanitarian gesture, our officials allowed Chinese students entry to Australia. After everything that went on, I agreed it was the least we could do. I believed the majority of Australians felt the same.

What most Australians didn't know was that the foreign pilots were piggybacked to this legislation. The Federal Court injunction by Justice Keely was circumvented and effectively nullified. These foreign pilots were coming to our country as strike breakers. Did they gather to defy and challenge in a passionate pursuit of freedom and liberty? Would they go without food or risk their lives for these ideals? Was theirs a commitment so strong that with only the clothes on their back and shopping bags in hand, they'd stand unyielding before a column of moving tanks?

Our latest offer to resume full services wasn't with the Kelty contracts, but with our old agreement, without the manufactured pay rise. The airlines refused this offer, as was their right. But if I shut down my business, I shouldn't complain about a lack of cash flow. And it's reasonable to assume that my lack of cash would not be subsidised by taxpayers.

Behind the scenes, meetings were held with both Bill Kelty and Simon Crean. The attitude was summed up by Mr Crean. He thought we were stupid; we could have had the money. All we needed do was play the game. You'd be amazed at just what they can fit within those guidelines.

Others joined the chorus. Sections of the press bleated: stupid pilots — air traffic controllers got 12 percent, others more. All those labelling us as such had a right to their opinions. But, if intelligent enough to think us stupid, then they should have had the ability to make a distinction. If the money was there for the taking, but refused, then it obviously wasn't about the money.

It wasn't about the money for the airlines either. The Kelty contracts were a closely-guarded secret. If a pilot was considering this option, then the document could only be viewed at the airline office. You couldn't bring a representative, have it checked by a lawyer, or even take it home. Why such secrecy?

Eventually, the contract was leaked. Pre-dispute, pilot salaries averaged $80,000 per annum (considering both Mainline and regional operations), with 68 stick hours in a typical month. My last flying block had been in April, with Frank. Pre-flight and post-flight duties added 21 hours. Another 12 hours for 'between sectors' preparation, and factoring simulator time and the rest, added more. I was away from home for 11 days and did early morning and late-night duty.

I'm not complaining; it's part of the job, but something ignored by those touting our productivity as 8, 10 or 13 hours a week.

With innovative scheduling, productivity could increase, but pilots didn't produce the rosters. If our claim was used as the starting point, then my first suggestion would be for composite blocks. Get rid of the reserve patterns, and incorporate a few days of standby duty into all the blocks. With everything on the table, the company and pilots were free to explore benefits for both.

The Kelty contracts allowed for the old salary, plus the IRC determined six percent. As an example, Captain McCarthy's $85,000 would become $90,100, a perfect fit for the guidelines. The fiddle was that the Kelty contract was based on 55 hours a month. If a pilot flew the average 68 hours, then the extra 13 hours were calculated at the new rate. This would then become $111,396. Adjusting for standard annual leave (as a pilot would not fly extra hours while off), the annual income would become $110,759. A tad more than six percent, this pay rise was closer to the politicians' hike, and more than the 29.47 that, by this stage, we admitted was an ambit claim.

It gets worse, or better, depending on perspective. Any hours above the base of 55 (say 13) paid an additional $60. This would add $8,287 (considering annual leave) and bring the total to $119,046. It was one mean piece of conjuring by the sorcerer's apprentice, and as our Pilot Executive Brian McCarthy noted, Kelty's contract would have increased his salary by a fraction over 40 percent.

Bob Hawke plunged into attack mode. Our greedy grab for money was capable of not only wrecking our national economy, but it challenged our country's very existence. We showed complete contempt for others. A bitter cocktail of bile and vitriol spewed from his gnarled mouth. We would rape the Australian community.

In times such as these, the returned pilot could fly 75 hours per month, sometimes more. I wondered if they provided a calculator at the private viewings? David Jull, the aviation spokesman for the opposition, happened to have one. Punching the buttons, he estimated the Kelty contracts delivered increases of between 32 and 46 percent.

As Brad Norington noted, Mr Jull's drawing such attention prompted the airlines to offer him a private briefing (they seemed to like closed doors), but Peter Abeles preferred a more direct approach. David Jull recalled the telephone conversation (Abeles' recollection differing slightly). After identifying himself, Sir Peter continued, "I'm very disappointed with you, Mr Jull. I'm going to ring Andrew and have you removed and I'm going to ring Rupert and have you scrubbed out."

CHAPTER 22

Matthew turned three in September. Despite the stress, we were determined to celebrate his birthday as normally as we could. Our good friends Coralee and Dave drove down with their two children, and Jenny and Michael arrived with their little daughter. Sherry and Kris, with their young daughter, also dropped by.

The children ran around playing games and having a wild time. We shared a few drinks as the adult conversation centred on the Dispute. Time for chocolate cake, and Matthew blew out his candles and led the charge, ending with not just cake delivered to mouth, but all over his face. A huge chocolatey smile followed, and games resumed.

This was our first gathering during the turmoil. Over the following months, our four families formed our own support group, a subset of the wider group. There were BBQs, meetings, phone calls and other functions. We filled the picnic area at Bribie Island one Sunday, and attended regular get togethers in Brisbane. Our telephone group met midweek for a sausage sizzle, and we became friendly with an Australian Airlines Captain and his family who lived nearby. Although this period conjured up a pretty dark cloud, it had the silver lining of getting to know people we would otherwise not have met.

Stephan and I started home brewing. Brewing day was Thursday. Stephan arrived and we prepared ingredients, which we added to the big plastic bucket. Downstairs we had a cupboard in the laundry. I fitted a shelf at just the right height, dubbing the cupboard 'The Brewery'. After seven days, Stephan returned, although he dropped 'round several times a week, and we'd attend to bottling. Two weeks later, we held the ceremonial tasting. As the Dispute dragged on, our prowess increased. We became quite proud, even fixing a label to the bottles offered at our gatherings. Brewed by Stephan & Paul, we called it *Dispute Draft*.

Bob Hawke wrote me a letter. He wrote to us all. At his prime ministerial desk, pen poised thoughtfully in hand, the news cameras zoomed this into our family room. The next day, I read it in *The Australian*. The letter was later delivered to our home:

> "I am writing to you personally in order to communicate to you directly, free of media clamour or distortion from other sources, my government's position in this traumatic dispute in which you have become ensnarled."

I didn't need a letter to know his position. He went on to say he was convinced neither me, nor the overwhelming majority of my colleagues, deliberately intended or envisaged the damage caused by the current dispute. He did have nice things to say about my distinguished (if a little glorified) profession, then continued, at length, about damage to our country and what he called a 'national emergency'.

He was right. I didn't intend to cause harm. I worked office hours for six days, and the inconvenience caused was my fault. But that was hardly an emergency and inflicted far less damage on our economy than the now weeks long airline shutdown.

Turning to the second of his three pages, his thoughts verged towards catastrophic. He gave his opinion should we be allowed the choice not to renew our agreement:

> "But what is at stake — and has been from the beginning — is the future of the Australian economy; and that means the future welfare and hopes of every Australian family, including, of course, your own."

If that was not enough, he continued:

> "Success for the Federation's claim would have destroyed the wage and salary system of Australia. That is not an exaggeration; it is not some sort of best guess about the consequences; it is an undeniable fact."

And then where should we be? One of my hopes, as an Australian, was for the freedom to make my own choices. Was their house of cards this fragile? I disagreed with this 'undeniable fact', and wondered how an agreement between the government and ACTU could be destroyed by a small group who were not even affiliated.

Hawke continued:

> "It would have placed in jeopardy all the benefits for the future made possible by the restraint and responsibility of the Australian workforce over the past six years. The key to Australia's future represented by the tremendous achievement of unions, business and Government in restructuring the Australian industrial award system — now at the threshold of an historic success — would be nullified. The serious costs currently involved would be minimal compared with the disastrous consequences, had we succumbed to the Federation's claim."

The six-year plan in tatters ... our golden future nullified... Here I felt he missed an opportunity. If our ambit claim could cause Australia to slip, submerged below the blue waters, and thus create another dispute (where exactly did the Indian Ocean stop and the Pacific begin?), then how could it be that 36 percent slated for his pocket, and a greater percentage for Peter Abeles, would not result in a reprint of the world atlas? This opportunity, as with many others, slipped by. The PM summed up:

> "That, simply, is why my Government has had to take its unshakable stand — not because we like it but because we have no alternative. There we stand. We can do no other."

Did this beast that Mr Hawke was promising to kill even exist? By such logic, if, at any stage, the Accord was discarded and enterprise bargaining resumed, we'd face disaster. I didn't think so. Without the chicanery of the Accord, it may even produce moderate wage outcomes, and a low level of industrial disputation. I also felt that it was the Australian peoples' government, not Bob Hawke's. Mr Hawke carried on about regretting the Dispute. His whole career had been dedicated to the resolution of conflict and national conciliation, and he abhorred the very idea of Australian being set against Australian ('Hit as hard as you can, quick as you can, carte blanche from me').

By the third page of the PM's letter, we approached the crux of the matter. Any role the Federation may have played in resolving the Dispute had been erased by our leadership's 'instruction' to resign:

> "As a result the Federation has no members employed in the industry. In that situation the employers, the airlines, had no alternative but to proceed to re-hire through the individual contracts. That has been, and remains, the only course available to them and the proper course for them."

I resigned because my family and everything we had was threatened. We followed simple advice that, in the fullness of time, proved correct. Perhaps, recalling Peter Abeles' thoughts at the 15th of August meeting, the former ACTU leader continued:

> "The way is open to your re-employment through the contracts with individual pilots being offered by the airlines."

Continuing in this vein:

> "Not all pilots will be able to be re-employed because, as I have said, we shall certainly have in future an industry characterised by higher productivity. But very many can find a place in the industry again."

So, this is where the sorcerer's apprentice got the good oil on individual contracts. Psychological nuance, the master's speciality, was reserved for a future lesson.

The Australian people's government included the Department of Foreign Affairs and Trade. A quick check with Gareth Evans, the Foreign Minister, would confirm: "Australia's approach to human rights and freedoms reflects its liberal democratic ideals and a belief in the inherent dignity and the equal and inalienable rights of all people, as set out in the Universal Declaration of Human Rights." It may have been a good idea at the time, if Mr Evans expanded: "The rights of freedom of expression, association and assembly are enshrined in the International Covenant on Civil and Political Rights, to which Australia is a party."

Mr Hawke and the then ACTU leader may have thought individual contracts were a proper course, but I disagreed and wished to be represented by my association. I'd learnt the hard way how far 'the feeble strength of one' went when dealing with a company or corporation. If I chose to freely associate with my colleagues, then I felt this was my decision, not Mr Hawke's. What Mr Hawke was suggesting came straight from Peter Abeles' playbook, 'Eliminate everything we want to eliminate.'

I kept the letter, but not the envelope. I crossed out our address, and wrote "RETURN TO SENDER". Turning it over, I resealed it with sticky tape and wrote:

THE FEDERATION IS THE PILOTS – THE PILOTS ARE THE FEDERATION

The taste of contempt sat bitter in my mouth. Our ambit claim was submitted in a similar manner to so many when Mr Hawke had headed the Council of Trade Unions, and for an increase less than he pocketed. What did he hope to achieve, this former ACTU leader, extolling the virtues of individual contracts and denying representation? Did he think I would fail to notice his gross hypocrisy, or the perceived benefits flowing to his friend Sir Peter Abeles? Dropping the envelope in the red letterbox, I vowed to fight these people with everything I had.

So many years have passed. The pages are framed and hang on my wall. It's not every day a letter arrives from the Prime Minister, special delivery. There are four frames. The first three hold the letter and the last is one I typed.

From *The Courier Mail,* dated the 24th of December 1988, I noted Mr Hawke's salary ($128,790). This was before the first instalment of the IRC sanctioned 36 percent pay rise. This instalment increased his salary to $143,526 (excluding electoral allowances). Next, I checked *The Courier Mail* of the 1st of June 1990. This gave the new salary after the final instalment that fitted so neatly within the guidelines ($169,052). Converting dollars to an overall percentage, I typed this on my page. From the TNT Annual General Meeting, I noted Sir Peter Abeles' surging remuneration (upped by 40% to 5.1M). I typed this below Mr Hawke's. Beneath this, I poured forth a diatribe, starting with Mr Hawke's own words:

> "The simple and undisputable fact is that if Australia was to cop a 30 percent increase to pilots, then the whole wage system would break down and the economy would be fractured and I believe irreparably."

I continued my vicious keyboard attack, with increases for airline executives, judges and others who qualified for the IRC 'magic pudding' formula. In no time, I filled the page with toxic anger. Fitting the sheet into the frame, I hesitated, then returned to the desk. Mulling it over, I removed the page, screwed it up, and threw it in the bin. Reading Mr Hawke's letter again, I deleted all but the top two lines. There was nothing I could say that would add anything to these, both ending in a percentage sign.

MPs' pay up 17.8% to $65,000

From GLENN STANAWAY in Canberra

FEDERAL MPs will get a 17.8 percent pay rise, taking backbenchers' salaries to about $65,000.

The pay push sparked angry scenes in the Labor caucus yesterday because Cabinet had rejected Remuneration Tribunal recommendations for a higher, backdated rise.

The caucus met twice yesterday before Labor MPs approved the rises.

The Industrial Relations Minister, Senator Cook, said Cabinet approved the smaller increases so politicians could set an example by accepting the same rules that applied to ordinary workers.

He said there would have been a general wages breakout had the Government not applied strict wage-fixing guidelines to MPs' pay.

The Government decision acknowledges pressure from the Australian Council of Trade Unions, which was unhappy with the original proposed rises.

The Opposition last night decided it would not oppose the increases. The Government had said that no rises, including those for judges and public servants, would go ahead if the coalition tried to block the legislation.

Backbenchers' pay will go from $55,000 to $58,300 on July 1, $61,798 on January 1 and $64,798 on July 1 next year.

Ministers' salaries will go from $93,709 to $99,332 on July 1 and to $110,367 a year later.

The Prime Minister, Mr Hawke, will get a wage rise from $143,526 to $169,052 in July next year. The pay of the Deputy Prime Minister, Mr Keating, will go from $112,439 to $132,431.

Departmental and authority heads will get a 19 percent rise from July 1. Federal Court and Family Court judges will get a 12 percent increase in two stages and Industrial Relations Commission members will receive a 6 percent rise.

Many Opposition MPs were furious that Cabinet had overturned the independent Remuneration Tribunal's recommendations, which met wage guidelines.

Labor MPs complained that they believed Mr Hawke had backed down on a promise last year that pay rises would be backdated to January 1.

The High Court Chief Justice's salary will go from $160,852 to $180,733 in July next year. High Court judges' pay will rise $20,000 to $164,290.

Federal and Family Court judges will get increases of $15,000 over the next year to take their salaries to $139,638.

From July 1 this year, salaries for departmental and authority heads will range from $111,004 to $126,848.

Flow-on to State MPs, Page 2

Above: Article by Glen Stanaway in *The Courier-Mail* dated 1 June 1990, indicating the final instalment of the IRC approved 36% increase (wheeled out on Christmas Eve 1988). Although trimmed, slightly, the total amount gave a more than 30% pay hike for both the Prime Minister and MPs.

Justice Maddern, very quiet for some time, wanted to see us back in the IRC. The airlines agreed, but our representatives wished to consult us first. Our meeting in Brisbane may have been the last in the series. In the usual format, AFAP Executive Brian McCarthy outlined recent events, the others spoke, and then he moved back to the microphone. He advised the floor would open shortly but, just before, business needed attention. McCarthy outlined the IRC raising the possibility of cancelling the general aviation awards. He then passed on Justice Maddern's request, or direction, or whatever it was.

The same person who cancelled our awards, opening the way for common law writs against us (but only us, despite all going on around him) and could see 36 percent for politicians fitting within the guidelines, thought we may care to share his company.

> Brian McCarthy posed the question, "Do you want to go back to the Industrial Relations Commission?"

Sharon and I headed up a family and this decision was for both of us, but no words were needed. I wrote on my paper in letters filling the sheet. The ballot box came around and I dropped it in. This would be a tense wait.

> I turned to Sharon. "If people vote to go back there, I'm walking out the door."
> Sharon looked straight back. "If you don't, I will."

I didn't know where we'd go or what we'd do, but one thing was for certain — we'd never again have anything to do with that institution. My stomach felt like the fermenting brew bubbling away in our laundry cupboard. Maybe, we could go overseas. There were plenty of jobs, which made me wonder. These foreign pilots ... If Australians could walk into jobs all over the world, why could these pilots only get a job here, and under these circumstances?

Up the front of the room, the votes were counted. Ours correlated; it looked as though they were through. Brian McCarthy, mobile microphone in hand, stood right of centre on the dais.

> "On the question of the IRC," he took a breath, "We won't be going back there."
> The 'no' vote was in the high nineties.

Dirty tricks ensued, and neither side acquitted itself well. In one incident, a greyhound was skinned and placed on the bonnet of a returned pilot's car. What was the significance of a skinned animal?

As Australians, we have our symbolism, but I'd never heard of anything like this. The finger of blame was levelled at us.

Greyhounds are racing dogs. I would have thought some sort of registration was necessary. Not that one skinned would be traceable, but records may show correlation. How did you get hold of one? Did people keep them? I didn't know, but hadn't seen any around our suburban streets. If so, then someone needed to slay the family pet. How would you do this? The dog would probably not have taken kindly to such malicious intent as the owner ran around the backyard trying to bop it on the head. If euthanized, you'd probably need a vet. There should be a record. Who would know how to skin an animal? Maybe a butcher? "Could I have two kilos of BBQ sausages, six T- bones, and if you wouldn't mind, could you please skin this greyhound?" And how did they transport it? In the family sedan? More than one person was probably needed to manipulate such cargo. Even in the dead of night, there'd be the need for stealth. This act would take someone who was well versed and skilled in such an operation. A car, if seen, can be traced, posing another risk, and if not under the streetlight, torches were needed. Laden footsteps and then the plonk on metal — it was all so bizarre.

Not to cast aspersions on my fellow pilots, but I really didn't think any of us capable of such sophistication. It was more like something out of one of those mafia movies. Even so, I couldn't imagine any of us dropping into the local pub to share a couple of beers with our mate, Jimmy the Weasel.

At one stage, Peter Abeles returned from a trip to Perth. He told of a fear conveyed by several returned pilots. Apparently, there was a threat to "break hands and legs". This, again, was strange. Who talks this way? Sometimes, we may offer encouragement, "Go for it, mate. Break a leg." But no one I knew thought of hands and legs. Maybe hands and feet, or arms and legs, but this was so foreign. Of all the people involved in this dispute, who had dealings with those who did this sort of thing, or worse?

Returned pilots received anonymous phone calls; their content and intent inexcusable. A young boy heard how his father was a despicable piece of garbage. No child should be subjected to this.

Among the 1,647 pilots who resigned, there were bound to be a few hotheads. The Federation disowned these members and warned against such actions. The stakes were as high as the emotions, but this is no excuse. Such low acts weren't limited to any one side — although, from reports, one could be forgiven for thinking so. While John Raby was away for a Federation meeting, his teenage daughter answered the phone and heard how her home would be blown up.

There were instances more in line with an industrial dispute. Those who take a certain path in industrial situations can be known as 'strike breakers'. Even though we weren't on strike, 'strike breaker' suffices, but, universally, there is another term; thus, negating the need for semantics. The foreign pilots were called by this derogatory term. They appeared upset, but as opportunists taking advantage in another country, they may have expected a negative response. Those from our ranks who returned to work were known by the same term. There were verbal altercations and heated exchanges. I recall one returned pilot gloating over the pay rise. Affecting a posh accent and waving invisible dollar bills under our noses, he carried on about the 'Rolls' and his high life under the Kelty contract.

Then there were the 'click beetles'. I don't know where this gadget originated, but I suspect North America. When America's system was liberalised, there were many strikes and disruptions. One infamous event concerned an equally infamous character, Francesco (Frank) Lorenzo. Frank Lorenzo used his company, Texas Air, to take over Continental Airlines. The battle was long and bitter, but in a nutshell, Lorenzo drastically cut conditions while slashing and burning the company. The result was strikes and mayhem. I remembered that time; our donations were passed on through the Federation. The company almost went under, but after Lorenzo's departure, it was nursed back to health. Gordon Bethune became the new CEO, and he involved everyone, using a simple formula — look after your staff and they'll look after your customers. Continental went *From Worst to First* (the title of Bethune's book).

Lorenzo moved on to Eastern Airlines. This time, luck wasn't with the staff. There was no white knight, and for Eastern, no happy ending. The company was eventually bankrupted; this once proud entity was gutted and torn to shreds. Ours was a re-run of the Continental saga, and as in that case, some broke ranks.

Bitterness occurs in every industrial situation when strike breakers emerge. Maybe born from one of these, or perhaps another, but somewhere along the line, a children's toy came to symbolise those who chose this path. The 'click-beetle' took flight and crossed the Pacific.

Up until now, I've used my logbook to jog my memory. For this time in my life, there are no logbook entries, but as the events were life changing, there's no problem remembering what happened. I thank Brad Norington for his book, which had provided what my memory cannot — exact dates. While I disagree with Norington's opinions and most of what he wrote, this resource, along with old newspaper articles, has helped to order events of the Dispute, and provided quotes.

In covering the nuts and bolts of IRC hearings and such, and in an account spanning 250 pages, Norington did not once mention what the Dispute was about. One article on the 6th of October 1989 in *The Herald* by Terry McCrann, however, nailed it:

> "... the war in the air has gone beyond an industrial dispute, however seminal.
> Beyond even a government legitimately defending its economic policy structure and has become a direct assault, in our case, by the government itself, on some of those basic rights which are the very fabric of our society. We have a government which has declared total war on an employee association and the individual rights of its members and is prepared to use its financial muscle to force unconditional surrender without regards to the costs imposed on bystanders."

McCrann went on:

> "... To cut through all the confusion and disinformation, there is one central issue — the right of any employee to be represented by a person or organisation of their choice in discussing employment with their employer. And what would seem obvious to a dim-witted five year old: the rather basic need for employer and employee to talk to each other to settle any dispute."

The airlines pushed the line that 'the system was approaching normal'. It was far from normal, but we faced the same old problem. We decided to log departures and arrivals ourselves. Each taking a four-hour shift, we moved about the terminals, noting aircraft as they came and went.

In the Ansett section, I was recording a departure. As I moved towards the lounge to check aircraft particulars, someone tried to gain my attention. It was Geoff. I last saw him in Perth, before he moved across to Melbourne. I remembered when he was my safety FO on the F28, but also that he later picked up a 737 slot in Melbourne. What was he doing here? As I approached, he smiled and swapped his Pax Travel Card from right hand to left to shake hands. The colouring caught my eye.

> I looked from the card to his eyes. "Geoff, what are you doing?"
> "C'mon Paul, I had to do it."
> My eyes burned into his.
> "They're only so many jobs; I have to look after my family."
> As if fire from my mouth, I spoke, "And I haven't got a family?"

Geoff knew Sharon and Rebecca from Adelaide, and that our family number had grown in Perth. I walked away. As I did, he yelled my name. The further I walked, the louder he yelled. Nothing he could say would make me turn. I finished my shift, dropped the log at the office, and drove home. During lunch, I told Sharon.

"Why would he do that?"

Sharon has a thing about phones. She hates telemarketers or anyone we don't know calling. Since our first phone connection, we've had a silent number. An hour or so later, I was upstairs when the phone rang. After picking it up and only saying hello, Geoff went off, not even giving his name.

> "We didn't get to finish our conversation this morning."
> I interrupted, "I thought we did."
> "Look, I just wanted to tell you there are only so many jobs, and you need to get back soon to get one."
> "Geoff, I'll go back when everyone else goes back." The speed and volume of my words increased. "You see, my family is one of 1647 other families, and every one needs taking care of." I took another breath. "And what about Brian McCarthy, John Raby and the others? They're out there on a very long limb because of a vote that came out at 95 percent. You've left them for dead, as you have my family."
> Geoff started to say something, but I cut him off. "Geoff, you made your decision. I wish you well and I wish your wife and daughter well, but you know, I really don't want to talk to you anymore."
> He started to speak again, and again I cut him off. "Geoff, goodbye."

Sharon asked who it was. I said it was Geoff; he must have arrived from his positioning flight and then called. She was concerned.

"How did he get our number?"

The irony of Geoff and several others was that they came through Northern Airlines/NTAW. The Federation originally *lobbied* for their jobs in Ansett.

The next week, I was back logging arrivals and departures. My shift had an hour to run when an aircraft arrived to the Ansett lounge. Having moved from Australian Airlines to Ansett several times, I stopped at the window. The aircraft chocked in. Having sat in that position, I knew it gave a good view into the terminal. My clipboard was black. In a casual manner, my hand moved to my right pocket. Palm covering the object, I ever so slowly positioned it atop the clipboard, facing the recently arrived aircraft. I could see both pilots and knew they could see me. Even such a small device, but brightly coloured, would be visible. Every pilot in the world knew its significance. I planned to stand there until the pilots left the cockpit. However, not 30 seconds after my inconspicuous action, two security guards and the Ansett ground manager sidled up. The security guards said nothing, but the manager spoke.

"What do you think you're doing?"
"Watching the aeroplanes."
The manager pointed to the top of my folder. "What's that?"
"What's what?"
He pointed again. "That."
Understanding now, I replied, "That's my clipboard."
"I'm not talking about the clipboard." He now pointed directly to the offending object, but I was still having trouble. Exasperated with our lack of communication, he directed, "Come with me."

I knew the terminals were leased, but not the legality. As a member of the public, I felt I had a right to be there. Despite my reasoning, this wasn't a polite invitation, and the security guards moved in closer.

“We can do this the easy way, or, if you like, the hard way.”

Despite my difficulties of only moments earlier, I grasped his meaning. We walked to his office. Inside, he dismissed the guards.

“Look at these monitors.”

I did, puzzled.

“Look, all these aircraft. You know it’s over; why don’t you come back?”

We weren’t strangers. As ground manager, he and I had shared polite conversations when working together.

Pointing at the monitors, I observed, “It’s only a fraction of when I worked here.”

“There’s more every day.”

“Sure, but look outside; all those foreign charters. Park your own aircraft and rent someone else’s, crew and all. Thousands of dollars in leases, then charter costs on top, where’s the logic in that?” I asked.

“It’s just short term.”

“One day of a business plan like that’s too long.”

The manager changed tack. “Why don’t you go downstairs, sign up, and start flying again.”

I told him I would, if afforded the basic freedoms and democratic processes of our country.

He raised his eyebrows. “Gawd, another one! Principles won’t put food on the table.”

“Then it’d be a pretty scabby meal.”

Returning to the monitors, he said it wouldn’t be long before operations were back to full strength. I asked what he thought about flying with the new and inexperienced pilots. I learned that he was of the Bob Hawke School of Aviation — apparently, it takes less than 10 hours to learn to fly. It didn’t really matter who sat up front. His kids had Nintendo; “They picked it up so quickly; what’s so hard about flying a plane?”

I inquired if there was any reason to hinder my leaving. There wasn't.

That weekend, I had another shift. With my constitutional right to bear click-beetles as yet unclarified, I left it at home (they did seem a little childish, maybe for good reason). Back at the Ansett terminal, a 737 prepared for departure. The Captain performed the walk-around and checked the nose cone. Even with his back turned, I recognised him. As he walked towards the right engine, my eyes burned into the back of his head. Maybe, he felt my stare, as after he'd inspected the cowl, he turned. Our eyes met. His compacted hat sat on his squat head above his squat body. He raised his right hand in a wave as his caterpillar moustache sat uncomfortably beneath his pudgy nose. If looks could kill, he'd lay prone on the ground. Another wave met my icy stare before his pudgy hand fell to his side. He was still looking when I turned and walked away. Under normal circumstances, I would have felt sorry for his FO, but these were far from normal times. Maybe, with a lashing of karma, the FO would have to fly with Frank again next month.

CHAPTER 23

Keith Williams wanted to access our Federation's membership list. A developer well known for major projects, including Sea World on the Gold Coast and the Hamilton Island resort in the Whitsundays, Williams went way back to the old Joh Bjelke-Peterson days in Queensland. He was one of several known as the 'white shoe brigade'. This brash group of developers were responsible for many Queensland projects that caused irreparable environmental damage and loss of heritage. They were also a force in the push to send Bjelke-Peterson to Canberra. The 'Joh for PM' campaign failed; as did Williams' bid to access our membership. Hamilton Island, along with many tourism ventures, was bleeding. Mr Williams wanted to sue us individually. He managed to serve writs on our Federation leaders, arriving by hand on Christmas Eve.

Sir Frank Moore of the Australian Tourism Industry Association advised their intention to ask the Governor General to intervene. Moore said that, as the crisis was crippling the nation's second largest earner of foreign exchange, drastic action was required:

> 'The crimes act provides the Federal Government with its ultimate weapon in a strike affecting interstate transport … the Commonwealth's powers are not limited in the way they are in most ordinary strikes.'

Apparently, penalties included jail terms. I wondered why airline executives weren't threatened in the same manner.

Mr John Dart, CEO of the Australian Federation of Travel Agents, advised that his members were calculating the cost of the Dispute. They intended to file a compensation claim against individual pilots under section 45D of the Trade Practices Act.

Each of these men, along with many journalists, missed an important point. Had we been on strike, then the little used section of the Crimes Act may have applied. But refusing to sign a contract was a basic right, and while this may have been a personal boycott, it wasn't covered by section 45D. I understood their frustration. The tourism industry was just as locked out as we were. As innocent victims, they weren't even considered when compensation was touted for the airlines. The tourist industry applied pressure through Clyde Holding, Minister for The Arts, Tourism and Territories, and did, in the end, achieve recompense. The original rationale of a disjointed industry, incapable of political clout, was eventually overturned by Sir Frank's relentless agitating.

Mr Holding added another to his list of threats. He floated the idea of cancelling our licences. My licence was the only qualification I had. Taking that would certainly limit options, but why such extremes and why only us? Awards cancelled, writs, threats of jail and now licences endangered. All as a result of our 'go slow' for six days. Did they think all this would entice me to do something I didn't wish to do? Although I resigned to protect my family, the reason makes no difference. I didn't work for the company anymore. I'd go back any time, but only with the rights and conventions of our country upheld. What was next to bludgeon me into submission? Marched off to the Gulag?

Several pilots elected to return. Only a small trickle, but with these and the foreigners, the airlines returned a few of their aircraft to service. Questions surrounded safety, methods of training and an accompanying increase in incidents. So much so, that a Senate inquiry opened. Minor incidents included French pilots requesting wine with in-flight crew meals and other European pilots smoking in the toilets. More serious was when a foreign aircraft risked passengers' lives by not following the published, stepped descent. A pilot with poor English skills failed to respond to air traffic instructions, and a B737 crossed an active runway without a clearance. Another jet followed the wrong departure route from a major centre, jeopardising not only its passengers and crew, but those of other aircraft. Other 'bottom of the trade' flying involved an Australian Airlines B737 reported by a Cairns resident to have hit powerlines on an approach to runway 15. Yet another incident involved an East-West BAe 146 narrowly avoiding collision with terrain on an instrument approach to Hamilton Island. Disaster was averted at the last minute by the Ground Proximity Warning System.

Three senators tabling the Majority Senate Committee interim report thought the Australian airline system "has not been made unsafe", while two felt that "clearly air safety has been affected." In an unkind thought, I wondered when the three senators thinking things were fine and dandy were due to fly out of Canberra.

With our original agreement cancelled, the airlines proposed a new award based on the Kelty contracts. Justice Maddern assigned Justice Alan Paine the task of ensuring these contracts fitted within the guidelines.

At last, the scam was laid bare. Justice Paine could do the calculations as easily as David Jull. The fiddle would finally be exposed. Justice Paine reported back, and I waited for those words: 'outrageous', 'ridiculous', 'incredible'. But Paine advised that the contracts fell within the guidelines. 'Loath' and 'despise' were now relegated to the politest of conversation. While Paine did note that aspects were missing from the current contracts that could be reinstated at a later date, the rubber stamp was applied.

We withdrew our claim — the new award exceeded it. At least, this document gave us the opportunity of a starting point. Seniority and the standard terms of our old award could be bargained back, perhaps in a trade-off, reducing the Kelty pay rise. Features were modernised and scheduling updated to increase productivity — a chance for all to gain.

The new award, although interim, posed legal questions. These took us back to the IRC, but only in the sense of who would be respondent. The airlines opposed any role we may play, and so a series of hearings, or whatever went on in this institution, began.

My contempt for the IRC increased. Even before the latest antics, I felt the basics hadn't changed. The airlines needed pilots, and pilots needed to fly. If the door was opened allowing each to talk to the other, the whole mess — without the perils of legal action, targeting individuals, or threats of jail — could be sorted.

As the end of October approached, we hadn't worked for more than two months. In a conciliatory measure, we offered to return to work, on our old agreement, for the Christmas holidays. After that, there could be a cooling off period and, hopefully, negotiations. I thought it a good opportunity. It could be construed as a partial back down, saving the companies' face and a chance to get Australians where they wanted to go over Christmas.

Two days later, Transport and Communications Minister Willis rejected our offer, labelling it ridiculous. Getting people around for the break, working for at least 30 percent less than the current salaries, and putting the airlines back into business was ridiculous?

Next day, the Prime Minister claimed the Dispute was over. He reasoned that, if we no longer worked for the airlines, we couldn't be in dispute with them. At least, that's what I think he meant. Anyway, the Dispute ceased to exist. As luck would have it, we still existed. But I wondered what Sir Frank and the other tourism associations thought of such logic. For them, this day wasn't all that different to yesterday.

A day later, on the 31st of October, the damages case commenced. As we feared, the airlines were deadly serious about pursuing us in court. While most of us were safe, 67 individual writs remained valid, along with those against our Federation and officials.

With bases in different states, writs were served in each of these. To tidy things up, the judge agreed to join the four airlines' actions into one and deal with the interstate writs in the same court. In the Supreme Court of Victoria, Justice Bob Brooking presided. Just like Justice Maddern of the IRC, Brooking wasted no time. Argument went back and forth, lawyers picked over the finer points of law, and witnesses provided a picture of events. The airlines based their claims on industrial and economic torts covering several issues. Their central theme: six days of working between 9:00 am and 5:00 pm had breached our contract.

I was grateful for the legal advice passed on during the evening of the 23rd of August. Our resignations meant the writs against individuals ceased. Bludgeoning those 67 pilots who received theirs before the barrage halted wasn't worth the trouble. The airlines decided to drop these and honed their sights on our officials and the Federation as a whole. If 1,647 files had spilled across their table, I wondered how different this picture could have been.

The airlines claimed our resignations were induced by Federation officers. Apparently, we could be trusted with passengers' lives and millions of dollars' worth of equipment, yet could be led up the garden path. While they used an assortment of psychological tricks, they couldn't read my mind. The writs were the reason we were now before the Supreme Court. If the writs against our Federation and officials resulted in this action, then it's fair to assume one against my family would have a similar effect. The companies' barrister vigorously prosecuting these very writs from the same batch destined for my front door, kind of knocked their argument, I felt, but I wasn't a lawyer.

The telephone call I had received from crewing arose. Airline executives were tendering refusals by pilots to fly outside of office hours as evidence. The final claim against us referenced newspaper and magazine ads taken out by the AFAP. Strike breakers were warned they would not be part of any negotiations when the Dispute was resolved. The airlines claimed that these ads had proved a disincentive to apply for a Kelty contract. Our newsletters throughout 1989 reached their mark, and these were also presented to the court as evidence. The threat of applying for a 55-day credit card, or starting a lawn mowing business, was taken very seriously indeed.

A former Ansett Captain, Ken White, took the stand. He'd spoken with Graeme McMahon. They had travelled on the same flight, and the next day he visited the general manager in his office. McMahon alluded to the meeting he attended in the Prime Minister's office on the 15th of August.

> Captain White told the court, "The tenor of the conversation with Mr McMahon ... was that the pilots' union would be destroyed because of the forces arraigned against it."

Peter Abeles was called but, sadly, his memory failed him throughout. His time before the court wasn't encouraging. If a TNT shareholder, I would have been worried. How could someone in his position have so little knowledge as to the running of his company? While the minutes of the 15th of August meeting hadn't yet surfaced, our officials were aware of it. Sir Peter confirmed a meeting took place, but could not be sure as to the date or venue. On the question of Government compensation, he didn't think any benefits flowed to his company during the period. He was also "terribly hurt" by such a carte blanche suggestion that he wanted to eliminate the pilots' representative body.

Ted Harris, the Chairman of Australian Airlines, had scant knowledge as to how many pilots the company employed. I wouldn't have expected someone overseeing the airline to have exact numbers, but perhaps a ballpark figure. He was also asked about the 15th of August meeting. He didn't remember if notes were taken, and indicated that the deal to compensate the airlines that he and Abeles had pushed, occurred at a later date, as it wasn't finalised at this meeting.

A former Ipec pilot gave testimony. Captain Terry Seedsman recalled bumping into Len Coysh at a football match two months before the Dispute. Captain Seedsman previously made a sworn statement, and when questioned, he recalled the conversation. Coysh: "The Fatman, Abeles, has put away so much money it would frighten you blokes. We're going to crush you bastards. We're going to teach you c---- a lesson."

The case concluded with the airlines aiming to extract maximum damages against our Federation leaders. Their legal representatives argued their common theme: "We don't necessarily say that the pilots were led into it, but it is the closest you will see to that." Their lawyer was another who'd never attended our meetings.

Federation officials, aware of the 15th of August meeting in the PM's office, requested a copy of the minutes. Together with Captain White's and Captain Seedsman's testimony, the minutes would have helped to debunk many of the airlines' arguments. And they would have shown the correct order of events and planning, in place of the many back-to-front versions reported.

Unfortunately, and even though pursued through proper legal channels, the meeting minutes did not arrive in time. Delivery took two and a half years. After two weeks of sitting days, Justice Brooking reserved his decision until the 20th of November.

Leading up to the court case, we thought about contingencies. I believed we'd be fine if we all stuck together. I felt that no matter what they threw at us, this would be repelled by our united shield. But Ansett worried me. Running a business this way didn't make sense. Deregulation was coming, and the money wasted so far could have been spent strengthening and shaping the company to face the challenging times ahead.

Looking back, I can see the plan was to hit hard, with the expectation we'd crumble. Signed up fast, the whole thing short and sweet — just as when Abeles had used the technique before. It hadn't gone that way. Where was the evaluation?

In an aircraft emergency, we perform checks, drills, and procedures, then decide on a course of action. All crew members must be involved, using all the resources available. But it doesn't stop there. The plan is evaluated, and if not achieving the desired result, then it's back to square one and a new plan is devised. Hurtling towards the ground and shovelling more coals onto this same fire serves only to propel the vehicle faster in this direction; it can only end badly.

Where were the board, general manager, department heads and specialists? Didn't anyone think continuing the lockout was counterproductive? They disrupted the network, lost millions of dollars and shed the most experienced workers, in a field where experience is essential.

The same went for the government. Where were the ministers, back benchers and local members? Didn't any politician see this vicious attack as wrong, unfair, un-Australian or immoral? And how did they perceive this strange brand of 'fairness' and 'equity', as they opened their own pay packets?

And what of the ACTU, an organisation based on the concept of representing people collectively? Like sheep in a children's song Don Spencer could have penned — as *Bill the Kelty* barked, union leaders, with barely a bleat, were herded to the industrial relations shed. Dragged across the floor, they exposed themselves to a fleecing of rights and conditions won from the blood and sweat of generations. I guess by now they knew, it wasn't worth upsetting Bill.

Was there no one who regarded individual contracts as 'a race to the bottom, undermining rights and conditions'? Apparently, not a solitary soul thought the Kelty Contract 'a damaging choice for a workplace agreement'; 'a total repudiation of the basic Australian philosophy of the fair go'; or something that, 'if allowed to succeed, would change the character of our country'.

The chartered course unaltered, Abeles thrust Ansett and the other airlines towards their eventual destination, as did Hawke, leading the government in tandem with Kelty's ACTU.

I thought "all we want to do is negotiate" was a fairly big opening. Who knew what paths or directions this may have taken, but at least we'd have worked together. Instead, all they'd accept was total capitulation. What would have happened at Sioux City if Captain Al Haynes and his three DC-10 crewmembers had capitulated?

The paperwork continued. News reports focused on our productivity. The time we spent working was the same as most airlines. Our problem was the complex scheduling needed for all the different aircraft. On the major trunk routes, Ansett ran four types; for regional services, three; Australian Airlines, a couple less. Engaging only one or two types on the major routes would have cut costs, increased efficiency and enhanced productivity. Something proved not only by predecessor Reg Ansett, but the successful entrants after deregulation. Even without Monday morning quarterbacking, operating so many different aircraft was plain stupid. Attempting to utilise these efficiently far outweighed the cost of pilots. The companies pursued a policy of cancellation and substitution. When one type was substituted for another, so were operating and reserve crews. Crews either idled or needed to complete ongoing flights, so positioned as passengers. Two sets of crew served one aircraft, and the same applied to reserve.

I thought it a little cheeky when the companies colluded to produce an 'independent' report demonstrating less than optimum stick hours. A passenger sitting next to deadheading pilots could have come to the same conclusion.

When jets were introduced in Reg Ansett's day, both companies ran the DC-9 and B727 on Mainline. Our hotchpotch fleet belonged to Peter Abeles. Juggling these was company policy, with rosters compiled by a dedicated department. Reproducing this report as newspaper ads, the airlines somehow apportioned blame to pilots, and I felt that went beyond cheeky.

Journalists appeared to unquestionably swallow the airlines' line. On the 9th of September, Peter Bowers of the *Sydney Morning Herald* wrote an article. Discussing objectives, he lampooned suggestions that the 'de facto father-son relationship' between Abeles and Hawke may have been a factor in Hawke backing the dispute:

> "That would make Bob Hawke a mug, and whatever his faults, he is no mug."
> Some disagreed but, regardless of how he got there, Hawke's backing of Abeles was in no doubt.

> Mr Bowers, offering his thoughts as to Abeles' aims, continued:
> "Abeles to opportunistically break the power of the pilots' Federation which has had the airlines on auto-control, establish a new wages regime by individual contract, in the process shed a few hundred pilots, making Ansett a lean mean flying machine in readiness for deregulation in October — November next year."

Journalist Bowers expended the same amount of print as his colleague, Brad Norington, on democratic rights and freedoms, and appeared to misread his calculator. A few hundred pilots equated to about 25 percent of our number. Culling these, while adding more than 30 percent to the remaining pilots' salaries, did little more than reduce the workforce to 75 percent. When factoring training costs, this looked to me like less bang for more bucks.

Fewer pilots spread over so many aircraft types was certainly a lean exercise. As a passenger, Mr Bowers may have appreciated the meanness. Perhaps, enough to find himself in that distant queue snaking from the airline counter, behind 'Mr 13 hours a week'. Peter Bowers died a few years ago. With no disrespect, just as a pilot's responsibility is a safe operation, a journalist should check and report facts. The theme of 'lean and mean' was parroted by many. If only Dracula could get his restructuring through, everything would run much smoother down at the blood bank.

Did these journalists think I had such control, auto or otherwise? Doing their best to utilise all the different aircraft efficiently could result in a call from crewing the night before a rostered flight to Perth:

> "Tomorrow we've made some changes. Instead of crewing to Sydney, we've put the A320 on. Now you'll pax that sector. We've also taken the 737 off the Melbourne leg, substituting the 767. You'll need to deadhead. We've kept the 737 on Adelaide, so

> crew that one, but the Perth leg's been canned, the 727 takes over. We're updating your Pax Travel Card, so you can pick it up in the morning. After the Overnight, the 737 operates back to Adelaide, so you and your Captain remain on that. We're still running the figures for the return to Brisbane. Once through yield management, we'll update you."

It was amazing we managed the stick hours we did, and the productivity. As noted in a company memo, this was achieved with: "the patience and cooperation of all our crews."

Did those compiling 'independent' reports do so in the early hours of a Sunday when originally rostered for this time off? How would they respond after yet another change? "There's no one else to do it — if you don't, then the flight can't go."

Years later, Rod Eddington became Ansett's Chief Executive. From his vantage point:

> "I described Ansett publicly and internally as a great airline, but a poor business. Qantas had a fleet that was all Boeings. Ansett had a Noah's Ark fleet — one of almost every aircraft known to man. The disadvantages of that are obvious."

How could a journalist think this was my doing? Really, I had the same influence over this Abeles' craziness as I did over everything that happened after the 24th of August. I may as well have been a member of the Bankstown Bowling Club.

Now was a perfect opportunity. Paring down the fleet to just a few types would cut out the duplicated and overlapping rosters that plagued crew planning. Several senior pilots decided to retire, several more accepted career positions overseas and the others working offshore could slot back as needed. Streamlining rosters was another factor; with all on the table, there was a chance for 'lean and mean'. All the airlines needed to do was open the door.

Virgin Blue, a successful entrant after deregulation, was capitalised with less than $50 million. Accounts later showed TNT Dispute losses in the order of $50M. News Limited, as an equal partner, must have suffered the same. It could be assumed Australian Airlines was in a similar boat (it turned out to have sunk even further).

Just looking at Ansett, with the money wasted, they could have started another two airlines. This would have been almost as stupid as beating their pilots about the head with a hundred-million-dollar baseball bat. Instead, Ansett could have become much stronger — an ideal way to start out in a newly deregulated market.

With these sorts of tools in our executives' kit, how would our companies fare? How could a few bruised and bloodied pilots transform operational clumsiness into 'lean and mean'? Was flushing a hundred million down the lockout toilet a sound business practice? And, the bleeding obvious, had Dracula not been taking care of that side of things — with these problem-solving techniques, would any of these four airlines even survive?

By this time, we'd held several more pilot meetings and another was imminent. I spent time at the Federation office catching up on the latest and keeping in touch with colleagues. The coming meeting reminded me of our first. I had not seen the Captain who was previously so worried about the flaky young First Officers. I asked a guy in the office about him.

> "Nah, he's not around."
> "What do you mean not around?"
> "Went back weeks ago."
> My eyes widened as my jaw dropped.
> "Yeah, started to get wobbly. Made jelly look like building material — then went back."

As a senior Captain, his superannuation payout was substantial, with long service leave on top. Through his career, he rode the crest of the wave, progressing to the 767. At an age when financially secure and with children off his hands, he fretted about placing his trust in me, and walked his walk.

Coralee and Dave were visiting. As I was making cups of tea, Sharon rushed into the kitchen.

"Something's wrong."

Her skin looked pale and her face was drained of colour. Hurriedly, I asked our friends to watch the children as I guided Sharon to the car. Screeching onto the road, we raced towards the hospital. At emergency, they quickly settled her and inserted a drip. The doctor slipped behind the curtain while I waited outside.

After what seemed like an eternity, the doctor drew back the curtain. "She's lost some blood, but is stable now." He looked up from his clipboard. "Has your wife been exposed to a stressful situation?"

I guess, having your home threatened, the thought of someone wanting to lockup your husband, various groups preparing lists with threats to sue for millions, and newspaper and television journalists determined to extract maximum retribution for simply refusing to sign a contract, may have qualified.

"We'll keep her on the drip."

I looked at him, too afraid to ask my question.

"There's nothing to worry about. Your wife will be fine."

I stood completely still.

"And your baby will be fine too."

CHAPTER 24

Cathay Pacific was one of the first overseas airlines to realise the opportunity. Sharon and I discussed it. Cathay was an excellent company and many of our pilots were already on their way to Hong Kong. Buried in an old file, I retrieved my application. Finally filled in, I sent it off.

The phone rang. The lady sounded confused. The first thing she asked was my name. She was the one calling, so I asked her name.

> "I'm sorry; I have so many to call. If you tell me your name, I can find my place."
>
> I thought this to be an odd phone call and was about to say so when she spoke again.
>
> "This is Cathay Pacific; I'm arranging pilot interviews."
>
> Any comment about odd phone calls immediately discarded, I gave my name.
>
> "OK, I've got you now. Your interview is at 10 o'clock."
>
> She gave a day the following week, adding the venue at the Hilton Hotel.
>
> "Who was that?"
>
> "I've got a Cathay interview."
>
> "Well, we better dust off your suit then."

Sharon dropped me off and I made my way up in the lift. The procedure was to call a number. I dialled, and shortly after, a voice tinged with a British accent answered. He advised they were running a little late and asked me to come up in 15 minutes, giving a room number.

15 minutes later, I knocked on the door. I was greeted by the Personnel Manager who, in turn, introduced me to the Lockheed

TriStar Fleet Manager. An Australian, who after his RAAF discharge, made his way to Hong Kong and over the years had progressed to this management position.

Ushered to a seat behind a desk, the Captain asked me, "Have you read *Beyond Lion Rock*?" (The Story of Cathay Pacific Airways)

The Personal Manager checked licences and documents, and inquired if my 'medical' was still current.

> "Have you been to Hong Kong?"

I answered no, not volunteering that my sole experience of international travel was a turnaround flight from Headland to Denpasar.

Since filling in the application, I had grappled with a question, and now it came. The Personal Manager opened his folder. He withdrew an old page, my handwritten letter from when I was a student pilot at Cessnock. He then extracted my next letter, sent from Perth and typed this time. Giving the dates of both, he looked straight at me.

> "Why is it that although we sent you an application form in March of 1987, you have only submitted it now?"

For all my preparation, I still hadn't settled on an answer. I mentioned my interest while we were in Perth, but that moving to Hong Kong would be a big change for a young family. We wanted to be sure before responding. I left it at that, although it was obvious. It was the same reason two Cathay Pacific Managers were conducting pilot interviews in a Brisbane hotel.

> "If given the choice, what type would you prefer to fly?"

Everyone wanted to fly the jumbo, but the L-1011 wasn't without mystique. It was an enticing question, given the most sophisticated piece of mechanical equipment I could set my hands to these days was a Mazda 323.

"I'd be more than happy with either."

Neither face showed any emotion. Maybe they would have liked to hear, "747" or, perhaps, the Fleet Manager would shield an inner smile at the Lockheed. Who knows what goes through an interviewer's mind?

Technical questions came with the second interview, if lucky enough to get one, so the interview wrapped up. I thanked them and they thanked me for attending. We shook hands, and the Personnel Manager advised that letters would be sent in the next few weeks. Downstairs in the lobby, I passed a Captain I had flown with shortly before my last Ansett flight — logbook, licences and resume in his hands.

We were sweating on Cathay. We had made up our minds that, if successful, we'd go. Each day, I anxiously checked the mailbox. The letter arrived. I ripped it open. Cathay Pacific was pleased to advise that my initial interview was successful, and asked if I could continue to update my qualifications and experience. I was in the 'hold' file, with no second interview. It was disappointing, but not surprising. Cathay was cherry-picking; taking only the most experienced. The Captain I had passed in the Hilton lobby, and many more, were off to Hong Kong.

While the airline dispute in Australia raged on and the initial pilot exodus centred on Asia, other pilots headed to Europe. Several took jobs in Germany, where an event grabbing headlines was celebrated around the world. After 28 years, a city, a country and a people divided, were reunited. After the Second World War, Germany and its capital, Berlin, were split into four zones. The relationship between the Allied powers and the Soviet Union later deteriorated.

As time moved on, people in West Germany flourished, while those in the Soviet-controlled east foundered. The gap widened, and people fled to the west. Many of those leaving were specialist and skilled workers. Two and a half million had left by 1961 when the authorities decided to forcibly stop the drain. During the night, between the 12th and 13th of August 1961, soldiers and workers erected poles with barbed wire strung between, blocked roads leading across the border and cut telephone lines. Wherever you happened to be on this night was where you'd say for decades. The initial barrier was later reinforced with concrete blocks, upgraded again in 1965, and again between 1975 and 1980. Eastern border guards were authorised to shoot anyone approaching the wall. Nearly 200 people died in their struggle for freedom.

By 1988, Communism was on the wane across Europe, and in 1989, new exit points were opened. An official announcement on the night of the 9th of November effectively opened the border. Glued to the TV, we watched people from both sides flock to the wall. Impromptu celebrations sprung up as people stood atop, while others began chipping away. The wall came down, hammered and chiselled, then dismantled. Less than a year later, on the 3rd of October 1990, East and West Germany were formally reunified.

After reserving his decision in our damages case on the 20th of November, Justice Brooking handed down his judgement on the 23rd:

> "In the absence of protective legislation [as in Australia] trade unions and their officials who instigate industrial action likely to cause heavy losses to employers may themselves be destroyed by powerful forces they unleash ... So it has been said that in the normal situation the union organiser who persuades workmen to "down tools", has procured a breach of their contracts of employment unless he

> also makes sure that they terminate the contracts by giving the legally effective period of notice ... and that all Australian unions and their officials who call out their members on strike, will almost inevitably be found directly to have induced breaches of their contracts of employment ... Whether this is a good thing or bad, is not my concern but if it is understandable then the remedy must lie with Parliament."

As with every other union or association that had ever downed tools, we had breached our contract. There's no denying we caused disruption and inconvenience, but business hours worked for less than a week was not the biggest industrial sin ever committed. Even Justice Maddern could have seen that, had he looked out his window while cancelling our awards.

The part about making sure 'they terminate the contracts' was salutary. Once again, I was grateful for our legal advice. If everything we owned was added to Justice Brooking's damages bill, it would be a lash too great to endure. And what if his meter had not stopped at six days?

Finally, the penny dropped. Somewhere, deep in the bowels of the ACTU, what should have been obvious became so. Obscuring clouds parted and the heavens burst forth in a brilliant display of blinding enlightenment. As if Quasimodo was swinging on the ropes in Paris' Notre Dame, the alarm bells rang so loud that even the blinkered eyes of ACTU officials widened. It may not taste so pleasant, this medicine of our own making, should someone try and shove it down our throats.

Scrambling, they made a mad dash to the airlines. "Please, please, don't collect the loot." If the final step was left undone, then perhaps the genie could be shoehorned back into the bottle. Alas, it was too late. Sitting on the opposition benches, the Member for Bennelong, the industrial relations architect who added the fission of section 45D to his party's IR arsenal, looked on with an approving smile. As Hawke and Kelty swung their crushing weapon, it went even further than John Howard's beloved Section 45D, and was enacted in a way previously thought possible only in his dreams. Not only this, but, when it came to the Kelty contracts, Howard had blunted several pencils as he filled his notebook.

A man transformed. Instead of the whiny, sarcastic voice speaking of olive branches neatly and tidily inserted in inappropriate places, the ACTU secretary talked of "support against the damages claim".

Like a rare breed of leopard, Mr Hawke chimed in:

> "What has happened is a matter of deep regret. Everything on the record shows that Hawke, the conciliator, the person who's built his whole life trying to get conciliation, consensus, negotiation, that was why I pleaded stay in the system. I am deeply hurt this situation has arisen. It's not the Hawke style."

I must have misunderstood (my French proved to be only a marginal improvement on Latin). As for staying in the system, Mr Fred Chaney, the Opposition Deputy Leader, in plain English and without resorting to the third person, clarified:

> "On one hand Mr Hawke had stated the airlines had his Government's full support for their damages action against the Federation, but had now expressed regret at the use of financial penalties against the pilots. It is nonsense that Mr Hawke says the pilots exposed themselves to such action by going outside the system. The pilots' Federation did not become liable because it stepped outside the Accord. The Accord is only a private agreement between the Labor Party and the ACTU, and has no legal standing."

Justice Brooking was meticulous. He scoured statutes, not just dating back to the arrival of the First Fleet, but before. He referenced

British law not yet tidied from our books, and some laws from medieval times. Later, I read an article from *The Journal of Industrial Relations*. The author discussed the Brooking ruling:

> "Such statements of judicial sanctimony are not uncommon, but it should not be forgotten that much of the common law applied in this case was created by a demonstrably anti-union British judiciary. Justice Brooking claimed that he had 'a duty to apply the law as laid down by the House of Lords', but even if this is so (which is arguable), one wonders how long it will take the Australian judiciary to less uncritically apply British common law."

Justice Brooking had yet to determine a date for a further hearing, to set the amount for damages. The airlines' estimate for our days of working executive hours was $10 million. On the question of our resignations, not surprisingly, Brooking found against the airlines. He worked diligently, a stickler for detail, and his judgement took hours to read, an indication of his effort and time invested. Here was a chance to ease his workload. Perhaps, between sips of tea, it must've been a no-brainer. He was a judge — he knew what a writ was.

As for our newspaper and magazine ads, Justice Brooking found no evidence that these dissuaded applicants. These were our two small victories. Our organisation, but more importantly our leaders, were at risk. Brian McCarthy, John Raby, Tony Fitzsimons, Noel Holt, Terry Seedsman and Terry O'Connell were all liable. We owned offices in Melbourne, Sydney and Brisbane, but even if these were sold, there'd be a shortfall. Our leaders had carried out our wishes and acted on our behalf. Our resignations protected us, but not them. They stood to lose everything.

Had the minutes of the 15th of August meeting arrived in time, would these have made a difference? Probably not. The law was instilled by hereditary peers. All were expected to know their place, and if not, they would be put into it. As it transpired, the minutes were entered into the public record years later, in our immigration case.

Our case was a question of industrial action lasting for those six days. As a coincidence, the ruling on the 23rd of November fell exactly three months after the airlines began their action. The shutdown and lockout, 92 days (to date), had caused far more distress than we had by working only office hours. The tourist industry lay in chaos and our economy was damaged, with many innocent victims. Could these people claim against the airlines?

The Boeing 747 was one aircraft I would have loved to fly. The recently introduced model, the -400, was an updated jumbo. Its first Qantas delivery flight became an aviation record. London to Sydney, non-stop. The airframe was based on the -300 version, but with new features and materials.

For pilots, the biggest change was the 747's new generation flight deck. Flight engineers saw a bigger change; they were replaced by automated systems. A longer wing made of lighter alloys was fitted with winglets to reduce drag. An extra fuel tank added in the horizontal stabiliser increased range, as did more fuel-efficient engines. Despite its significant technological improvements, this was still a 747, and it flew at around the same speed, carrying roughly the same payload.

On the 29th of November 1989, Qantas pilot 'structural efficiency and work value claims' were processed through the IRC. You could restructure awards within the 'principles', and examine work value and structural efficiency until the cows came home, or talk of wishy washy, manpower productivity improvements, but the 747 was still governed by the same principles of flight as the Wright Flyer. The electronic flight instruments simply provided a different way of doing the same thing, albeit enabling easier operation. The IRC found that by pilots gleaning information from cathode ray tubes rather than mechanical instruments, and by using a third of the switches, gauges and lights of the classic 747, they had somehow restructured work value efficiencies by 17 percent. Or, so it appeared, as the Qantas pilots were awarded an increase of this amount.

Some in the press were shrill. How stupid were we? We could have had the same. Yes, we knew that — we could have had more. Both Simon Crean and Bill Kelty made that clear, as did Kelty's contracts, now rubber-stamped into the new awards. Baggage handlers, traffic officers and other airline workers under the Accord's repression were allowed six percent wage rises. How could six times this percentage for politicians fit within the guidelines? The income tribunal covering the judge who presided in our case thought a multiple of 12, with a little change for his other pocket, was fair. If you didn't wish to play this game, the results were now glaringly obvious.

Some among officialdom felt that nothing should be spared in forcing us to submit. To me, this went against everything our country stood for. The damages ruling, added to Bob Hawke's letter, and everything else they threw at us, only strengthened our resolve. Tom Petty released a single that year. Spinning it on the turntable, I gritted my teeth and sang along as Tom's determined voice hammered from the black vinyl — there was no way either of us would back down.

CHAPTER 25

Sallyanne Atkinson, the Brisbane Lord Mayor, called a public meeting. Brian McCarthy was up for our AFAP meeting and was invited to speak. It seemed people from all walks of life were interested, as many gathered at the Brisbane Town Hall. Captain McCarthy presented our position. It was simple; all we wanted to do was negotiate.

As I was leaving, an older couple approached. Behind the last row of seats, they moved closer.

> "Are you one of the pilots?"
>
> By now, I was getting used to stock-standard responses when I answered yes, such as, "Just go back to work, ya bastard." On other occasions, the response was more encouraging. I wondered which this would be.
>
> "We are but two." The lady reached out and held my arm. "We are but two; we cannot fight, but you can." She spoke with what sounded like a European accent. Her husband, in a similar accent, explained that they owned a small motel on the Gold Coast. "We have driven up this morning to hear Captain McCarthy speak and give him a message."

They explained that their motel was almost empty. My heart sank. A small family enterprise, they would have little to tide them over in hard times like these. From Eastern Europe, the couple added a piece to the jigsaw of their lives. To escape an oppressive regime, they told their version of swimming the river to freedom. After making their way to Australia, they eventually settled in Coolangatta.

"You have such a beautiful country; we wanted to make it our own."
In recent times, though, they'd become concerned. "We didn't give up everything and come to Australia to see the same things happening." Once again, the lady reached for my arm. "We are but two; we cannot fight, but you can." Her eyes penetrated mine. "Fight for us, fight for us. Don't ever give in."
Just two words I spoke, but from the same place as hers. "I won't."
Her husband looked across to Brian McCarthy who was talking with a small group. "Captain McCarthy is busy. Maybe you can give him our message."
I nodded.
"Please tell him that, if any of the pilots need a break, then they are welcome at our motel. They will be our guests, no charge."

These two, perhaps in their late fifties, I imagined could barely afford the petrol to drive there that day. The group around Brian McCarthy dispersed.

"C'mon, why don't you tell him yourselves?" I asked the elderly couple.

As I walked away from them, I turned. The lady reached out. I could no longer hear her words, but knew what she was saying.

After picking up Sharon and the two little ones, we drove to the Brothers Rugby Club. As we took our seats, I noticed the Captain I had first flown the Melbourne freighter with, Geoff, sitting behind, with his wife. We'd flown together many times, both on the F27 in Adelaide, and then the F28 in Perth. He had moved to Brisbane after us, and was also on the 737. I asked how they were.

"We're fine. And how about you?"
"We're fine too."

> He smiled, "We'll all be fine, as long as we stick together."

The meeting opened, following the usual format. Just before handing over to us, Brian McCarthy gave an outline of the comments from the town hall meeting. He also passed on the message from an Australian couple, originally from Eastern Europe.

Ari dropped through Brisbane on a trip and rang to invite me for dinner. He and Jack, his Captain, were meeting at an Indian restaurant. I drove the van to the city and met them there. Ari loved the 767, and Indian food. It was ironic, but if not for the '82 recession, he may have joined Ansett. If I had taken his advice, I would have applied to Qantas.

Eyes watered as beef madras blasted my taste buds. The different flavours tantalised and were worth the mouthful of fire. Occasionally, we spoke of the Dispute, but each time I steered the conversation away. Sometimes, my emotions ran away with me, leading to a lengthy monologue. Among us, this was fine, but to others who had their own concerns and problems, I found that sharing only a brief outline of our aims and the current state of play were more than enough.

After the last piece of garlic naan, Jack discreetly excused himself. Ari had slipped him notes and, without me knowing, both took care of the bill. Time to leave. As I reached for my wallet, Ari stopped me.

> "No worries. It's all done."

I protested, but Jack added, "It's on us. I hope everything works out and you'll be back at work soon. But maybe things are a little tough for you at the moment."

He wasn't wrong. In some ways, we'd been lucky. When I resigned, I had three months of leave owing. By giving short notice, we forfeited a month's salary, but when I had joined the company, we were kept a month behind. The two cancelled each other out. Initially too, our superannuation was withheld, but later released on the grounds of hardship.

It'd been three months, and my leave pay was all but gone. Superannuation compounds and is designed to mature after a lifetime of work. Seven years in Ansett was a little shy of that. I calculated that, with what we had, we could pay all our bills and make the minimum house repayments until about April of the following year. It would be a shame to lose our house to the bank, after keeping it from Abeles and Murdoch. Surely, this dispute would be resolved before then. The only problem was, we had nothing left to live on. We also had to think of our new family member, due in February. We had baby stuff, but we'd need a few new things.

The Federation advised we were entitled to certain benefits. I imagined this was because of the lockout. I felt there'd be no way someone on strike could claim compensation of any kind. It was an unpalatable decision, but if the people's money was used to subsidise the airlines in their fight against us, then maybe a fraction of that could go to our families.

With our two littlest ones in tow, Sharon and I fronted the Commonwealth Employment Service (CES). Ushering us into an interview room, an officer began the paperwork.

> "What are your qualifications?"
> "I hold an Airline Transport Pilot's Licence."
> "Have you been employed in this capacity?"
> "Yes, I spent seven years in an airline, and before that several in the light aircraft industry."
> He wrote this down as we danced around. Maybe he'd been directed not to bring it up. "Have you been applying for positions?"

I showed him the Cathay letter and copies of others I'd sent to various airlines. He made a note. The Airline Dispute was one of the biggest in our country's industrial history. It was the reason we were there, yet no one in the room thought to mention it. As we walked out, an unpleasant feeling came over us; it wasn't something we relished. We were on the dole.

My colleague Kris and I'd been talking. We felt the Federal Opposition should be doing more. After all, employers and employees negotiating was basically *their* industrial relations policy. John Moore was our federal member. As it happened, Sharon and I had plonked ourselves in a blue-ribbon Liberal seat. I made an appointment to see him. He was brash and to the point.

> "What do you want?"
> I wasn't expecting him to be so direct but followed suit. "Well, for a start, the Liberal Party could do more."
> "What can we do?"
> "We're trying to accomplish what is basically one of your platforms; you could do a lot more in pointing this out. And a little support wouldn't hurt either."
> "We can't be seen to be taking sides."
> "Why not? Hawke's backing his mate Abeles and the airlines?"
> "What's in it for me?"
> To the point and, being a politician, I could only think of one thing that might sway him. "Votes. There are a lot of pilot families, and despite what most of the newspapers are bleating, we do have some support."

I was a novice at this game. It would take a lot more than a few pilot families and supporters to change the government, but I couldn't think of anything else.

> "What do you want to do, then?"
> I wanted the Liberal Party to do more, but I had to think of something specific. "We can have a public meeting. You can state your party's policy, and we can put our case. We could invite local business leaders and people from the area."

A group of pilots had gone out into the community, visiting workers' clubs and RSLs, and they had attended public meetings, presenting our side.

> "Alright, but I'll pay for the hall. We can't be seen to be accepting anything from your Federation."

That was fine by me, as my mouth had gotten a little ahead of my brain. I had no idea how to organise something like this. I called Kris and we met, before speaking with the branch chairman. He suggested we contact Ray and John. Ray was a former 727 Captain with Ansett, and John was a senior First Officer, formerly with Australian Airlines. They were part of the speaking group, and agreed to talk at the meeting.

The Toowong RSL hall filled. John Moore invited Terry White, a state politician, and Dick Holt, a former Federation president, drove up from the Gold Coast. Local business people and others gathered, together with a contingent of journalists with TV cameras. I had no idea who notified them. The rest of the crowd were pilots and their families.

Captain Ray began. He outlined the AFAP's history and emphasised the many safety innovations lobbied for and introduced. First Officer John was ex-Air Force where he'd flown the C-130 Hercules, a type used when the government drafted the RAAF during our dispute. John pointed out that the sideways seating didn't comply with public transport standards. In an emergency, civilian aircraft must be able to evacuate all onboard within 90 seconds. If the Hercules had an abnormal landing, or suffered a problem that jammed the rear cargo door, then passengers may not be evacuated in time.

He also noted that the government was unable to insure military aircraft for the carriage of civilians. The government was not only risking passengers' lives, but exposing itself to multi-million-dollar lawsuits, if anything went wrong.

John Moore gave an outline of Liberal Party policies, then Terry White added to this, from a state perspective. Dick Holt also offered his view, before the meeting wound down.

Kris and I thanked Mr Moore, and he thanked us for the attendance. It was all very cordial. I'm not sure if it achieved a great deal, but we felt better for it. There were times when it seemed that the whole world was against us. We were all we had, so whenever we got together it was a good feeling.

The Federation needed volunteers to work the office phones. If everyone gave a day here and there it helped. Two of us sat behind the desk as a senior officer gave a quick brief.

> "Just answer, and take it from there."
> "But I have no idea what to say. I'm not up with all the technical stuff."
> "Don't worry. If it's the press or someone needing more, then one of us, or Maurice, can handle it. Usually, it's a pilot ringing to chat."

Maurice Ritchie was the branch chairman. Every time I'd visited the office, he was there. He was ex-Australian Airlines, and before that, he'd flown the Lockheed P-3 Orion with the RAAF. This aircraft is used for maritime surveillance and based on the L-188 Electra. Like Brian McCarthy and John Raby, Maurice was another who'd received a death threat and he was concerned for his wife's safety. She worked at a local hospital, so each morning, Maurice drove her to work. She then waited until he picked her up each evening. He was usually first to arrive at our office, and the last to leave.

Luke was on the line. Luke and I went way back. A couple of years younger, he'd done the GA thing and joined Ansett on an intake before mine. I first met Luke when studying for the senior subjects at Bankstown where I sat next to Paul and where I first met Ari.

> "How long do you think this thing'll last?"
> "Luke, to be honest, I have no idea. I'm just answering the phones. If you want to talk to Maurice, I can get him."
> "No, it's alright. You know my wife's pregnant."

I said I could understand the strain and, if needed, there was always the welfare fund. I also suggested Luke find a group of friends to meet regularly. It was a good way of extending mutual support.

> "Is this your first?"
> "Yeah."
> "Luke, there's one thing I do know. If we all look out for each other and stick together, then we'll be fine."

My passion for music extended to following the careers of several musicians. There were those who hit the highs, and then descended to the lows. The Beatles were popular when I was young. Later, they branched out as solo artists. I liked the way John Lennon challenged perceptions. Ringo got a bunch of the greats together and toured with his 'All-Starr' Band. My children know his voice from our library of Thomas the Tank Engine videos. George Harrison tended towards the mystique of the east. A big influence was the maestro, Pandit Ravi Shankar. Ravi composed a piece for George's memorial concert in 2002. He called it, *'Arpan'*, a magical blend of east and west, especially created for 'Jairaj'.

As I passed by a TV years ago, *Concert for George* was playing. Ravi's daughter, Anoushka, conducted the mixed group of Indian and western musicians. Whatever I was doing stopped, and wherever I was going became unimportant. I stood before the screen, frozen. I chased down the DVD, and to this day, every time I slot it in life halts, and as the piece moves a surreal feeling washes over me. For just under 24 minutes this gift for George becomes a gift to me. In 1971, George arranged the *Concert for Bangladesh*. He amassed a group of top musicians, including Ravi Shankar, who donated their time for the benefit. The gift passed through UNESCO to the Bangladeshi people. In an interview, George spoke at length of his philosophy. He quoted the Maharishi Mahesh Yogi, "For a forest to be green, each tree must be green." Sometime after that day of answering phones, I learnt we had another parched tree — Luke had gone back.

Our officials created a fund for those in need. Several senior Captains contributed a portion of their superannuation, and pilots now overseas sent back a percentage of their salaries. The Welfare Fund was open for anyone to contribute, and I was surprised at the varied donations.

Kris was an administrator who needed a lift to the office. I wanted to check the latest 'Go-Around' (our newsletter), so I offered to drive him in. After his shift, one of the others would drop him home. On the way, Kris explained the practical aspects of the fund. He also mentioned several instances of people walking in off the street and dropping a wad of notes or a cheque on the table.

Arriving to the building, Kris and I arranged to catch up after Christmas. Sharon and I had decided to spend this special time with family, and we planned to drive to Sydney. It would do us all good.

In the large back room of the office, which housed a fax machine and several notice boards, I checked for any newspaper reports or articles I hadn't seen. One of the boards displayed a host of letters written in support, many by hand. I spent time reading these. Out the window, the 'Brekky Creek' meandered by, on its way to join the Brisbane River.

Several others browsed the notices, and a former Ansett Check Captain stood by the fax machine. I hadn't flown with him, but had seen him around. Certain Check Captains acted puffed up with self-importance, sort of 'legends in their own lunchtime', and this Captain came across as one. I said hello and walked past.

A group of people walked through the door and asked if this was the pilots' Federation. Three among them were older, while the other two were, perhaps, in their twenties. In the main office, everyone was busy, so the group was ushered through to the back.

> "These people dropped by to find out first-hand what's going on. Could you have a chat with them?"

The last time I'd seen this former Check Captain, he'd been blathering on about some figjam incident where his superior skills had saved the day. I have a friend who calls this sort of oratory, 'hero stories'. Our Wiley hero stepped up.

> "There's currently a hearing in the IRC ..."

The IRC! What planet was this guy on? Who among us had anything but contempt for the IRC? By this stage, mine was a bottomless pit.

The Check Captain continued, "As we speak, in the IRC ..."

I really didn't know what was going on in the IRC, nor did I care, but maybe it was something to do with the Award. He kept harking on about a hearing and some judge. When he paused, I thought to add relevant issues. In all his IRC bluster, the Captain had failed to mention one, but he started up again. He had the conch, so I didn't interrupt. With a satisfied look, he finally drew to a close. The people thanked him and started to leave. I took a few steps towards them.

> "You've taken the time and made the effort to come by. There are important issues. Even though the newspapers carry on about our initial claim, it's not about money." All five in the group looked straight at me. "I think very few people would put everything on the line for a few extra dollars."

"But we thought you wanted a huge pay rise. More than anyone else," said a visitor.

"No, we want the right to negotiate with our employers. And besides, I could go back tomorrow and pick up even more."

My media baron former boss hadn't done a good job in pointing this out.

"Then, why don't you go back?"

I shook my head. "I could spend the rest of the day talking about rights and freedoms, but there are others far more articulate."

The visitors followed me to the middle of the room.

"If you were to read just one, then I'd recommend this." I pointed to the *Herald* article from the 6th of October:

"… To cut through all the confusion and disinformation, there is one central issue — the right of any employee to be represented by a person or organisation of their choice in discussing employment with their employer."

While they read, I looked across to the Breakfast Creek Wharf. A place to 'be seen', this new complex featured an intricate water clock, and top-notch restaurants and speciality shops. They finished reading, and I moved back.

"There's one more. A letter to the editor. This one discusses the role of the RAAF as part of the Australian Defence Force. As you'll see, the author is well qualified to comment."

Defence misused in air strike

SIR – I write concerning the use of the RAAF to provide commercial airline services for the public during the dispute between the airlines and its pilots.

I do so in desperation after waiting for some public spokesman either to tell the public the legal basis for using the RAAF in this way or to question the use of the RAAF for these purposes.

As a former service officer involved in this area of administration of the Australian Defence Force (ADF), I am so concerned at this misuse of the ADF that I believe it is time that the authorities concerned answer publicly the questions I pose in this letter.

Some commentators have expressed mild concern that all might not be kosher in this matter, but they have failed to grasp the full implications of this misuse of the ADF.

There are two instructions to the ADF concerning the use of the ADF in support of the public; these instructions are issued on the authority of the minister. The first concerns the use of the ADF in giving assistance to the civil community and the second concerns aid to the civil power.

In the case of assistance to the civil community, the ADF can assist civilian organisations under a cost recovery policy which is subject to the minister's prerogative. The main circumstances under which such assistance can be given are:

- It must be of training value to the ADF, or
- There must be no suitable alternative, or
- It must be in support of an event of national significance.

It is clear that in the pilots' dispute, the first two conditions do not apply. With respect to the third condition, it should be made clear that an "event" does not mean an industrial dispute but an event as the Bicentennial celebrations.

For example, the minister has made a judgment that the Adelaide Grand Prix is an event of national significance so that FA18 and F111C aircraft of the RAAF are made available to the organisers to provide a flyover at the event.

The Prime Minister, in his letter to the airline pilots, talks of the "national emergency created by the federation of Australian airline pilots". Perhaps, then, the ADF is being used in aid to the civil power, i.e. to maintain law and order by assisting the civil authority, i.e. the Government, in action against an unlawful action of a section of the community.

If this is the case then the ADF would have to be "called out" by an order of the Governor-General-in Council. Was this done in this case?

If it were – and the public deserves to know – then the Government must advise the public of the reasons that an industrial dispute is considered a national emergency since it has not declared the airline industry an essential industry.

If the dispute has been adjudged a national emergency and the ADF has not been called out in accordance with the Constitution, then the public needs to be seriously concerned at the implications of such use of executive power.

The Governor-General, as the Commander-in-Chief of the ADF, is the only protection the public has against the abuse of power by the executive arm of the Government. In the past, constitutional experts have stated that the reserve powers of the Governor-General were merely formal, but the use of the ADF in the airline dispute should bring home to the Australian public the dangers of adopting this view.

As your perceptive columnist, Des Keegan, pointed out (16/9), "Would he (Mr Hawke) launch the military against striking power workers? Would he fight the wharfies?" Under exactly what circumstances would the ADF be used to settle industrial disputes?

Without answers to the questions above the public can only believe that the ADF is now an arm of the executive for use against sections of the community who do not toe the industrial line of the incumbent government – the precedent certainly appears to have been set in the present airline dispute.

I write this letter as a concerned citizen who happens to have some knowledge of the practical aspects of the administration of the Constitution with respect to the employment of the ADF in civil occurrences.

The use of the ADF in the present airline dispute seems little different from the use of the military in industrial disputes in Eastern Europe or South America. It would seem that Mr Keating's concerns at Australia becoming a banana republic have already been justified.

It seems to me that some basic freedoms are under threat in Australia as a result of the way this dispute has been handled, not the least of which is the freedom of association. The ADF exists to protect the Australian public against the loss of such freedoms due to action by external enemies.

In this dispute, the ADF is instead being used to assist the Government in suppressing such freedoms.

AIR VICE-MARSHAL
B. H. COLLINGS
RAAF (Ret'd)
Farrer, ACT

Above: Letter to the editor by Air Vice Marshall, B. H. Collings, RAAF (Ret'd) Farrer, ACT, *The Australian* newspaper, 22nd of September, 1989.

From the first time I read this letter to the editor, I felt the strength within it. The issues that both the *Herald* piece and this letter raised presented our argument in a nutshell. Adding favours for privileged mates, and forcing capitulation, more or less summed up what the whole dispute was about for me. If I went back, not only would I be condoning this, but I would become a part of it. The last few paragraphs packed the punch:

> "It seems to me that some basic freedoms are under threat in Australia as a result of the way this dispute has been handled. Not the least of which is freedom of association. The ADF exists to protect the Australian public against the loss of such freedoms due to action by external enemies.

In this dispute the ADF is instead being used to assist the Government in suppressing such freedoms."

Air-Vice Marshal B.H. Collings
RAAF (Ret'd)
Farrer, ACT

I thanked the visitors for dropping by. A younger one spoke for the first time.

"I guess you won't be going back."

Picking up a copy of the 'Go-Around', I walked past the glass partition of the first office. Admin Officer Kris sat inside. Across the desk from him, the Captain with a greater faith in the IRC than me (which wouldn't have been hard), was making a point. Kris looked up and smiled as I waved. Where had the time gone? Christmas was upon us, and then the New Year. We'd catch up again then.

I wound down the windows. Buckling my seat belt, I felt a damp strip where it crossed my chest. As usual, it wouldn't take long to cool down once we got going. Turning the key, I coaxed the old engine into life.

CHAPTER 26

We packed carefully. Even if we could afford them, there was no room for fancy children's presents. We had each bought something simple and took the minimum of clothes. At least it was summer.

Taking the New England Highway, we left Queensland. Rural New South Wales passed by. We shared the driving, and Sharon sat behind the wheel with her tummy almost touching it. Further south, we drove through Tamworth. Memories flooded back of my days training for my commercial licence at Cessnock. I had cut my aviation teeth winging over these roads that we now traversed.

There was a navigation aid at Scone. I used to sit with Indonesian cadets as they practised let downs for their instrument ratings. Looking down, the countryside had looked lush. From ground level, the grass was still surprisingly green, and it smelt of recently cut freshness. Out of town, the road eased by several race-horse studs, with long driveways and training tracks. In the distance stood stables and graceful buildings. Owners' names were often written below those of the properties; familiar names from our lists of the rich and famous. Another, with bright white fences and an elaborate gate, left no doubt — property of the United Arab Emirates.

Our little car scuttled along. The engine turned at a higher rate than the van, but it wasn't nearly as thirsty. Maybe it was nostalgia, but after passing Cessnock, I switched from the highway and took the backroad to Sydney. It'd been years. As we wound through the dirt track, we tasted the dust that seeped through the window seals. I still remembered each of the turns.

At last, we arrived to Sydney. Up Mum and Dad's driveway, the question that'd been asked ad-infinitum from the backseat for the last 12 hours was finally answered in the positive. The lights of the Christmas tree twinkled in the lounge room, and we carried the children up to bed. It was Christmas Eve.

The next morning everyone was up early. Presents waited under a silver tree, a convenience these days. Childhood memories returned of a house filled with the scent of pine, presents underneath, and a special one at the end of my bed. Eyes opening well before sunrise, I'd nag my parents until they relented. This morning was no different, except it was our sheets tugged, in time with imploring mouths. Mum's, Dad's, and Maree's presents joined the three from the back of the Mazda. In our pyjamas, we were dragged to the silver branches, and little eyes lit up. Small hands shredded paper and scattered it about the lounge room floor.

After breakfast, Dad drove Mum to mass. Preparations for the day began, and Auntie Joan and Uncle Bede were up from Goulburn, always arriving first. Uncle Bede's idea of fashionably late was around half an hour early. Cousin Peter had driven up from Canberra the night before, and he arrived with Auntie Pat and Uncle Alex.

This Christmas was different. Our age-old tradition of not discussing current events was broken, with Uncle Alex the first into the breach.

> "That Brian McCarthy's gotten you into a lot of trouble."

I started to explain that it was the other way around, but this view conflicted with everything Alex had read. Uncle Bede didn't like that we'd challenged the government. Here we had two staunch supporters of each major party. How had we managed to upset both? Maybe, an astute student of political science could analyse our actions. Applying the opposite might be a good recipe for a successful political career.

I could understand Uncle Bede's view. We were challenging his party, but only the Bob Hawke version, not the traditional Labor values. Uncle Alex was an avid reader of the *Sydney Morning Herald,* and the industrial editor had his ear.

No matter what PR we attempted, or how many times pilots spoke at community clubs, or what we said as individuals, we could never counter the weight of the mainstream media. But this was

Christmas Day, and not a time for disagreements. I was too fond of these uncles anyway, so the subject was passed over. Uncle Bede had an uncanny knack for winning things. Each year he supplied the ham, which, more often than not, he'd won in the RSL raffle. Cold chicken, pork and Uncle Bede's ham graced the table, with coleslaw, potatoes and salads. Mum thought our Australian summers too hot for the traditional roast, so our feast was in keeping with our climate.

The children sampled everything, then ran around the yard. The afternoon passed sedately, and evening approached. While leftovers sat out, we were still full from lunch. Our guests left, and we bathed then put three exhausted children to bed. Sitting in the family room, we relaxed and chatted. Our plan was to stay until after the New Year. Mum wanted a special celebration for our (almost) two year old. Following that, we'd return to Brisbane.

In the time between, we visited friends. Roxanne and Ari had built a new house. The builder went bust three-quarters of the way through, so Ari took over, turning his hand to owner building. We shared pizza and quaffed red wine.

Gemma and Paul asked us around, where we joined Liz and Carl. They were all interested in developments. Sharon and I briefly outlined recent events, but didn't want our troubles dominating the evening. They were all supportive, with Liz thinking that one Prime Ministerial comment was particularly ignorant.

> "He must know how much training you go through, and how much responsibility you have."

We weren't a special case when it came to lengthy training and responsibility, but none I knew were required to consistently demonstrate their proficiency. Doctors, lawyers, architects or even politicians didn't face six-monthly simulator checks to renew their qualifications. Fires, failures, depressurisations, jumping from buttons on the side control panel. The proverbial axe discreetly disguised as a Check Captain's pen added to the already-high tension.

Gemma's Dad was a surgeon, and active in the Australian Medical Association. The AMA had their stoushes. During one, a small group broke away. When I spoke of "those who elected to return" Gemma looked at me with knowing eyes.

"Come on. I think you're being far too polite."

After their stint in Port Hedland, Louise and Johnno had moved back to Sydney. Johnno was on the F27. We joined them for dinner on Saturday night. This evening was different than with our other friends; our four sets of Federation feet being pretty wet by this stage. We talked freely about the Dispute. East–West had sold the F27s so, even if everything was settled, John would have to slot back somewhere else in the system, and maybe have to wait until something became available. Things were tight. They were thinking of leaving for overseas if something didn't happen soon.

Sunday was the last day of 1989. We saw in the New Year quietly, wondering what 1990 would bring. In the morning, our youngest princess was already up. Nanna and Grandpa wished her happy birthday as she sat eating her Vita Brits. We added our "happy birthdays", each with a hug.

Dad's face darkened with a worried frown, and Mum's bearing also clouded. "We've just heard bad news."

First thing every morning, Mum and Dad tuned the radio. I couldn't believe it ... 25! Until now, only dribs and drabs were returning. I always thought that, once the few waverers detached, we'd have our solid base. I asked Dad if I could use the phone. Dave may know more, I thought, not that anything could change how this affected us.

"G'day Dave, what's going on?"

There wasn't much he could add. "25 from Brisbane, that's about it."

I had trouble getting my head around the number. A former Ansett Check Captain was the ringleader; they held meetings and went back as a block. When Dave said the name, all I could think was, "... As we speak, in the IRC..." Dave gave other names. The Captain with whom I had flown my first Melbourne freighter was another. So much for: "If we all stick together..." Several more names had a familiar ring; some I'd flown with, and others I'd seen around.

My hand froze as I gripped the phone.
"Are you still there?"
I managed a faint, "yeah", but couldn't say anything for several seconds. My mind refused to accept it; all I could do was repeat what Dave had just told me.
"Kris?"
"Yeah. Kris was with them."

Kris? I had only seen him the other day. The line fell silent. The many plans for when both of our families had moved to Brisbane — children's birthday parties, BBQs, and the times we'd sat, talked and shared a beer. Our friendship reached back to those early Adelaide days.

If this news was not bad enough, we had lost another 15 pilots from Perth. I knew most of them. This swag of defections was a significant blow, especially coming all at once. It meant we slipped below 90 percent holding out the ranks. While 90 percent was still impressive, every time even one went back, it weakened the rest of us.

This breaking of the line was another of many major life experiences compacted into the tempest of this short period — a book is not judged this way, nor a personality. As the blow torch scorched, some brazen and loud of mouth crumpled. Others, thought of as meek and mild, towered. They made their decisions, and we made ours.

A few of them threw this line in our faces, but … hadn't a certain percentage *changed* their decisions?

I needed time. Sitting on the bed in my old room, I thought back to that night I first drove to the AFAP office. My mind drifted and flashed through a kaleidoscope of the last four months. Tumbles of colour from our lives, as if painted walls under a falling sky, finally settled on Kris and the others who'd plotted his same course. The ink on my resignation was a promise. An old Angels song ripped through my head, *'Am I Ever Gonna See Your Face Again'*.

Mum cooked a roast dinner and baked our family chocolate cake. We all sat at our dining room table. With so many birthdays and celebrations centred on this room, I remembered a special dinner, with a key-shaped birthday cake topped with 21 candles. All of our relatives had raised their sparkling-wine-filled glasses. Was that really 13 years ago?

Our little girl sat atop cushions mounted on the end chair. Her eyes sparkled as she blew out her two candles. Her personality had long shone through. Bright and happy like her big sister, both also showed unique traits. She laughed often, and hugged anyone who ventured close enough.

It was time to leave. We packed the car, with its rear bumper displaying our sticker: 'Pilots fight for Democracy'. Back in the garage in Brisbane, the 'Outback Australia' stickers on the back window of the van were joined by: 'Hawke Dis-Abeles Australia'. Another of these graced our garbage bin. At a rally, an older lady walked past a banner displaying the same message.

She had turned to one of the pilots holding an end and said, "You spelt it wrong."

Dad took me aside. He had that look on his face I'd come to recognise from so many years of passed down wisdom.

"Son, I don't think you're going to win this one."

I protested. Finally, we must have "shed our deadwood", and now, with the rest of us sticking together, we'd be fine. Dad just nodded. Abeles, Murdoch, Hawke and Kelty could throw whatever they liked at us, but nothing worried me more than the look I saw in my father's eye. I recalled another of his many sayings, "Son, the spectator often sees more than the player." He said nothing more.

Back in Brisbane, the mood had changed. The block defections were a blow but, as the year clicked over to 1990, attention focused on politics. Opposition Leader Andrew Peacock announced that, if elected, he'd order the government airline to negotiate. With the Accord scrapped and enterprise bargaining resumed, Ansett would follow suit, and that would be the end of it.

On the 19th of January, I did something I'd never done before; I attended my first demonstration. We gathered outside the Australian Airlines building in the city. What were you meant to do at a demonstration? I'd seen student protests, and workers parading down thoroughfares, nurses and even doctors angrily waving placards, but that was abstract, through a TV screen.

Someone brought a banner. As we unfurled it, we raised our voices in chorus: "NEGOTIATE – NEGOTIATE – NEGOTIATE."

New at this, we stood on the footpath, but we didn't stay long. News journalists with cameras showed up. 40 minutes after they arrived, we felt we'd made our point, and left. Over the next few months, we held many more demonstrations.

In early February, Bob Hawke called the election. Australians would be sent to the polls on the 24th of March. When Hawke campaigned in Queensland, we followed him; our members did the same in the other states. The police directed where we could and couldn't stand, with a set of rules. Our own rules were far more strict. At the slightest hint of violence, the offender would be handed to police.

On one of those 'meet the people' jaunts, Bob Hawke was out and about in Brisbane. By this time, we'd dug up bits and pieces of uniforms, or improvised. I wore old airline shirts, dark trousers, and my out-of-date, two-bar epaulettes. I found an old hat that shed pieces of brown-orange matter, and wings from my graduation day at Cessnock. One Australian Airlines pilot didn't have a cap, so instead wore a bowler hat. Another had the most impressive set of wings I'd ever seen, although I hadn't heard of Harley-Davidson Airlines.

If Bob Hawke was out to meet the people, then I was one. In my rag tag uniform, and nursing Matthew and Amelia in each arm, I moved briskly towards him. Something deep inside drove my legs. I had no idea how to express my disgust in just a few words; I wanted to let him know we were still here and, no matter what he chose to hurl at us, we wouldn't give in.

Noticing my strident progress, Mr Hawke stopped and looked straight at me. I looked into his eyes, the venom toxic in his snarl-twisted face. One of his minders noticed, and rushed towards us.

> "THAT'S CLOSE ENOUGH."

I was thinking the same thing. That night on the TV news, the PM recalled the incident. Apparently, I was "an irresponsible pilot, putting my children in harm's way" — maybe carte blanche to chuck them into the street was Mr Hawke's idea of the occasional need for some tough love?

Next, he accused us of "stealing" our uniforms. The companies owned the uniforms. That's why we had given them back. I was angry. I called the station and was put through to the producer. "Don't you check what you put on your news?"

> "What are you talking about?'
> I launched straight in, my mind a little ahead of his, as he picked up the phone.
> "I just saw a report. Bob Hawke accused pilots of wearing stolen uniforms."
> "So?"

> "I'm one of the pilots, and that's not true."
> "But I've seen you. You're all wearing uniforms."
> "Yes, but they're not stolen. They're bits and pieces we put together ourselves. I have a release for my Ansett uniform."

Sir Peter Abeles was one of Bob Hawke's closest friends. There was a time, as Abeles told Pru Goward, when 'he paid Hawke's mortgage and his children's school fees.' It was hard to imagine that his mate didn't know something as basic as this.

> "I can bring the form in tomorrow."

I could do that, and wear my uniform at the same time. He told me "not to bother", which probably saved me another explanation (maybe, he'd wonder what I had to do with the space program).

Another 737 FO lived nearby. He was senior and in the pipeline for his second Cathay interview. Like us all, he was frustrated by the mainstream media's stranglehold. He had his own idea on how to get around it. He'd been on one foray, and planned another. It worked better with two. He called and said he'd be around a bit after midnight.

At 12:30 am, Frank knocked on our door. I invited him in and we chatted and sipped tea. An hour later, I asked if the time was right. He felt "not yet", but that another half an hour should do it. Around two in the morning, we set out. I moved the wooden cutting board, paint brush and wallpaper glue flakes in the old ice cream container to the floor, next to the water bottle. A stack of leaflets sat on the backseat.

Stealth was essential. At each site, I took one of the pages and laid it flat on the cutting board. Frank slipped out of the driver's seat, and by the time he was around to my side, the paint brush dipped in glue had covered the back of the page. He moved quickly. Backwards and forwards, we worked with precision. The train station, bus shelters, fences around building sites — all the while, we both kept a look out. Our sheets were only affixed in appropriate places, next to notices of bands playing or upcoming social events. We didn't want to suffer the same fate as William Posters (did I really use that one?).

At around five in the morning, we returned home, red-eyed, but with the satisfaction of a job well done. People catching trains and busses, or passing makeshift barricades, could expand on the limited pages of their tabloids. Our message, as if it were the wallpaper of life's surroundings, was plastered along the way.

February was a special month. It was Dad's birthday and, just as our New Year had changed its significance, so would one day this month. Valentine's Day approached. Coralee and Dave drove down to look after the children. I ferried Sharon to hospital and spent all morning at the Wesley. I offered encouragement, held her hand, and felt just as useless as the times before.

Years earlier, something inside told me that Rebecca would be Rebecca. Four years later, whatever that feeling was returned, and I knew that any offer of a traditional girl's name was probably not needed. On this day, however, and for a long time prior, whatever it was inside me, also told me that my choice wouldn't be a priority. Sharon had a boy's name, and I liked it too.

After lunch, I dropped by home to check on the children. Then, I returned to the hospital. At around three that afternoon, Nicholas arrived. For the fourth time, I held a little human in my arms whose blood pulsed through both our veins. Cradling his warmth, I looked into his eyes. That timeless feeling once again soaked through my being.

That afternoon, I didn't think about our little boy joining his brother and sisters, with a father who was unemployed and on the dole. Tomorrow was another day, and I could worry about that then. I had rung that afternoon, but that night, after arriving home and putting the children to bed, I called again and spoke with Mum and Dad. They had another grandchild, and just as on each of these occasions before, they were thrilled.

> "When can we see him?"

We no longer fitted into the Mazda, but we couldn't drive two cars to Sydney. I didn't know what to do. Maybe, my parents could drive up? We'd work something out. Mum passed the phone to Dad. He was excited, but I could hear concern in his voice. Our alliance hadn't stopped haemorrhaging. While not the big numbers as over the Christmas break, dribs and drabs were still returning. I guess, he was thinking the same thing that my mind had touched on earlier that day.

> "Son, I don't think you're going to get your job back."

It was one of those moments when something harboured deep inside is only realised when spoken out loud. I'd worn my Ansett uniform with pride, and I'd given my best. I could sign back up anytime, and they would give me more than 30 percent. What they wouldn't give was something that should have been basic. Asking for that right threatened to take away everything we had.

While I strongly believed that locking employees out and incurring huge losses wasn't a smart way to run a business, especially with the skies shortly opened, it was the sense of betrayal and resentment that hurt most.

> "You know, Dad. I don't know whether I want it back."
> Dad paused. "Sometimes, good comes out of bad, Son. You know, I never really warmed to the idea of you working for Abeles and Murdoch."

In all my years with Ansett, this was the first time Dad had even hinted at such a thought. He then said that they'd "try and get up next month", or perhaps the one after.

CHAPTER 27

Justice Brooking handed down his damages ruling: SIX POINT FIVE MILLION DOLLARS! We absorbed the news in stunned silence, two days before our little boy arrived. Our five pilot leaders, Terry O'Connell, and the Federation, as our organisation, were liable.

This ruling would wipe us out, eliminate us. Initially, Peter Abeles seemed in tune with Bruce Springsteen & The Seeger Sessions Band, '*Pay Me My Money Down*', but, perhaps with a little urging, he relented. The airlines advised that they didn't intend to pursue individuals. It was only verbal, but the threat remained. Abeles could have collected at any time, or if Ansett changed hands again, the pilot leaders would still be on the books and at the mercy of any new owner. The writs would remain valid for 15 years, and they would hang over six people's heads for this entire time.

Sadly, Tony Fitzsimons is no longer with us. Several years after the Dispute, he suffered a debilitating stroke that left him a quadriplegic. To ease the immense pressure on his wife, the Federation appealed to have his writ removed. This request was refused.

The airlines did intend to recover around $2,000,000 in legal fees and left open the option of collecting against the association. The AFAP owed over $1,000,000 of its own legal fees. The calculated figure was to cover losses in August, when we had mimicked executive hours. What of the losses in all the months since? What of the tourist operators, small businesses and the elderly couple with that small Gold Coast motel? There was no need for salt in these people's wounds, but it must have stung when the airlines were allowed a five percent fare increase to help recoup their losses from the lockout.

When Justice Brooking ruled months earlier, disquiet rumbled within the ACTU. Then, it had been too late. Now, the horse had well and truly bolted. It seemed all this wasn't the 'Hawke style'. Obviously, this particular style had many facets. If I wasn't so angry, I may have seen a lighter side. Working out the implications for the union movement wasn't rocket surgery. Two of the prime movers were a former ACTU leader, and a current one — talk about turkeys voting for Christmas.

With an election in the offing, we started a door-knocking campaign. The action began with Clyde Holding's Melbourne Ports. His was a marginal seat, and as he was the one who suggested cancelling our licences, one good turn deserved another.

We weren't campaigning for the Opposition necessarily, but rather against the government. We gathered in a suburban park within a marginal Brisbane seat. We worked in groups of two. I went with Bob, a former Australian Airlines Captain.

In just six months, I was losing track of all my new experiences. I didn't know what to expect when I approached that first door. Fortunately, the locals were receptive. They wanted to know why I didn't give up and go back to work. It was an opening to talk about what we were fighting for. At subsequent doorsteps, the baptism of fire I had feared burst forth.

> "Get off my property, you greedy piece of s---."
> "I guess a cup of tea's out of the question," I remarked to the slammed door.

Bob and I compared notes. At least, we had as many positives as negatives. After a couple of hours, we had left numerous leaflets with those interested. I tapped the knocker on another. The front door stood on a wide patio. To the right were French doors, maybe off a lounge room. Both were open. I guess he was in in his mid-fifties. He pleasantly asked what he could do for me.

> "I'm one of the pilots and …"

All semblance of pleasantness left the man's face. Saying nothing, he pushed past me. I started to speak but, for him, I wasn't there. He unlatched the right French door and closed it. I wanted to tell him what I was fighting for, why our families had risked all, but his face was a stone wall. He did the same with the left door, then turned the key in the lock.

I stood there bursting. I wanted to talk about rights trampled underfoot, freedoms, democracy. Frustration welled up inside. My feet wouldn't move, so I remained standing there until my legs obeyed my head.

I'd attended 13 years of school, but these past six months had rounded out my education. We doorknocked for hours. All these years later, I have one overriding memory — a lesson dispatched as two doors closed and locked. Sometimes, nothing cuts as deep as nothing.

The Prime Minister was up in Brisbane again. The day after Sharon and Nicholas arrived home, we went to another demonstration. Staring down their onslaught, Sharon had carried Nicholas as he formed. Now she held him in her arms as he slept.

Another of the wives in our group of protesters walked past. Noticing Nicholas, she stopped.

> "Oh, that's right. Last time, you were bulging. So, you had a little boy! Well, I guess he's a boy, all rugged up in that blue jumpsuit."

I looked around. Many wives held placards in one hand and a small palm in the other. Several younger pilots' parents were also there, as were entire families. Unable to dissuade grandparents, they gathered together as several generations. Our families were the rock on which our defiance was built. 31 years old, the young woman standing beside me yelled in anger. Her maternal instincts were to protect her children while, at the same time, her convictions never wavered. She faced the ferocity of Abeles, Murdoch, Hawke and Kelty's storm, and didn't flinch. 'Come hell or high water', we would look after our little ones, and 'come hell or high water', she would never give in. My eyes swept the sea of angry faces, hodgepodge uniforms, and banners and placards. A Bette Midler song filled my thoughts as my eyes rested on Sharon as she stood by my side, her strength flowing through my grounded wings.

Our problem remained. We, the pilots, could not get our message across. We decided to print our latest points on flyers, and go to the airport and hand them out. Many people took them, and many stopped to chat. Others heaved abuse, "Greedy pilots!" If these people believed half of what the media was dishing up, I admired their restraint.

Paul Everingham was Chief Minister when I lived in the Territory. On this day he walked across the pedestrian crossing.

> I offered my page. "Good morning, Mr Everingham. I was in Darwin when you were …"
> He walked straight past.
> A guy screeched his Jaguar to a halt and jumped out.
> "You're one of the pilots?"
> I nodded.
> "Can I talk to you?"
> "Sure."
> "What's it all about? I know what's in the papers, and I've seen Brian McCarthy on TV, but how about from a grunt on the ground?"

I guess I was a 'grunt on the ground', so I told him something of what I'd been banging on about. Ongoing news of the Dispute was probably far too much for many people, but for us it was a major event. Australian pilots think of our lives in two parts — that which occurred before the 24th of August 1989, and everything that happened as a result. When I drew to a close, the man nodded. He muttered thanks and thoughtfully slipped back into his Jag. It was a nice car.

Our direct approach angered our antagonists, so they employed a new tactic. While outside the Ansett terminal handing out my sheets, two bozos rolled up. One had a video camera. He pointed the lens and started recording. I ignored them. Next, he moved so close that the camera was just centimetres from my face. Instinctively, I raised my hand as a shield.

> The other guy yelled, "THAT'S ASSAULT!"
> I was startled. His voice was so loud and close.
> "I didn't touch you, and you can get that thing out of my face."
> He ramped up. "YOU LITTLE SHIT. I'M CALLING THE POLICE."

He made a call on his mobile phone. I was shaken. The whole thing happened so quickly and out of the blue. Did I touch the camera when raising my protective hand? Was it *possible* to assault a video camera?

A Commonwealth police officer arrived.

> "What's going on here? Has someone been assaulted?"
> The guy pointed his finger almost in my face again. "This little shit assaulted my friend."
> The policeman turned to him. "That'll be enough of that kind of language."
> Outraged, I fired back. "I didn't touch him." Looking straight at the guy, I added, "If anything, it was you who assaulted me, arsehole." (Oops)
> The policeman turned to me. "And you can mind your manners too, son."

The police officer was a big, burly guy. Perhaps in his late fifties, not only did he tower over me, but also over these two. "Can we get to the bottom of this?"

The aggressive one, in a calmer voice, explained that he and his friend were just happening by with their video camera when his friend was assaulted.

> I couldn't hold my tongue.
> "Son, you'll get your turn in a minute." The Officer then asked the video taker, "Did he hit you?"

There was talk of my hand brushing the camera and other fluff, but the officer wanted specifics.

> "Did his hand, arm, foot or leg contact your body in any way?"

A straight question. Amid much mumbling, the two admitted that "no", no bodily contact was made.

The policeman then asked for my version.

I explained I was handing out my leaflets when these two started videoing. As they zeroed in, close to my face, I raised a protective hand (I thought this had a nice ring).

Summing up, the officer noted nothing constituting an assault had occurred, and he believed it best if we all went our separate ways.

As the officer walked off, the aggressive clown had one last go. "Get you next time, you little shit."

I didn't say anything, although, in a gesture of farewell, I did raise my index and middle fingers.

> The policeman saw the last, turned, and shuffled back. "Got a family, son?"
> "Yeah, we've got four kids. The youngest is just a couple of weeks old."
> "You're only a young bloke. If you get yourself a record, it's going to make life even tougher."
> He was right.
> I nodded, and the officer moved away again.
> Out of the corner of his mouth came "Don't let the bastards wear you down."
> I beamed from ear to ear. "Not a snowflake's chance in hell."

On the way home, I dropped into the Federation office. A warning had come in, hot off the fax. In Melbourne and Perth, pairs of goons were videoing pilots handing out leaflets. The procedure commenced with videoing, but then became aggressive. The warning: 'Don't take the bait'. I suggested a fax south; the intimidation was not only happening in Melbourne and Perth. Not long after, similar reports came in from Sydney.

The airlines had engaged psychologists. They had instigated the cycle from the beginning: first, newspaper reports and TV items dealing with us that followed a pattern. It had begun with small articles and mentions, and the tension slowly built. Then, a major blow up was orchestrated. With the big shake, hopefully, a few more pilots would drop to the ground.

Jan Marsh was a psychologist, married to an IPEC pilot. She alerted us to the airlines' strategy. Apparently, it was a fairly run-of-the-mill psyche technique. No wonder we felt as though we were riding an emotional rollercoaster. Jan pointed out other tactics and offered her advice in our regular newsletters. During these months, I learnt more about human nature and how our country really worked.

Jan also noted another feature: the simple strategy of Herr Doktor Goebbels — keep the message short and sharp, and say the same thing over and over and over. It was in all the media, but I first noticed the routine in a television interview.

> "The planes are flying; it's all over."
> "How many aircraft are back in the air?"
> "The planes are flying; it's all over."
> "When will the airlines be back to full strength?"
> "The planes are flying; it's all over."

The choir, in perfect harmony, bleated the same message. A quick look out the window easily disputed this repeated statement. Ansett had a few aircraft up, and Australian Airlines even fewer (You should see us now?).

After significant repetition, the message was changed. Another theme was 'pilots, as if lemmings, are following a stupid leader'. Many of these people sprouting this common message travelled by air. If to Sydney, Melbourne, Canberra, or any port in the domestic network, they may have flown with me. Had they ever put anything on the line for something they believed in?

"Stupid pilots; stupid leader" blasted through the airwaves. As pointed out in a letter to the editor by Qantas pilot, Mark Sullivan, the cockpit of a modern jet, an example being the B747, has "2,150 instruments, levers, switches, warning lamps, safety devices and other pieces of control equipment." Stupid pilots; stupid leader? Operating in a sometimes hostile environment, these same people asserted that I was so dense as to be led by the nose to a splattered fate at the base of a cliff, yet they slipped nonchalantly into their seats in the cabin behind me. Pilots stupid; ... passenger?

B747 flight deck

Where had I seen this before? Short bursts even danced with syncopated rhythm, da da da, da da dada. Herr Doktor may have got it down pat, but it hadn't gone unnoticed by a favourite author. The short, sharp media snippets had the same tempo, "Four legs good, two legs ... *better*!"

One ABC reporter stood out. Everyone has their perceptions, and mine were of someone doing nothing more than mouthing the government's line. Dominic was with a group of pilots who left for overseas. Reporting their departure, she implied that these pilots were disillusioned and giving up. This, I felt, was typical of this reporter's slant. If she spoke to at least one of them, she would have found the complete opposite. Financially strapped and on the brink, close to losing all, far from surrendering, pilots were prepared to forego living in their own country rather than give in. All of their woes could be solved with just one signature. Instead, they would fight on from overseas, replenish the welfare fund and deny the one thing our antagonists needed most.

Others *had* given in, but these wore uniforms retrieved from plastic garbage bags. This journalist interviewed AFAP executive Brian McCarthy. Despite her disparaging tone, Captain McCarthy remained unfazed. She also interviewed several of those trying to force our capitulation. Did any of these perhaps consider that if one person or group in our society is denied their democratic rights — then those rights are denied to us all? We may have known, had Heather Ewart thought to ask. Perhaps then she could have reached for Samuel Johnson: "An injustice anywhere is an injustice everywhere."

Jan Marsh was prolific with her psyche analysis. Apparently, various studies concluded that, in difficult situations such as ours, one in five people took the course of least resistance, equating to about 350 from our ranks. From our initial intake in 1982, we lost just three. Our record was slightly better than the average, but how 'Mother Steve' must have fussed. A pilot I hadn't seen for years returned to work, as did Paul Bum (name now modified to something a little more descriptive). From the intake ahead, I wondered if Mark was still doing his own washing.

We were just under 80 percent solid, and holding. After all this time, even our detractors thought our solidarity impressive. But it wasn't enough. Reaching a statistical norm, we'd lost too many. Out of the 1,647 forced to resign, 1,300 remained strong.

The only chance we had was if the Opposition won government. The opinion polls were neck and neck, with Bob Hawke as the preferred Prime Minister over Andrew Peacock. Putting all our eggs in the election basket was far too big a risk. We faced an agonising decision.

Looking back to our time in Sydney, I could see the one straw too many for our burdened camel's back was the 'New Year block defections'. Dad had seen it, others had seen it, and now it stared us in the face. The chill engulfed us. All our ideals busted apart, the debris falling to the ground. There was only one way to save jobs and, even then, only some jobs would be saved.

Rain pelted down on the Valleys Football Club. Everything was lost; even our seniority was incinerated, and the ashes strewn to the wind.

On the 7th of March 1990, we returned to the Industrial Relations Commission. Several hearings lasted more than a week. It was time for retribution, and allowing even some jobs was an unsavoury sandwich served up to our reluctant mouths.

The excesses of the Accord years had come home to roost. We were descending into the darkness of the "recession that Australia had to have". The demand for travel had softened and with the foreign pilots, new GA recruits, and those returning from our own ranks, there were only so many jobs going. The Commission listed several conditions, and adding a hand to the grip, gave the steel of their knife a twist. They not only expected each of us to apply for these jobs, but wanted to see those applications.

The following day, Bob Hawke launched the ALP campaign. The faithful attended the Lyric Theatre at Queensland Performing

Arts Centre on Brisbane's South Bank. Outside, the unfaithful also gathered. At previous demonstrations, most of us just turned up. This time, the chain message asked us to bring placards. Banners were held aloft blaring 'Aviation Safety Is No Accident'. What could I write? I bought a white square of cardboard from the newsagent and a small piece of wood from the hardware store. With one glued to the other, I had my delivery vehicle. As much as I had hated my years at school, I tolerated English and I loved to read. Books portraying human frailties became favourites. The first of this genre was *Lord of the Flies* by William Golding. Next, I devoured *Brave New World* by Aldous Huxley.

I lost my copy of *Catch-22*, first read on a trip to Darwin. Recently replaced, I again marvelled at Joseph Heller's genius:

> "Some men are born mediocre, some men achieve mediocrity, and some men have mediocrity thrust upon them. With Major Major it had been all three. Even among men lacking all distinction he inevitably stood out as a man lacking more distinction than all the rest, and people who met him were always impressed by how unimpressive he was."

Another literary favourite was just the number of a year, now past. During the Dispute, my 'thoughtcrimes' were immense, but it was a small book by the same author that, to me, captured the moment. As much as I tried, I could find no words of my own to better express Bob Hawke's upwards redistribution of the Accord. George Orwell's view held just as much relevance as when written in 1943. Texta in hand, I wrote on the cardboard:

ALL ANIMALS ARE EQUAL
BUT SOME ANIMALS ARE MORE EQUAL
THAN OTHERS.

We assembled beside the theatre. We weren't the only ones out that day. Mr Hawke had also upset farmers and small business owners.

Members of the National Farmers' Federation and the Australian Small Business Association were out in force. The Small Business Association even hired a light aircraft with a banner: "Same Failed Policy — Same Hawke Government".

At the police briefing, we were allocated our respective areas — small business and farmers to the left; pilots, in our mishmash of uniforms, to the right.

After dropping Rebecca at school, Sharon and I joined our colleagues. We pushed a stroller, held a small hand, and carried our new arrival in what the lady in the Adelaide baby shop had called 'a cocoon'. We hadn't used it all that much, but it protected our baby boy from the wind. With our three little ones, we stood towards the back of the crowd. TV cameras waited at the entrance to capture the Prime Minister's arrival, and our reaction out to the side.

Arriving in plenty of time, as we waited, an olive-green Falcon sedan pulled up. I wouldn't have thought anything of it, except that when the bloke got out, he acted strangely. Dressed in a flannelette shirt and dark trousers, he held a brief case. He plunked this onto the bonnet and took out a mobile phone. Slipping out papers from inside, he studied these. At various intervals, he spoke on the phone, looking up and around. He wasn't with the other group, and he definitely was not one of us. It was his 'out-of-placeness' that caught and held my attention.

About half an hour later, word went around that Bob Hawke had arrived. We started to move into position. The police warned us to stay away from the entrance, but we felt we could make as much noise as we liked.

> "AUSTRALIAN JOBS FOR AUSTRALIANS! AUSTRALIAN JOBS FOR AUSTRALIANS!"

The bloke from the Falcon sprinted past me, and ran to the centre of our group. "VOTE FOR HAWKE! VOTE FOR HAWKE!"

I held my breath. In all our briefings, we'd been told "No violence". I felt the thrust of many menacing eyes, and took another breath.

I knew how emotions could ignite — a fire lit with just one spark. The police kept an eye out, but the TV cameras moved in. Like that old saying, a bulb flashed in my brain, and its light illuminated what I'd thought of as strange behaviour.

Someone told the agitator to piss off. With that, he jumped up and down, punching the air with his right fist. "BOB HAWKE! BOB HAWKE! BOB HAWKE!"

Since our first demonstration, we'd grown into adept protestors. No one touched him. Eventually, he gave up, but rather than slink away, this hired gun ran into the thick of the other protesting groups and started again. "HAWKE! HAWKE! HAWKE!"

As adept as we'd become, our co-demonstrators were pros. Although this goon's minders must have been close by in this tightly organised operation, the farmers and small business people surrounded him. Ten deep; a piggy in the middle. Completely cut off, he was like a deer in headlights. As if shuffling in the dark, his eyes flashed, he couldn't get out and no one could get in. He fell silent. Eyes as sharp as knives met his furtive glances and a deathly hush settled on the circle.

A chant started. Reverberating from what sounded like the bowels of the earth, soft at first, it gathered pace.

"Out! Out! OUT! OUT!"

The volume increased with the tempo.

"OUT–OUT–OUT!"

Desperation etched his face before the sea of humanity parted and into the midst he bolted. Running to his car, he yanked the door open and flung himself behind the wheel. The engine raced as the tyres laid two impressive rubber tracks on the bitumen and the Falcon fishtailed off. Things hadn't gone how they were meant to go — perhaps a bit of a bloody nose for the cameras, minders would shield him from any real harm, and dancing off he'd collect his cheque.

After the rally, we came together with our fellow protesters for a bite, before Sharon and I shepherded the children back to the car. As Coralee and Dave had parked nearby, we walked together. Standing at the lights, Sharon held my decaying cap as I loosened my tie and pressed the button. A chauffeured Ford LTD crossed the intersection, heading towards the city. It must have been a Commonwealth car, as the Minister for Telecommunications and Aviation Support, Ros Kelly, and some others sat inside.

The limo's colour matched the board she later used to keep records of grants to various sporting bodies. This was the last of several events this day that remain seared into my consciousness. As the limousine turned from Grey Street towards Victoria Bridge, Minister Kelly pointed at our two families and laughed as she remarked something to the other passengers.

The phone rang. It was Graham, a senior FO, formerly from the 737. Before joining Ansett, Graham flew Hercs in the air force. A member of my telephone group, as the Dispute lengthened, we rotated positions. I was second and, as his surname began with 'W', group leader duties had worked down to his turn.

> "I've got a message, but you're probably not going to like it."

Graham then read out the IRC stipulations. They had imposed a 'good behaviour period', along with their desire to see our applications for the few jobs going. Graham was right; I didn't like it, but I wasn't all that surprised, as the stipulations had been shared at the recent meeting.

The industrial commission demanded my good behaviour. It was just another impediment shoved up my already congested nose. Over the previous seven months, my 'industrial behaviour' could be measured in days.

"What are you going to do?"

I told him this would make no difference; we'd made up our minds months ago.

> "Yeah, Jan and I are the same. We're looking at Singapore Airlines. How about you?"
> I still had no idea what we'd do or where we would go, but one thing was certain — we'd have nothing to do with the IRC. "I've got some friends with MAS; maybe we'll look into that."

Conferences continued in the IRC, as did our foreign pilots' immigration hearing. We continued to demonstrate and doorknock as the election drew closer. It was a long shot, but if Peacock's party won, then the IRC would become irrelevant. It was a precarious thread from which to dangle, but it was the only thread we had.

CHAPTER 28

The morning of the 24th of March 1990 dawned. We voted early. On tenterhooks all day, we handed out 'how to vote' cards for Mary Lou Heath, one of the pilot's wives who was nominated in a nearby seat.

The polling booths closed, and Sharon and I quickly prepared the children's dinner and baths. Sitting fixated on election coverage throughout the evening as the numbers were tallied, it was as if we counted each vote ourselves. Rocketing interest rates were set to peak at around 18 percent, and a recession loomed. People had more to worry about than industrial relations.

As the hours dragged on, we became more deflated. Well before midnight, it was over — for the election, and for us. Despite losing the two-party vote, Hawke won an historic fourth term, albeit with a reduced majority. It made no difference to the chasm we now faced.

We considered Singapore Airlines. The lure for me was flying the jumbo 747-300, but it would be for five years. SIA took on a lot of senior Captains. They didn't care about new generation glass cockpit time, and they recruited pilots from the 727 and the DC-9 that used the older mechanical instruments. Singapore Airlines were also looking for First Officers. Graham, Michael and Stephan were among the many applying.

Jobs were on offer in the UK, but Sharon and I didn't have 'right of abode'. We were ineligible by one generation, as my great grandfather had travelled to Australia. Sharon's family tree was the same, although her great grandad wasn't as lucky. He had to pay for his ticket. Jobs were going in continental Europe too, which we thought was a little too far away, and the Middle East was too foreign.

My long-time friend and colleague Dominic had joined Malaysia Airlines, or MAS, for a three-year stint. MAS were in the midst of an expansion program. If I built up hours, I could update with Cathay.

As Dad said, "It's an ill wind..." If not for the Dispute, Malaysian would have aircraft stuck on the ground with no one to fly them. MAS had already taken on a greater number of Australians than any other carrier and were looking for more. I gave Dom a call.

The MAS Narrow Body Fleet Manager, Captain Ooi, was heading back to Australia in April. Dom advised that I apply. I updated my resume and added a copy of my last logbook page.

Despite developments in the IRC, I had no interest. The immigration case continued in the Federal Court. It would run for years. With the election over and no rallies or demonstrations, or door knocking or duties at the AFAP office, I had plenty of time to think about my family's future.

If we couldn't find a house payment by May, the bank could start repossessing it. We knew that it took three months of missed payments, as others had learnt by bitter experience. We didn't have two brass razoos to offer the bank, so the meter was ticking.

Coralee and Dave dropped in. Dave had decided to apply to MAS as well. Their family was in the same situation, but a month further in. We needed to get our houses up to scratch if we had to rent or sell. Coralee and Dave borrowed money from family, and the following weekend I helped Dave to concrete over the dirt to form a front veranda, previously planned but unaffordable. Their deck ran the full length of their rectangular house, so care was needed to pour and top just at the right times. For Dave, it was a breeze. Of the many jobs that had paid for his flying training, concreting was one.

At our place, I replaced flyscreens and took up the old carpets. We had a wooden pergola with peeling paint down the back. Stephan dropped by, and sweating in the midday sun, he climbed up with a paint pot. He spent all afternoon and by evening, as we prised the top off a home brew, he'd given it a liquid overhaul.

Malaysia Airlines liaised with the AFAP. A couple of weeks later, their April interview list came out. Dave had one; Stephan had another, but when I reached the end, my name wasn't there. I called Dom, and he rang the office. Captain Ooi advised that my application had been reviewed, but they felt that relocating with four young children would be too difficult for us. We'd lose it all if we stayed, so I called Captain Ooi myself. With all the diplomacy I could muster, I inquired if, perhaps, my name was inadvertently omitted. He recapped what Dominic told me. I assured him that, given the opportunity, we'd come.

All interview spots were filled. I knew Stephan was leaning towards SIA, and others had several interviews lined up. One Captain had three interviews over two days.

> "Captain Ooi, would you mind if I came to the briefing? If, perhaps, someone doesn't show, there may be a vacant slot."

Over the years, I'd developed another skill. I was good at clutching at straws. The Captain said that was fine, but an interview depended on time availability.

After driving the van to Stephan's, parking at Toowong station, and catching the train to the city, we walked to the Hilton. MAS were set up in a conference room. In another coincidence, the room was next to the room where Sir Peter Abeles had held his little gathering, now a lifetime ago.

The room filled with pilots, all familiar faces. Approaching the Personnel Manager, I explained that my name wasn't on the list.

> "Captain Ooi said that I could attend on the off-chance of an interview."
> The Manager turned to Captain Ooi who nodded. He checked the times on his list. "After the briefing, you can come back at 1:30."

Captain Ooi presented an outline of Malaysia Airlines, their fleet types and route structures. He then hung a map on the white board. I hadn't realised Malaysia had an eastern component across the South China Sea, and on the island of Borneo. The 737 ran domestic services on the peninsular and across to East Malaysia, as well as international routes to Singapore, Thailand, the Philippines and Indonesia. Standard operating procedures differed, as did the aircraft. We'd all flown the 737-300. We were being recruited for the older, -200 model. The aircraft was similar to fly, but lacked the glass cockpit. With different engines and other handling differences, it was still a 737. All we needed was a short conversion course.

Malaysia's population is made up of three main ethnic groups: Malay people who are known as Bumiputera, and smaller Chinese and Indian populations. Regarding the cultural differences, Captain Ooi shared a few tips: "Don't point with index fingers, or bare soles of your feet in anyone's direction, or use your left hand to accept or offer anything."

The briefing lasted an hour, after which tea, coffee, cakes and biscuits were wheeled in. With nothing else for me to do, and a couple of hours to kill, I returned home. Not only was I nervous about the interview, I was nervous about whether I would actually get one. Butterflies swarmed in my stomach. I hadn't had anything to eat and couldn't keep anything down if I tried. Retracing my steps, I arrived back to the conference room with 10 minutes to spare.

Back in November 1983, two young Australians were caught trafficking drugs in Malaysia. The laws there are strict, especially in the case of heroine. The penalty was capital punishment. The parents of these two young people went through hell. Their long-distance attempts at legal recourse proved a nightmare, and the heartache on their faces showed every time this aired on TV.

As Dad was fond of saying, "There are two sides to every story." The other side was the depth of misery and often death that resulted from addiction to this vile substance. This misery had touched our Prime Minister's life. It was a private matter and not anyone else's business. However, emotions travel with us, and whether sitting quietly at home or in a national television studio, bottled up feelings eventually reach the safety valve. In an unguarded moment, this private family matter became public knowledge. As well as being Prime Minister, Bob Hawke was a father. In a television interview, his anguish, grief, distress and everything else welled up, and tears filled his eyes. Bob Hawke was far from my favourite person, but one thing bound us together. We were both fathers, and we both had daughters. Hearts went out to the Hawke family. Thankfully for Hawke's daughter and her family, this story had a happy ending. But not so for those who chose to traffic drugs in a foreign country.

The Malaysian people believed the horrors brought about by trafficking heroin should be punishable by death. This is spelled out graphically at every immigration point and in every information pamphlet, as is the case in many South-East Asian countries. In Bahasa Malaysia, the word for drugs is 'Dadah'. In a slogan as simple as it is sinister, the results of both using and trafficking warned, 'Dadah is Death', and it was posted at every entry point to this country.

These two young Australians were at the bottom of this despicable drug 'food chain', but Kevin Barlow and Brian Chambers decided to traffick in the misery of heroin, for their own benefit, in a country that was unforgiving. The executions of Chambers and Barlow on the 7th of July 1986 created diplomatic furore. Malaysia was a friendly country, yet the high state of emotions was inflamed when Bob Hawke abandoned accepted country to country protocols and, without regard for cultural differences or sensitivities, used the term "barbaric". Hawke's words sparked outrage, and Malaysia–Australia relations plummeted.

The Personnel Manager, Kamil Wahib, sat waiting in the conference room, beside the remnants of earlier refreshments. He offered me tea and cake, but I was still too pent up to oblige. For differing reasons, he refrained as well. I later learnt that it was Ramadan.

Mr Kamil inquired about my family, and we made small talk. I replied politely, all the while with my heart pounding. Would I even get the chance of an interview? In the most casual fashion, he asked what I thought of Bob Hawke. Following my measured response, he inquired if I'd heard of the Chambers and Barlow case.

"Yes, it was a few years ago."

"Do you remember what your Prime Minister said?"

I did, and said so.

"Do you think Australians agreed with him?"

"I can only speak for myself, but my feeling is no."

It must have been the nerves, but I went on, "I have

> four children. One of my biggest fears as they grow older is the scourge of drugs."

The Personnel Manager looked at me as my nerve-driven voice rattled on about wasted bodies, with wasted, mainline-pocked, riddled limbs, and pathetic, wasted lives that, without suppliers, pushers and peddlers could have unleashed who knows what.

> "Instead, the oxygen thieves of drug cartels live luxurious lifestyles built on those subsisting in the gutters of addiction. Maybe, these two Australians were victims too, taken advantage of by those at the top, desperate for their next fix. How many more young lives, however, would have ended as prematurely as theirs, had their heroine made it through?" I added that I believed Australians respected other cultures, and the laws of other countries. "We have our views, as does everyone, but we shouldn't try and force these on others."
> The Manager's eyes remained riveted to mine.
> "Malaysia is not Australia," I concluded. "I think our Prime Minister should have held his tongue."

The phone on the table next to the conference room entrance rang.

Mr Kamil picked it up. Then, he turned to me.

> "They're ready. I'll take you up."

Relief flowed through me, but, at the same time, my muscles tensed. At least, I had a chance. Mr Kamil escorted me to the lift and into an upper floor room where a long table stood, chairs either side. Capt Ooi and another Captain sat behind. I turned to Mr Kamil to thank him for showing me up, but instead of leaving, he moved to the other side of the table. I hadn't noticed that there were three chairs.

"Please, take a seat."

Undoing my coat, I settled into the chair as Mr Kamil spoke to the others in Bahasa Malaysia. Politely I waited, as the three men opposite engaged in a lengthy exchange. Nerves simmering, I waited some more. They finished chatting, and the two Captains turned their attention to me.

I'd been through several such interviews, and I always dreaded the first question, as it set the tone. I felt a good opening carried weight in the overall process. I steeled myself. Instead of Captain Ooi commencing, the Assisting Captain spoke. He asked if he could check my licences and logbooks. I handed these across and after a short time, he nodded to Captain Ooi. Checking licences and logbooks was standard, but it served only to prolong my mental nail biting.

Captain Ooi looked up. I prepared to face the first real question. He looked down again and checked a sheet of paper. He looked up, and my nerves became a rollercoaster, in harmony with his upward and downward gazes.

> "We have a course in May, and one in June. Which would suit you best?"

This interview had none of the traits of any that had preceded it. As it was, things were starting to get a little grim at home. Whatever happened next in our lives, needed to happen soon.

> "If it was my choice, then the earlier date would be fine."

Perhaps the technical or other probing questions were next. Instead, Captain Ooi turned to Mr Kamil. "Put him down for a May start."

The Captain then smiled and said he looked forward to seeing me in Kuala Lumpur. Rising, he shook my hand, as did the other two. I thanked them for the interview and left, thinking this was the strangest one I'd had. Even so, it had ended with the desired result, and I was relieved, to say the least.

In the lobby, I took coins from my pocket and rang home.

> "We're going to Malaysia."
> "What? How do you know? Don't you have to wait until they send a letter or something?"
> "They'll send a telegram, but they said I could start in May."

Two days after the interview, the phone rang.

> "I have a telegram for you. It'll be delivered tomorrow, but I can read it now if you like." The lady read out the short note before adding, "You must be one of the pilots; I've had several of these today. All the best to you."
> I thanked her. The next day, the 16th of April 1990, the telegram arrived.

We only had a couple of weeks to get organised. First off, I called the real estate agent. We wanted to keep our house. We would return, at some stage, and when we did we'd have a home. Meanwhile, we could rent it out. The same thinking applied to our little car. Sharon suggested we loan it to her dad. He had his motor bike and an old Datsun. You could see the road through the rust in the Datsun's floor, so it would be nice if he had a newer car to get around in. When we came back, we'd have a house and a car.

We didn't have much stuff, but planned to take our table and chairs, lounge suite and children's beds, which would half fill a container. We had met Jeanette and Mark in Perth, but got to know them in Brisbane during the Dispute. They were leaving at the same time, so we decided to share a container. The elephant in the room was the contents of our garage. I didn't want to talk about it, but knew something had to be done. We couldn't take it with us, and it couldn't go to Darwin. We'd accumulated junk. When we left Adelaide, everything fitted in the van, trailer and boxes. Leaving Perth, we had needed to cull some. We'd been in Brisbane for less than 18 months, but couldn't take everything with us. At least a vanload had to go. I loaded up; one trip to the tip should do it.

I opened the garage door to find a pool of water under the van. On lifting the bonnet, it was obvious; the water pump had blown. We didn't have any money to fix it, and the back of the car was full of junk. Even with the seats folded down, the load was too bulky to fit in the little car. I grabbed the plastic jerry can from my planned Nullarbor crossing, and filled the container, placing it on the passenger-side floor. So many years ago, I'd done the same with Port Lincoln tank water, and again for the trip to Port Pirie. I took the cap off the radiator, and held the hose, filling it to overflowing. Scrambling to the driver's seat, I turned the key.

When I arrived to the tip, steam was gushing out. I lifted the bonnet and began to unload. By the time I had emptied the tray, the engine had cooled. I poured in more water and secured the radiator cap. Back home, steam hissed as I parked in the garage. My car deserved better. In all these years, it had only faltered once, and then it got us up the hill. I gently closed the door, sorry.

The agent called.

> "I've got some friends looking to rent in the area. Can I bring them by tomorrow?"

Following a cursory look through, the tenants were quick on the uptake. They'd move in the weekend after we left.

Time was getting away. The removalist came to plan the load. With our stuff packed first, he'd transfer the container to Jeanette and Mark's place. On leaving, he noticed the blue car in the garage.

> "What are you going to do with the van?"
> "To tell the truth, I don't know."

"I need a van for our smaller jobs. Do you want to sell it?"

"No, I don't, but I'll probably have to. I've had it since new."

He stopped and looked at me. "It's a one owner?"

"Yeah, the water pump's blown, but apart from that, it runs fine."

"How much do you want?"

I had no idea what it was worth. I never thought of it in monetary terms.

"Would you take 800?"

He could've said one dollar, or several thousand, it made no difference. "I guess so."

He looked at the back. "It's even got a tow bar."

I'd forgotten, but I had another problem. "It's got a trailer."

"Can I have a look?"

"Sure, it's down the back."

We walked down to the back gate. He pulled another figure from his hat, which I again accepted. Walking back through the garage, he noticed the surfboard.

"You certainly like blue. My son surfs. What about the board?"

"For another 50, I'll put it in the back of the van."

A couple of days later, the removalist was back with a tow truck. The car was towed straight to the shop and fitted with a new water pump. It'd get a good going over, and any other parts in need of replacement would be fixed at the same time, before a new paint job. My treasured ride would start a new life, doing what it was originally designed to do.

Over 15 years earlier, I drove that car from the dealers, with its Deauville Blue glittering in the sun. Since then, we'd traversed one side of Australia to the other, and north to the Top End; not to mention all the places in between. These shared trips provided me not only transport but, at times, a temporary home. After thousands and thousands of kilometres, several sets of number plates, and hours upon hours listening to the no-longer-functioning stereo cassette, most recent trips involved sedate drives to the airport. Rebecca even used the car as a cubby house while parked in the garage. It'd seen better days and my plan was to refurbish it when funds allowed. Really, I just didn't want to part with it.

On taking everything out, I found things behind and under the seat not seen for years. The original warranty card remained in the glove box, and I jokingly handed it to the new owner. "If anything goes wrong, give General Motors a call." Manoeuvring chains were secured, and the front raised, and my steed was hitched to the back of the tow truck. With the new owner, tow truck driver, and Sharon all in close proximity, the void inside me was something deep and dark. Even if I wished to share, no words could explain. I just stood there. A gentle touch on my upper arm, and Sharon walked back through the garage; the lump inside me formed by sadness. Adding salt to my wound, an old Dylan song traced through my mind, '*It's All Over Now, Baby Blue*'.

The loss of my car, towed down the street, not even afforded the dignity of leaving under its own power, epitomised every other loss. The loss of my job, my career, and almost the house, combined with the loss of being able to live in our own country.

As the blue van disappeared, never to be seen or driven by me again, my thoughts honed in on everything that had happened. I remembered Dad's words: "Whatever happens, Son, always take responsibility for your actions." Throughout Dad's life, he had medical problems, enduring heart bypass surgery, twice. He had also lost his left eye. While adding a room and expanding a kitchen on a complex at Wollstonecraft, one storey up, Dad had a sight problem. The job stopped, and we explained to the clients why, and when we may resume. On the day he went into hospital, Dad took me aside. "Son, if things don't go so well, you'll finish that job for me." It was both question and statement. Barely 20 years old, I had no idea of the work involved, and his words were a shock. Although extremely serious, Dad's doctor described a fairly 'routine' operation. There was no need for grave thoughts.

It was only years later that I understood Dad's meaning. Under stress and feeling such anxiety, there was still time for a father-son lesson. I was already an adult, but a young one. Just as in this hypothetical case where responsibility would pass to me, so it was with life.

I knew, as the red taillight of that cherished vehicle disappeared around the corner, that everything that happened was a result of decisions we had made. We chose to stand for something we believed in, even if few outside our group understood. We chose to support our friends, colleagues and their families; we chose to fight in the streets, and we chose to counter the onslaught garnered by two of the most powerful businessmen in our country, coupled with the might of the Hawke-led government and the seething resentment of Kelty's ACTU. And we chose not to back down.

As I turned to walk inside, I knew this day marked the beginning of a long process. We had fought the good fight, finished the race, and kept the faith. It was time to start picking up the pieces, and get on with it.

CHAPTER 29

The time to leave drew closer. The MAS flight left from Sydney. We planned to go down a few days before and visit Mum and Dad. They could get to know their brand-new grandson, at least fleetingly.

We arranged to catch a Qantas flight on the return leg of an international sequence. It was inconvenient, but there was no way we'd set foot on a domestic aircraft. Many tasks concertinaed into the last few days. I needed to renew my medical certificate. Usually, I went to a local doctor. He was busy and I was running short on time. I looked up another on the outskirts of the city, and drove in and parked in a nearby street.

Four other patients waited in the surgery as the receptionist confirmed my aviation medical.

> "Are you one of the Dispute pilots?"
> "Yes, I am."
> "Doctor asked me to check. In that case, there'll be no charge."

I didn't know this doctor. I'd never been to him before. Picking up a magazine, I flicked through. About to put it back down, a picture caught my eye. It was the TV reporter, Heather Ewart. There was no way I'd ever forget her. The article started out all warm and fuzzy, with Heather happy in her life shared with her partner. The picture included Barrie Cassidy. I knew the name and remembered he was also an ABC reporter. Nurses and doctors married; flight attendants and pilots did the same. Working in close proximity, I guessed it wasn't unusual for journalists to get together. But really, Heather Ewart's private life was none of my business. I started to turn the page when my eye caught the column under the photo. Flipping back, I read the paragraph.

"W-H-A-A-A-T!"

Slamming the magazine shut, I threw it on the table. Four sets of startled patients' eyes, and the receptionist's, turned my way. It was just as well it wasn't my turn. Part of my check-up was blood pressure. Barrie Cassidy had left the ABC in 1986. He was Bob Hawke's personal press secretary. Working with the Prime Minister, Cassidy was a senior public servant. Hadn't Bob Hawke proposed a substantial wage increase for this group? Wouldn't Hawke's proposal seek to place these people above and beyond the community, with an unacceptably greedy grab for money? Couldn't such an increase destroy the salary system of Australia? What about the future of the Australian economy — the future welfare and hopes of every Australian family?

There was no 'Blitzkrieg of these high-flying militants' nor declaration of war against these minion menaces; or carte blanche — "hit as hard as you can, quick as you can". Hadn't they shown complete contempt for others? And why no bitter cocktail of bile and vitriol spewed forth on 3AW radio interview — this coercive, physical invasion inflicted on the Australian community? Where was Heather Ewart with her verbal Molotov cocktails flung from her drive-by slot on the ABC news? And where the bloody hell was Brad Norington, his precious author's cap at the ready? With indignant outrage barraging readers from his first page — how could they even think to raise the Jolly Roger with such a huge pay rise — this 'highly paid, privileged group which sought to put themselves still further above the rest'?

From a *Herald* article of the 30th of April 1990 titled 'The game's the same: it's the ump to blame', Terry McCrann raised a point:

> "... The pilots? Remember them? Those guys who were going to destroy the country with their 30 percent pay claim?
> So dangerous were they and their claim that the government had to close the airline industry down, tear an enormous hole in our most prospective

> export earner in tourism, and initiate a whole range of unprecedented and draconian anti-worker measures to break them.
> Yet within six months the very same government, headed by the very same Robert Hawke, has proposed a 42 percent pay increase for top public servants."

A short time later, Alan Ramsey wrote of politicians' anger when the latest instalment to up their pay was delayed (*Sydney Morning Herald*, 2nd June, 1990, 'The MP's get theirs — in due course'):

> "... It hasn't helped matters that, under the new salary structure for ministerial staff, Hawke's press secretary, Barrie Cassidy, his political advisor, Geoff Walsh, and Paul Keating's senior advisor, Don Russell, all get big pay increases that lift their salaries to a maximum $96,000 a year, plus a government car."

As well as his book, written before the dust stopped rising let alone settled, Brad Norington covered the Dispute by writing a host of articles for the *Sydney Morning Herald*. One dated 21st of December, 1989, was titled, 'Workers restive as elite groups make pay grab'. The first line of his table started with the general workforce (six percent pay rise), and worked through several occupations, ending with top public servants (up to 30 percent pay rise). Norington wasn't one to let a chance go by:

> "A series of bigger pay rises which has flowed to some sections of the workforce exposes the folly of the campaign outside the wage system by the Australian Federation of Air Pilots to gain a 30 percent pay rise for 1,647 pilots."

Norington went on to say that, if we pilots had stayed in the system, we could have achieved at least half our claim and kept our "precious working conditions — now lost".

As Mr Kelty's contracts demonstrated, we would not have achieved only half of our claim; we could have *exceeded* our claim. So, bigger pay rises fudged through the Accord were good, but outside of the Accord, they were deemed bad. Maybe, like uranium.

While the Labor party had a policy banning uranium mining, in 1984 the Hawke-led government changed tack. Two uranium mines in the Northern Territory were now acceptable, as was one in South Australia. Did this same thinking apply to the Accord? While certain radioactive heavy metal could be deemed 'good uranium', the system disallowed the 'bad' type that could fuel a major catastrophe.

The battle was lost. A clear message was understood by all: 'shows what happens to those outside the system'. Simply punching my old salary and the Kelty contract into a calculator proved that the Accord could fudge big pay rises. While Mr Norington considered us dim-witted for not taking advantage, I thought his chiding reinforced everything that was wrong with the system. How could 30 percent for senior public servants be fair and equitable, while ordinary people got just six percent?

Unfortunately, this indecency did not die a natural death. Rearranging the industrial award system may have fostered the goodwill of ACTU leaders, but many fell by the wayside. As the pendulum swung in its ever-increasing arc, a young person who made one feeble choice could be left out in the cold, if faced with the threat of "take it or leave it." The greed and excesses of that time were not stamped out, and the bounds of common decency were not restored. The seeds sown in the fields of our industrial landscape bloomed and grew to a mature tree that bore fruit of a putrid obscenity.

Whenever working people threaten action to restore their living standards, or demand a fairer share, or even seek to retain conditions under threat, indignant howls rise to a crescendo. Cries of "greed", accompany belittling, at fever pitch. By contrast, when the manhole cover is raised on the sewer of executive pay rates, silence is golden. The stench wafts under these same noses as if it's Chanel No.5.

I kept a newspaper clipping which illustrated just how far we descended in this vile, spiral dive. On the 19th of December 2012, the *Sydney Morning Herald* reported the chief executive of the ANZ Bank took home a package of almost $20 million. The article quoted the bank chairman, Mr John Morschel:

> "In response to complaints about Mr Smith's package — worth about $26,000 a day — Mr Morschel conceded it was 'a lot of money'. However, he said it was 'perfectly reasonable' when compared with the pay of executives who ran similar sized banks overseas..."

If this one individual's remuneration was reduced to perhaps $1 million (a princely sum in anyone's language, but maybe not Mr Morschel's), then the remaining $19 million could be used to benefit other workers. Given that the average salary at that time was around $60,000 per annum, more than 300 other people could have been employed.

In Terry McCrann's 1990 article, he happened to mention the salaries of Will Bailey, Stewart Fowler and the other bank chiefs of those times — $600,000. If I divided my salary then, had I been earning one, into this figure, and applied this to what the chiefs of these same corporations achieved today, this ratio suggests an income somewhat excessive for a B737 First Officer — between $800,000 and $1.6 million.

If all the others gorging themselves at this same trough were awarded reasonable salaries, how many people could have kept jobs that were axed in cost-cutting, and how much better would the service provided have been?

One of our banks was formed to serve the Australian people's common good. It was privatised (commencing in 1991 and finalised in 1996), with the first stage under the stewardship of the person who introduced the Accord. A business must make a profit, and a bank must sit on a firm and solid footing. But do profits need to be excessive? And why should these institutions that once would have distributed wealth to the Australian people generate such enormous bonuses? If a company performs well, it's because every person in that company performed well. So, why, just as with the Accord, was one highly paid, privileged group put above the rest?

If still in the people's hands, perhaps, such excesses would be reduced and the benefits shared more equitably. Could these have flowed to help those that life's fortune had not shone so brightly upon? A chance, so the last shall be first? Or, through social programs, could these funds have helped care for our seniors, educated our younger ones, reduced our budget deficits, or simply contributed to our common wealth? If still in our possession, would we have allowed interest rate rises in excess of those set by our reserve bank?

What did ordinary men and women, ciphers in this calculation, think of such greed and excess? Obscenity had replaced a pay scale that rewarded service to the public. What of the ordinary people's thoughts when these same snouts attempted to justify such an indecency and became so red-faced and illuminated as to resemble a light on the hill? Alas, ordinary people seemed to have been forgotten.

The cheque from sale of the van, trailer and surfboard covered our final financial bits and pieces. I arranged for the car to be trucked to Darwin, Telecom to disconnect the phone, and I paid the electricity and other bills. We set aside money for Sydney, plus a few dollars for 'just-in-case'. $134 remained. We wished friends farewell and promised to keep in touch, and I made one last visit to the Federation office.

A goodbye to all and well wishes included a "Please pass on my good wishes to those missed." Frank was long gone, now in Hong Kong. Coralee and Dave were sorting their things to join us in Malaysia; Stephan was soon to depart for Singapore; and Jenny and Michael, and Jan and Graham were also packing for the Lion City. While many had already gone, and with more leaving in the next few months, others were destined to stay.

As I began to leave, Bill, an administration guy, formerly Ansett, asked if I'd filled in my application form. The storm inside me broke and thunder clapped from my mouth.

> "I want nothing to do with Ansett, and the IRC can rot in hell."
> Contrasting my emotion-charged words, he asked calmly, "Have you got a few minutes?"

United by our hopes and desires, we had stood together for months. I had more than a few minutes for him. We moved to a quiet corner.

> "You know, you're one of the more fortunate ones. You've got a 737 endorsement."

Our old friend Johnno had moved his family to Fiji. Although he flew the F27 with East-West, it was considered an 'old type', and John accepted a job flying light aircraft. Those without a 'glass cockpit rating' had a harder time. Even that graceful lady, the beautiful 727, had become old technology. Some couldn't leave due to family reasons, with kids in a crucial stage of school or frail parents. In a way, having young children was an advantage; we all up and left together. Bill, both friend and former colleague, talked of those staying behind.

> "The only hope they have is one of the few jobs going with our former employers." The boot was in and we had to eat every crumb of the humble pie

they dished up. "I know it's something you don't want to do, but some still need our care."

Anger flared within me again. He was right, on both counts. However, if there was one last thing I could do for those left, I would, no matter how distasteful the thought. Maybe, I could swallow without chewing, but not a skerrick more than needed.

"Have you got a form?"

Bill found one in the office desk. At the top was a dashed line, with space for name, address, telephone number and underneath that aeronautical experience, including aircraft types and total hours. I scribbled my name at the top and signed on the last line.

"But you've left it blank."
"It's for the IRC, right?"
"Yes."
"Then all they want to see is a stack of these on their table."
"Yeah, but you've only given your name."
"If it ever gets to Ansett, they'll have nowhere to send a reply. This is for us, not them."

I had climbed my mountains and made my journeys — all to join Ansett. I was about to embark on another journey that no longer involved Ansett, and I knew it would never involve them again. I returned Bill's pen; my form, along with the rest, added to the pile. Smiling, he offered his hand, with a firm grip.

For more than seven months, this coalition of Corporate–Government–IR might had swung their wrecking ball. With my pride momentarily blinding me to our foundation; everything we built was built on this, and now it was all that remained. The reminder, gentle, came from a friend — those who needed our care were our own.

The next day was busy, and the last in our home. I dropped Rebecca at school then drove towards the city, stopping off at Toowong. I hated this place. Joining the queue, I shuffled the papers in my hand. It was still early but the clerk looked dishevelled.

"Can I help you?"
"I've got a job. I want to cancel this."
I handed over the papers, file number in the corner.
"Okay. That's good news. When do you start?"
"Seventh of May."
"Still at the same address?"
"No, I'll give you a forwarding one in Sydney."
"All done. I'll put this in the system."
I always felt tense in this office and, although not my intention, I may have sounded a little gruff.
"Thanks for your help."
"No worries, and good luck."
I returned his smile. "Ta."

In the city, I found the international money changer that I'd walked past many times but never used.

"That's an even 250 Ringgits."

I thanked him and opened my wallet. The space recently vacated by Australian dollars was filled with red notes.

Stopping at the local supermarket, I bought chocolates, sweets and paper party hats. At home, the shipping container was out front and already a quarter full. We busied ourselves keeping the children out of the way and helping where we could. At around 2 pm, I placed the bag of sweets and chocolates on the passenger side floor, and drove to Rebecca's school. I left the plastic shopping bag with the teacher, then waited in the car.

When Rebecca was two years old, we signed up for a financial plan to cover her secondary education. Each pay, a small amount went to this account. With education on the backburner, a few months prior, we cashed it in. Fees and administration costs had swallowed any gains; we didn't even get our money back.

Rebecca's class filed into the playground. Rebecca handed out the sweets and chocolates as party hats slipped onto heads. Watching on, the lump in my throat threatened to deprive my lungs. She was happy and settled in school, and in the afternoon sun, she flittered among her many friends. They played games and sang songs.

Many of the 'Dispute kids' had copped abuse at school. It was usually the older children, but Rebecca was fronted by a boy in her class, too.

> "Your father's one of the pilots. They deserve everything they got."

Rebecca had a birthday coming up, and so did I. We later heard that our seven-year-old princess had stood to her full height and looked him in the eye.

> "You're a very stupid boy."

In some ways, Rebecca was like me, but in other ways she was very much her mother's daughter. The school bell rang. I held her hand and we walked to the car. I couldn't talk, I couldn't even swallow.

At home, the container was almost loaded. Dave arrived. Tomorrow evening we'd leave for Sydney, but this night was with our friends. We packed our six bulging suitcases in the boot and back seat of

Dave's Holden, and children's backpacks and other bits and pieces filled the Mazda.

With the remaining items in the container, the truck drove off. Sharon and I took a last walk through the empty house. Pausing on the front step, we closed and locked the door.

Sharon sat in the Mazda's driving seat, and with all others taken, I dropped into the Commodore, beside Dave. Dave and I'd been mates since we first met in Darwin. For one of the meetings, he came down by train. I picked him up at the station and later dropped him off. Two hours after bringing the van to a halt in the parking area, we were still talking.

I remember a story he shared with me from that time. His family had been out. On arriving home, they found a box by the front door. It was filled with groceries. Someone gave it a lot of thought, as there were special treats for the children and even a couple of tins of dog food.

Our family had experienced something similar. A Captain from the Federation called one day. I'd seen him about, but as he was from Australian Airlines, I didn't know him well.

> He began, "A flight attendant's husband was here this morning."
> As I wondered where this was going, he continued, "He slapped 2,000 dollars on the table and said it was to go to the FO families. We had a meeting and came up with eight. Yours is one."

As we drove north, our moods were sombre; the empty house fell into the distance. I wondered when, or even if, our children would bathe in the Queensland sunshine again. Thinking out loud, I said as much to Dave. Their house had a 'For Sale' sign out front. They'd join us later; he was on MAS's June course. We'd both been busy getting everything done before our departures. Until recently, Dave's family were living on bare floors. The new veranda had made a big difference, and the children scampered from inside to outside and back again. With more help from family, carpets covered the concrete. Their house, that otherwise would have taken years to upgrade, was marketable. We drove to Morayfield, two mates sat side by side in an old Commodore. Despite how we felt, we were lucky. At least for us, whatever lay ahead 'lay ahead'.

It didn't have to be this way. For me, the Dispute didn't begin on the 18th of August 1989. It began when Peter Abeles appointed Graeme McMahon as general manager. I remembered the taunts, goading, and verbal fists punching the air. Maybe, if we'd known then what we knew now, things might have been different.

A thug in a suit ... I thought of another in a flannelette shirt. The day that olive green Falcon pulled up at the Lyric Theatre changed forever how I viewed demonstrations. I wondered about the going rate for a tap on the nose. Did the remuneration paid depend on the results? What of the calculation when neither we nor our fellow demonstrators obliged? And what of a general manager with a similar set of skills? Would he one day fishtail into the distance?

We had pulled a 'go slow'. But I still didn't think our actions sat on a par with slamming the taps shut on our nation's fuel. Were the refineries shut down, workers locked out, and writs served? We didn't see foreign tankers imported from the US or Europe plying our Australian roads, or foreign drivers slipped under the table of our immigration laws.

Yet, we'd been eliminated, and at what cost? With the plan brought to fruition, and the wish fulfilled, in another glimpse through the Accord's dining room window, Peter Abeles even managed a huge pay rise. Bob Hawke received the same, and the airlines squibbed money from passengers, with their five percent fare increase. It's an old saying, and even though he wielded so much power and influence, our former employer was still a human being. Even he wasn't exempt; sometimes, we should be careful what we wish for.

In all the years since, whenever I think of the Airline Dispute of 1989-90, one thought overrides all others. The tragedy wasn't limited to those in our ranks. Innocent people, many in the tourism and related industries, were left decimated. Small businesses least able to withstand the pressures became bankrupt. Owners joined their employees and were left to wallow, aimlessly blown by an ill wind, in the tumbleweeds of an industrial wasteland. I feared for the older couple I had met at the Brisbane Town Hall. For some, it was too much, and the heartbreak too great. Innocent people became caught up in something beyond their control. A lifetime's work was snuffed out, and so a life.

Pilots lost careers and homes. Families were prised apart and friendships ended, but worst of all were the suicides. While some of us took the chance to start again and rebuild our shattered lives, for others, the loss was so great that it led to the ultimate tragedy. Tragedy is not thought of in degrees, but the loss of a child must be one of the greatest. Families were so disrupted that teenagers became consumed by hopelessness and felt unable to cope. They took a step that could never be retraced.

Years later, I learned that this heartbreak encompassed all sides. It brought home to me that there's no divide when it comes to tragedy. Geoff, who I'd met in Darwin and shared a base with in Adelaide and Perth, last seen in the Brisbane terminal after he elected to return, took his own life.

Dave and I loaded the cars. Tomorrow he'd drop the Mazda to the trucking yard. The adults carted overfilled suitcases to the check-in counter. I worried about excess baggage. Not only did we have all these bags, but a car seat, booster and capsule.

> "You're Malaysia Airlines staff?"
> It sounded so strange that I almost blurted out, "I'm Ans..."

This time, it was a 'see-ya-later'. In a few weeks, we'd catch up in KL. We crossed the tarmac and climbed the steps to the Qantas Boeing 767. Mum, Dad, and Maree stood waiting at Sydney's international terminal. Two cars sat parked in the parking area. Mum rushed forward, and Sharon passed the bundle from her arms.

> "And who have we here?"
> Rebecca stepped up. "Nana, that's my baby brother, Nicky."

We left most of the bags downstairs, and Mum and Dad fussed over Nicky (these days, "The name's Nick"). During those two days, we christened our baby in Mum's parish church, and visited Gemma and Paul. In the capsule, Nicholas slept through his introductions. Roxanne and Ari dropped by. The 767 did the KL run, so he'd probably see us there.

The days flew, and the time came for us to do the same. All our relatives gathered together. It was like Christmas at Kingsford Smith. With bags checked and boarding passes in hand, we fronted the departure gate. Outside immigration, we moved around the circle. Aunties shed tears as we hugged. Uncle Alex picked up a bit of a sniffle. Must have been the air-conditioning. I had one too.

> "I hope it all works out."
> "Thanks, you take care."

In some ways, Uncle Bede was like a big kid. He gripped my hand, but no words came. I tried too, but the same happened. He was my favourite. I thought of all those times he and Aunty Joan had taken us out, his sizzling BBQs, and his hot, brightly coloured cars. My hand gently squeezed his shoulder.

Tears ran down Maree's cheeks and we hugged. No matter how old we got, she'd always be my baby sister. I moved across to Mum. A tear slipped from her eye as she said something, the words too soft to hear. We hugged again. Dad was last. We faced each other, the grip tight.

"Look after them, Son."
"I will, Dad."

Inside the sterile area, Sharon filled in our departure forms. We had scrambled to get new passports issued in time. Three doors down from our house in Brisbane, two teachers were raising their young children. They were the only people we knew who were authorised to witness our signatures. Sharon entered the details of these brand-new documents along with the two older ones, one of those only used for the second time. I thought of all the years that passed without needing my passport, and the young age at which our children needed theirs.

Amidst all the sadness shone one speck of excitement. I'd never flown in a 747. At the end of the aerobridge, the MAS purser checked our boarding cards. Something must have been noted in her paperwork because she looked up and smiled.

> "More Australians joining us. Welcome to Malaysia Airlines." Then, "Please follow me."

As the aircraft doors would shortly close, so too would this part of our lives. I carried our baby boy, while Sharon guided the others. Lead pellets clustered in my stomach, fortunately, too heavy for an outward display. We felt like political refugees, leaving our country; denied our basic rights and freedoms. We would soon learn how differently our new employer regarded us, when compared with our old. As we ascended the spiral staircase, Sharon and I looked at each other. MAS had booked us first class.

The Malaysia Airlines jumbo rumbled down Runway 16. Nose gently lifting, we took off into the wind.

EPILOGUE

Time passes so quickly. As I sit and write in 2021, enough water has passed beneath the bridge for the aftermath to be viewed with more than a touch of hindsight. Looking back and putting keyboard to screen, I am also reminded that the wound I thought healed so many years ago can still provoke my anger. The baby boy carried aboard our Malaysia Airlines flight has turned 31.

Alex Paterson was one of the pilots involved. The first time I wore my Ansett uniform, observing from the Fokker Friendship jump seat, he was the First Officer. In the year leading up to the Dispute, Alex and his brother, Chris, were the ones who wrote the open letters detailing the failings of the Accord. Alex later published his perspective by building a website. Along with old newspaper cuttings and Brad Norington's book, in compiling this account, I used Alex's research extensively. The following is taken from his thoughts:

> "It should be remembered that, by definition, an 'Accord' is an agreement between willing partners. Further, the 'Accord' had no legal standing in industrial law; it was simply an agreement between the Federal Labor Government and the unions affiliated with the ACTU and with the support of some major employers like Sir Peter Abeles."

Over the life of the Hawke-led government, the Prices and Incomes Accord compressed wages and salaries, and as noted by journalist Graham Matthews, the Accord "reduced real income for workers by between 17 and 28 percent."

From Malaysia, we viewed the inevitable unravelling of the Accord. For years, high flying businessmen pummelled our monetary membrane. Awash with cash gleaned from the restraint of working men and women, and propped up by banks caught up in the exuberance, the combination of air and an inflatable rubber device could be used to illustrate what happened in 1990. One puff too many was forced into our brightly coloured economy.

Mr Ian Macfarlane, a former governor of the Reserve Bank, gave one of the ABC's Boyer lectures of 2006. His opening summed up the era:

> "In the early 1990s Australia went into a recession, the origins of which have been a matter of dispute and whose legacy remains with us. I believe that the financial excesses of the 1980s reached such a scale that the 1990 recession was inevitable."

Shortly after leaving our country, politicians' salaries were reviewed. The 36 percent seen as fitting within the guidelines by Justice Maddern was trimmed, slightly. Glancing through an Australian newspaper, I read the indignant justification of a minister's wife, "But my husband works odd hours and spends time away from home. Weekends and public holidays aren't always free and we often miss out on special family occasions."

With the latest adjustment, the total pay rise amounted to an overall 31.26 percent. When all was said and done, I found their hypocrisy breathtaking. Although, I may have alluded to this before.

Bob Hawke's destiny was to become, at the time, the only Labor Prime Minister removed from office by his own party. He was replaced by Paul Keating. During the Dispute, I had watched Mr Keating. Bob Hawke often ran off at the mouth, wordful in his peculiar brand of convoluted gobbledygook. Keating looked on and often made the same point, precisely and articulately. As the Dispute dragged on, Paul Keating had little to say. There were obligatory comments, but I found them few and far between. A Keating insult held such potence that a reputation could be shredded. His delivery was given with such precision that the recipient was unaware of their own demise until a careful review and several days had passed.

I disagreed with many of Paul Keating's policies and disliked his arrogance. Punishing interest rates and a recession to remedy the effects of greed and excess was not something ordinary people should "have to have". Despite this, I admired his intellect. Not just within refined sarcasm, a signature of the Keating insult, but when turned to matters of state. Of all the brilliant things Bob Hawke thought he said as Prime Minister, to me nothing came close to the power of Paul Keating's Redfern Address. When Bob Hawke spluttered one emotional outburst after another, so contrasted with Brian McCarthy's composure, my eyes drifted to Paul Keating. To me, Keating kept his own time, biding this until his jelly-backed leader became such a liability as to be tolerated no longer. That time came.

Keating unsheathed the political sword that was last gripped by his leader. Hawke was consigned to the political scrapheap in 1991. Had they been around at the time, the Bondi Hipsters, Dom and Adrian, may have caught the irony.

Over the years, Mr Hawke maintained a media profile, proffering comments and a torrent of unsolicited advice, along with the odd stone lobbed from his glass chateau. It reminded me of another of Dad's gems, "Son, no one ever learnt anything through an open mouth." At political events, Hawke was rolled out. Just when it appeared he'd gone away, up he popped again. There were some personal matters. On national television, joined by his new wife, a romantic side was revealed. I shied away from the TV, affording them the privacy I would have desired if in their situation. At the cricket, Bob reverted to an old practice, skolling a beer for the cameras. The empty cup in his hand joined a lop-sided grin on his face. During the 30th anniversary celebrations of Australia's America's Cup win, he attempted a lame joke, while dressed in a look-at-me jacket that could have been sewn from old newspapers.

Was his craving the limelight linked to the rejection that ended his Prime Ministership? Was it a manifestation of an inflated ego? Who would know? And, as the young ones say, whatever. At times like these, I couldn't help thinking, what a silly old bugger.

In 2011, Qantas tried the lockout stunt (did I mention what Ian Oldmeadow got up to after Ansett?). The CEO, Alan Joyce, liaising with Oldmeadow, attacked those providing the basics of the business — a safe operation. Incidentally, Joyce's multimillion-dollar pay was quarantined from any such assault and upped by 71 percent. Just as last time, locking the doors proved disastrous. The company lost millions of dollars and goodwill that, in some cases, were never recovered.

Paul Keating was moved to comment. Critical of the lockout strategy, he said a bargained outcome would have been better for Qantas in the long term. Enterprise bargaining stood the test of time:

> "It produced a 2.5% inflation rate for 20 years broadly. Notwithstanding the chicanery of Howard and Reith and others, it basically produced moderate wage outcomes and a low level of industrial disputation."

Sir Peter Abeles incurred the wrath of his shareholders. A couple of newspaper excerpts summed up the feeling: The *Sun-Herald,* dated the 4th of November 1990, reported:

> "The controversial pilots' dispute cost TNT $53 million which helped cause a drop in return on shareholders' funds from 24.2pc to 13.4pc and a 25.6pc drop in pre-tax profit to $223.4 million.
> Despite this downturn, Sir Peter picked up $5.1 million as part of his 'performance package'.
> This provoked a bitter protest at last Wednesday's heated annual general meeting from Jack Tilburn, a director of the Australian Shareholders Association, who said the total remuneration of $28.3 million to directors was unjustified given the company's performance.'"

And in a subsequent article in *The Sydney Morning Herald* on Boxing Day 1990:

> "In justifying the payment of $5 million to TNT chief executive Sir Peter Abeles, chairman Fred Millar said: 'That amount is large by anyone's standards but the remuneration paid should be dependent on the results.'
> Fair enough. But what the shareholders wanted to know was why, during a year in which TNT profits had fallen 40 percent, the directors had given themselves a pay rise of 40 percent — equivalent to 20 percent of its entire net profit. One called the whole thing obscene."

Like they say, pay peanuts and what do you get? Sir Peter suffered the same indignity as his friend Bob Hawke. He may have eliminated everything he wanted to eliminate, but his wish had a flow on effect. Peter Abeles was voted off the board of his own company. Saving face, he moved to concentrate on Ansett where he endured a similar fate.

Selling pies in Eastern Europe was another business venture with a member of the excesses of the eighties club, John Elliott. It didn't appear to go that well. I imagined both at the cart: John Elliott, "Poies, poies, come and get your poies!"; and Sir Peter, "You vill eat zis."

Abeles succumbed to cancer and died in June 1999, aged 75. Looking back on his friend's life, Bob Hawke was buoyant with emotion. Rising above the rest, he described his last moments with Sir Peter; one last kiss before such a life passed, this, on his forehead.

In 1985 Rupert Murdoch renounced his Australian citizenship to become a naturalised American. I remember a part of the ceremony on TV. Mr Murdoch stood in the room solemnly chanting:

> "I hereby declare, on oath, that I absolutely and entirely renounce and abjure all allegiance

> and fidelity to any foreign prince, potentate, or sovereignty of whom or which I have heretofore been a subject or citizen ..."

With this allegiance he pursued business interests in the US. Things had to be shuffled around a little with the Australian holdings, which worked out, and the UK arm still managed to tap away.

Bill Kelty left the ACTU in 2000. He moved to the private sector and took a job with a transport magnate. As to his time supporting the Accord, John Burgess and Richard Sappey noted in the *New Zealand Journal of Industrial Relations* in 1992:

> "Moreover, since 1983 average real adult award wages have declined in every year — the result has been one of the most significant redistributions of income from labour to capital this century."

Did Kelty represent Australian workers and their families? As the June 2004 edition of the *Socialist Alternative* noted:

> "With its reliance on union officials doing deals, the Accord also precipitated a decline in union organization, with membership dropping from 49 percent in the early 1980s to the low 20s today."

Simon Crean, the other wheel in the ACTU, joined parliament at the 1990 election. He served 23 years, half on the government benches and half in opposition. Rising to lead the Labor Party for a period, he had advice when announcing his retirement prior to the 2013 election. Choosing a replacement, he preached, should be a democratic practice:

> "You can't expect people to join a party if they don't have rights, and one of the most important rights that they should have is the ability to have a say in who represents them."

Len Coysh was moved sideways, and he and Ansett eventually parted company. Graeme McMahon saw a similar destiny, although he took a little longer. After bolting into the midst, Ken Cowley from News Limited took over, keeping the seat warm until Rod Eddington was appointed to fill the executive position.

The Dispute was assessed to have cost the Australian economy over one billion dollars, with estimates as high as four billion. At the end of the day, Treasury tallied the receipts. Government spending on the Airline Dispute was only exceeded, in recent times, by that of the war in Vietnam. With such expenditure, it's fair to say Australians have a right to know where all this money went. A cold case now, it would take a Royal Commission to uncover the truth. What we experienced altered the way we thought about politics and, for that matter, many aspects of our previous 'middle Australia' existence. The far-right tactics of Regan and Thatcher adopted by Hawke and Kelty forever changed our 'slightly right of centre' leanings.

I would never again take a newspaper article on face value, and I still avoid certain publications. We purchased a book by an author who, before our troubles, I would not have thought to read. We bought our copy of John Pilger's *A Secret Country* in 1990. Read so many times it has become dog-eared and tattered, recently, I bought a new copy; in print for the same number of years our youngest has walked this earth. Chapter 6, titled '*Mates*', deals with the interrelationships of many prominent people: Peter Abeles, Rupert Murdoch, Bob Hawke and even Bill Kelty feature. It was as though there were two Australias. One where ordinary people lived and worked, and one manipulated for the benefit of a few. Almost beyond belief, I came to regard Pilger's words as the truth. If someone wrote this about me, I would have sued for defamation. 31 years later, the words in this latest edition are not only unchanged, but added to.

The pilot leaders, written off as unemployable, resigned their AFAP positions in a gesture of goodwill. This allowed others to move into the executive positions and start rebuilding. With the new executive firmly in place, Brian McCarthy moved overseas and resumed his career with a foreign airline. In 2003, he returned to work in Australia. Passengers on Virgin Australia may have heard his voice. Not "All we want to do is negotiate", but, "Good morning ladies and gentlemen."

John Raby left for overseas to join a VIP operation in Oman. He then moved to a small European airline operating regular services and 'charter runs' to the Caribbean and Far East. His next move was to the UK where he became the Chief Pilot of easyJet. Recruited by Virgin Blue, Raby returned to Australia and was integral in setting up flying operations. He became the Chief Pilot and held this position until retiring a few years ago.

The Federation lay prone on the ground. With barely a pulse, the AFAP was not even considered worth one final kick, as our antagonists skulked away. But that is not the end of the story. For the first time, a general aviation pilot was voted to the president's position. Terry O'Connell returned to his office and began again; his and the pilots' efforts rebuilt the association to the point where the AFAP once more represents domestic pilots and retains general aviation members. Today membership stands at the highest in its history.

Sadly, Terry passed away on the 7th of October, 2012. After more than 30 years with the AFAP, aged 61, he lost his battle with cancer. Long time AFAP associate, Lawrie Cox, observed:

> "Terry demonstrated credibility and honesty in all his work and even his hardest opponents would concede he never wavered in getting the outcome for the AFAP members. The 1989 dispute placed great pressure on all involved but he continued to provide advice and good humour throughout. As a staff member, he was personally held liable for damages arising, along with five other pilot leaders at the time. Despite this pressure, Terry never wavered in representing pilots."

Considering our antagonists' aim was to eliminate the Federation, it's interesting to compare then with now. In 1989, the AFAP had 3,049 members. As of 30th of June 2021, the AFAP represented 5,420 pilots. And, it seems, Abeles, Murdoch, Hawke and Kelty achieved something that was 'diametrically opposed' to their aim. None of the airlines involved in the dispute exist today.

IPEC Aviation features on the *List of defunct airlines of Oceania* (possibly an old Ministry of Truth document). Operations ceased in 1993. East-West Airlines rates a mention in the same communiqué, ceasing operations also in 1993 (what was left was bundled into Ansett). Australian Airlines is another no longer with us. Posting record profits before the Dispute, it was crippled, with losses in the order of $150 million. There was only one solution. In 1992, Australian Airlines was absorbed into Qantas, forming Qantas Domestic. Qantas wouldn't wear the losses, so these were reconciled before taking control. Needless to say, and as had become the custom, taxpayers were asked to put hands in pockets again. Unfortunately, this request was in such a soft voice that not all were able to hear.

Ansett suffered similar losses; not quite the lean, mean, flying machine — mortally wounded, it limped on with its Noah's ark fleet. With cash to upgrade and renew flushed away, it struggled towards its eventual demise.

As Tom Ballantyne, Chief Correspondent, Orient Aviation, noted: "While Sir Reg Ansett laid the groundwork for a national icon, Sir Peter Abeles took it by the scruff of the neck and laid the groundwork for disaster."

So, what was it all about? What did it achieve?

Mr Jull calculated the returned pilots' pay rise in simple terms. There were allowances in the old, but not in the new, and other differences. As it turned out, it was a case of "what you lose on the hurdy-gurdy, you pick up on the roundabout", or, at least, they did. The base of 55 hours provided the guts of their pay rise.

After the dust settled, Alex Paterson sharpened his pencil. He made several calculations and comparisons. He used a block with 65.15 flying hours (as it as was closest to the average of 68 hours). Applying this month's flying pattern, he calculated the before and after. Referencing the old agreement (section 9, page 18, of Ansett Airlines Pilots' Agreement in 1988), he then applied the same flying hours to the new (section 8, page 6, of IRC Ansett Airlines Pilots' Award 1989). This typical roster gave an increase of 34 percent. Extra flying, as Mr Jull observed, widened the gap.

At various stages, the airlines offered to take us back; the first time with seniority intact. The condition? Sign the contract. If they could afford to pay us the new salary, it was obvious that the whole thing was not about money.

This point was reinforced from our side. At another stage, we offered to resume full services, but on the lower pay rate of our old agreement. The sticking point, from start to finish, was the right to freely associate, and negotiate through our representatives, directly with our employers.

During the death throes of the Hawke leadership, changes were afoot. Terry Vine observed in the *Herald-Sun* ('Cook flies in the face of fairness', dated 21st of October 1991):

> "Isn't politics a magnificent example of barefaced hypocrisy? The latest is the minister for Industrial Relations, Senator Cook, foreshadowing a government rewrite of the Industrial Relations Act. The rewrite would give employers and unions greater scope to negotiate agreements on wages and conditions as an alternative to the arbitration system. Now I think that is a marvellous thing and the quicker they do it, the better.
> So, I therefore pose one question — isn't that exactly what Australia's airline pilots were trying to do before Our Beloved Leader took to them with a chainsaw?"

Prime Minister Keating renewed the Accord one last time, in name only. We viewed the irony from Malaysia, as Keating ditched centralised wage fixing and, in another of life's organic twists, employers and employees negotiated terms and conditions through their representatives directly. In concert, the ACTU labelled the IRC irrelevant. An observer may well have thought the whole experiment turned out to be a crock. And so, the old way of doing things resumed. Dom and Adrian would have been blown away.

REFERENCES

Ansett Transport Industries (Operations) Pty Ltd. 'Writ', August, 1989.

A.T.I. (Ansett Transport Industries) Pilots Seniority List, 1st July 1989.

Australian Federation of Air Pilots. 'State of Play'. *Go-Around — Overseas Edition No. 57*, March 11, 1992.

Ballantyne, Tom (Chief Correspondent, Orient Aviation). 'What really went wrong at Ansett?' Australian Airports Association, Airports & Aviation Outlook 2002.

National Convention, Held in Adelaide, November 11-12, 2002-10-23.

Beams, Nick. 'Industrial relations and the trade unions under Labor: From Whitlam to Rudd', Part 3, November 14, 2007.

Bowen, Warren. 'Three Cheers for Bob', *Go-Around*, December 24, 1991.

Bowers, Peter. 'Spring brings out the egos', *The Sydney Morning Herald*, 9th September 1989.

Burgess, John, and Richard Sappey. *New Zealand Journal of Industrial Relations*, 1992.

Collings, B. H. 'Defence misused in air strike', Letter to the editor, *The Australian*, September 22, 1989.

Curlewis, Dick. 'The Australian Pilots Dispute in 1989'. *Radical Tradition: An Australasian History Page*, http://www.takver.com/history/pilotsdispute1989.htm, viewed 12 April 2021.

Evans, Jim, and Nigel K. Daw. *An Iconic Airline: The Story of Airlines of South Australia*.

Gosman, Keith. 'The wide world of Sir Peter Abeles', *The Sun-Herald*, (Pg 32) 4th November 1990.

Goward, Pru. 'Industrial reform will be PM's Everest — it won't resemble Hawke's Accord', *The Sydney Morning Herald*, May 28, 2020.

Hawke, R. J. L. 'Letter to Mr P. Edgley', dated 14 September 1989.

Heller, Joseph. *Catch 22*. Simon & Schuster. November 10, 1961.

Kelly, Hugo, Mark Metherell, and Jennifer McAsey. 'From the Archives, 1989: Chaos as Australia's domestic pilots resign en masse', *The Age*, August 25, 1989: https://www.theage.com.au/national/from-the-archives-1989-chaos-as-australia-s-domestic-pilots-resign-en-masse-20200821-p55nzh.htm. Viewed February 1, 2021.

Light, Deborah. 'Winners and losers of 1990', *The Sydney Morning Herald*. (Pg 32) 26 December 1990.

Macfarlane, Ian. 'Boyer lecture', *Australian Broadcasting Commission*, 2006.

McCarthy, Brian, (1990), 'The Airline Dispute: Wage Determination or Union Extermination?', Department of Economics, University of Wollongong, 15 October1990, 22p. https://ro.uow.edu.au/kirby/3

McCrann, Terry. 'Victory for pilots is vital for some basic rights', *The Herald*, Melbourne, October 6, 1989.

McCrann, Terry. 'The Game's the Same: It's the Ump to Blame', *The Herald*, Melbourne, April 30, 1990.

Norington, Brad. *Sky Pirates: The Pilots' Strike that Grounded Australia*. ABC Books, Sydney, 1990.

Norington, Brad. 'Workers restive as elite groups make pay grab', *The Sydney Morning Herald*, December 21, 1989.

Orwell, George. *Animal Farm*. Secker and Warburg, London, England. 17th August 1945.

O'Sullivan, Matt. Qantas chief's pay rise sparks anger, *The Sydney Morning Herald*, September 7, 2011.

Paterson, Alex. A Pilots Perspective of the Australian Pilots Dispute of 1989.

Pekol, Suzanne. 'Taxpayers give $6000 gift to MPs', *The Courier-Mail*, Brisbane, December 24, 1988.

Pilger, John. *A Secret Country*. Oxford: Clio Press, 1990.

Ramsey, Alan. 'The MP's get theirs — in due course', *The Sydney Morning Herald*, June 2, 1990.

Rintoul, Stuart. '13 hours' flying a week for $128,000', *The Australian*, August 25, 1989.

Smith, Graham, F. 'Consensus to Coercion: the Australian Air Pilots Dispute', *Journal of Industrial Relations*. June 1, 1990: https://journals.sagepub.com/doi/10.1177/002218569003200204. Viewed March 8, 2021.

Stanaway, Glenn. 'MPs' pay up 17.8% to $65,000', *The Courier-Mail*, Brisbane, June 1, 1990.

Stone, Deborah, and Penny Robinson. 'Industrial chaos hits Vic', *The Australian*, August 19-20, 1989.

Thuy Tram, Dang. *Last Night I Dreamed of Peace: The Diary of Dang Thuy Tram*. Translated by Andrew X. Pham. Published in the US in October 2008.

Vine, Terry. 'Cook flies in the face of fairness', *Herald-Sun*, 21st of October 1991.

Wood, Katie. 'The 1989 Pilots' Strike', *The Socialist Alternative*, 31/5/2004 (Edition 79 — June 2004).

Yeats, Clancy. 'Shareholders back pay for ANZ's Smith', *The Sydney Morning Herald*, December 19, 2012.